SIKH CHALLENGES IN NORTH AMERICA

PAST | PRESENT | FUTURE

Amrik Singh Chattha, MD

Author: Amrik Singh Chattha, MD

Editor and Publisher: Sayantan Chakravarty
India Empire Magazine

Cover Design: Jaydev Singh Bisht

Printed: August 2022

Publishing Agency:

India Empire
Apartment 340, Hauz Khas SFS
New Delhi - 110016, India.
M: +91-9899117477
E: Sayantanc@gmail.com
W: www.indiaempire.com

ISBN No.: 978-81-958108-1-9

*Dedicated to the Heroes of
Komagata Maru and Ghadar.
They sacrificed their
lives so we could live free.*

PREFACE

PREFACE

It was in July 1967 that I joined the Daniel Drake Memorial Hospital in Cincinnati, Ohio as a resident physician. At the time an entirely new world opened up before me, and not all of it was very pleasant. The children in the car park usually addressed me as a genie, almost like an alien that had landed on their turf. The three neurology residency programs showed ample reluctance in accepting me. Others simply chose not to show any interest in me after they saw my photograph with a turban. This new, uninviting environment also opened my mind to what difficulties my Sikh predecessors may have encountered when they had immigrated to North America at the turn of the 20th century.

The Sikhs had started migrating to various countries following the British conquest of Punjab in 1848. With worsening economic conditions in Punjab, the migrants took to various British colonies. The Sikh soldiers serving in the imperial army learned about Canada and the US from their counterparts during the Boxer rebellion in China and the diamond jubilee celebrations of Queen Victoria, and the coronation of King Edward VII. As a result of the abolition of slavery, there was an overall labor shortage. Businesses in North America were looking for cheap labor. Along with other Asian groups, the Sikhs too started migrating in search of greener pastures.

As a community, the Sikhs faced great hostility in both the US and Canada from white supremacist groups, labor unions and the official machinery itself. Still they struggled through the early period of the 20th century to settle mostly in the Pacific West. Those days, with porous borders in place, back and forth movement between the US and Canada was not too difficult. A series of articles have been written on the struggle of Sikhs who initially landed in Canada (Brar). No such effort, however, has been made to document the lives of the early Sikh settlers in the US.

Local authors have written about the difficulties and hostilities encountered by the early Sikh settlers, and also about the great successes many of them could make of their lives. Conferences, seminars and books have explored significant events such as the Komagata Maru and the Ghadar movements. Baba Gurdit Singh chartered the Komagata Maru ship to Vancouver, Canada and educated and patriotic Indians organized the Ghadar movement to get freedom from the British. They belonged to all religious groups and were supported mostly by Sikh labor at farms and mills in the Pacific West. They became the forerunners of the Indian freedom struggle.

The early writings on Sikhs are mainly scattered articles that appeared in the local press in the US and Canada. They are largely deprecatory in tone when it comes to the turban-wearing Hindoos, immigrants from Asia that followed the Chinese and the Japanese as cheap labor for serving the young, developing communities in North America's west coast. Most of the early Sikh migrants were less-educated, single young men, handicapped by their inability to communicate with the Anglo-Saxons of North America.

They came from a nation enslaved by the British, only to be humiliated by the white race in North America. They faced severe discrimination and riots on grounds of their race, turban and being people of a subjugated nation. While they were initially welcomed to make up for the shortage of labor, as their numbers began to grow, they faced raw hatred and violence. The white-nation movement in North America gained momentum and anti-Asiatic laws were passed to stop the immigration of Sikhs and others. Frustrated by the humiliation both at home and overseas, they seethed against the British and wanted them thrown out of India at any cost. They pooled together their resources and with planning and networking of the educated Indians in the west coast organized the Ghadar movement, initially by communicating anti-British, patriotic and freedom-loving sentiments and propaganda through multilingual publications known as *Ghadar, Circular-i-Azadi, Swadesh Sewak, Aryan, Pardesi, Khalsa Sansar, Free Hindustan.*

This book is an effort to summarize the history of Sikh settlers in North America for about one hundred and twenty-five years starting with the arrival of Risaldar Major Kesur Singh in Canada in 1897. It tries also to draw attention to the difficulties, hatred, discrimination and the harsh anti-immigration laws the early Sikh settlers had to face. These issues have been discussed in light of available information from earlier Sikh settlers and their families.

Apart from the articles published in the local press in those early days, the South Asian American Digital Archive (SAADA) and the Sikhpioneer.org have served as the backbone of information for this book. These two organizations have made serious and laudable efforts towards recording the oral and digitized history of the original Sikh settlers. Johanna Ogden looked at early Sikh settlements along the Columbia River, and their role in the Ghadar movement. The list of sources is long and does not include many scholars of Sikhism that are on the faculty of Sikh chairs in the US and Canada.

Most of the Sikh literature in the US started appearing in sizable numbers following the large-scale immigrations that took place after 1965. It was the 1965 Immigration Act that was signed into law by President Lyndon B. Johnson that opened the doors for Asian migration to the US. Mark Juergensmeyer, Norman Gerald Barrier, Kristina Myrvold, Verne Dusenbery, Eleanor Nesbitt, Paul Michael Taylor and a few others took a great deal of interest in the Sikh diaspora. Bruce LaBrack (1988) wrote about the Sikhs of Northern California. Karen Leonard (1992) gave elaborate accounts of Punjabi-Mexican relationships and marriages. Indian writers like Harish K. Puri wrote extensively on the Ghadar movement and its relationship to the Sikh diaspora in North America.

The world has changed since the days of those early settlers and Sikhs today are scattered all over the planet. The present generation of immigrant Sikhs are more educated than their predecessors and consist of physicians, engineers and business people. They are actively involved in community affairs and have established many

Gurdwaras and other social-interest organizations. Interest in Sikhism has gone up with the creation of many Sikh-study chairs in various leading American universities. The Sikh chairs and the Smithsonian Sikh exhibits under the tutelage of Dr Paul Michael Taylor have played a major role in introducing Sikhism to the host society. Sikhs have been able to engage with other religions through interfaith groups and the Parliament of the World's Religions.

Also, the community's current issues and challenges have been discussed, and likely changes that can take place going forward have been summarized in this book. The future of Sikhism is discussed in the light of the changing concept of religion. The new waves of agnosticism, atheism and the impact of globalization, acculturation and detraditionalization have been explored. The likely impact of these changes on the Sikh religion, its symbols, customs and Sikh *Maryada* is brought to attention as adaptation and assimilation happens in future.

In light of the above is there a likely evolution of a changed and newer Sikhism? The slow and subtle change is unavoidable and could lead to agnostic and atheist Sikhs, a movement towards Nanak Panthi philosophy with no visible symbols, and all-inclusive offshoots of Sikhism.

The road ahead, and the march forward, is not going to be one without thorns. It was not easy growing up with a turban in the US. Rampant and reckless bullying in schools has already taken a heavy toll on an entire generation. Turban and brown skin tone became objects of hatred and ridicule, exacerbated by Islamophobia. As a result, hate crimes have gone up markedly. Several Sikh organizations have become very active in promoting the respect and dignity of Sikhism and its most important religious symbol, the turban. It has been an object of mistaken identity, hate crime and discrimination.

America, on the other hand, is becoming less religious and less color conscious. Turban-clad Sikhs are today a part of the defense and police services in both the US and Canada. The assimilation in the host society is not Anglo conformity, instead it is a mosaic of cultures, colors and religions. The Sikh diaspora continues to progress economically and politically. Sikhs in the US are well-settled now. Canadian Sikhs are in a better position as they have a home away from home.

On the whole, this book is a candid effort at summarizing the various difficulties faced by the Sikhs who migrated to North America over the last one hundred and twenty-five years, and the possible challenges and changes in future. The views expressed in this book at places are personal and could become controversial and the subject of debate. Hopefully, it will serve as a history of Sikhs in North America for all Sikhs and provide an understanding of the past, present, and future for the young, and for posterity. ∎

Contents

A Sikh boy and his friend in Canada, 1959

" *Man's yesterday may ne'er be like his morrow, Nought may endure but Mutability"*

—Percy Bysshe Shelley

HUMAN MIGRATION

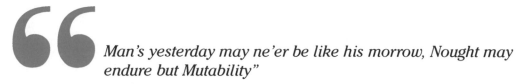

This book is an attempt to look closely at the past, current and future challenges to the culture and religious values of Sikhs in North America. In order to deeply fathom and understand the changes and challenges of a cultural and religious group that moves into a new country, it is quite important to understand human migration itself, and the challenges it presents

The earliest human movement started from Africa and spread to other countries. This movement, in all likelihood, was in search of food and for finding greener pastures and better livable environments. Many of the hunters and gatherers had mini-migrations in adjoining locations. With the improvement in agricultural techniques, they settled in small towns. The invention of the wheel further improved mobility.

Forced migration occurred during the Roman period when subjects of defeated territories and nations were brought as slaves. Similar forced migrations were seen many centuries later, during the time of slavery that was institutionalized by western nations. The law of diminishing returns also resulted in migrations when people from densely populated regions who were competing for limited resources began to migrate, and took over empty land mass.

With the birth of organized religions, religious persecutions resulted in forced migrations. The movement of human beings continued as newer modes of transportations were invented, first the ship and then the aircraft. This trend is unlikely to stop and exploratory trips are now being made to other planets. Industrial revolution, coupled with the invention of gunpowder and a tremendous growth in the shipbuilding industry led to the conquest of several parts of the world and colonization by western nations. Both the rulers, and the ruled, made migratory movements.

There was a long period in history when the Orient was far richer than the Occident. The GDP of nations like India and China were manifold that of Europe, and the New World was yet to be discovered by Spain,

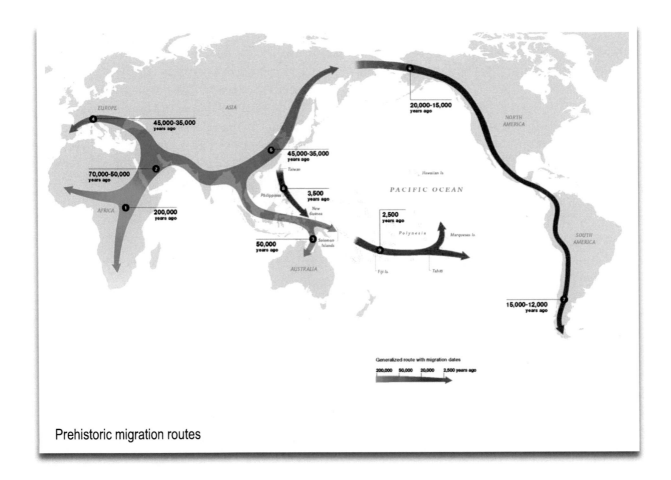

Prehistoric migration routes

Portugal, France and England. That was also a time when more and more westerners led expeditions to the east in order to create trading posts. There was also a scramble for Africa and the entire continent was colonized. Soon the process of colonization of the Orient also began. After the collapse of the colonies, migratory movements reversed from the east to the developed west. Migration, therefore, is an unending process.

Why humans migrate

In the long history of migration, one can see the following reasons and types of human migration.

1. **Push migration:**

Forced migration as happened during the time of slavery and earlier in Roman times when defeated subjects were brought as slaves.

Humans are pushed out by religious and political persecution, as well as natural disasters. Human history is full of examples of these movements. Puritans moved to America to avoid religious persecution and likewise Rohingyas are escaping from Myanmar. Syrian refugees migrated due to political persecution. The latest is from Afghanistan after the Taliban took over the country in 2021 after the fall of the Government in Kabul.

A slow and subtle migration also occurs due to climate change that results in global warming which in turn causes droughts, hurricanes, floods and rising sea levels. The processes of deforestation and desertification are a result of climate change that occurred millions of years ago.

2. **Pull migration:**

Humans move to places where there are better opportunities and quality of life. The indentured labor system was introduced by the European colonizers after the abolition of slavery. That resulted in the movement of Indian labor to different parts of the world, mainly to islands in the Pacific, Atlantic and Indian Ocean.

3. Sojourn migration:

These are people migrating for a short period with plans to return to the home country. Some of the Sikh migrants who were single, wanted to return home after earning enough money to purchase land and a brick home in their native villages in Punjab. They later changed their mind and became permanent residents in North America and elsewhere. Sojourn migrants have rarely been adventurers, explorers or missionaries. This kind of migration has been possible largely as a result of steamships in the 19th century and latter-day aircrafts.

4. Transnational migration:
This is the most recent immigration trend that has been brought into effect by globalization, the internet, better communication and transportation.

Many families are separated during migration and new classification of family relationships have evolved. They include terms such as 'astronaut fathers' meant to describe male parents who shuttle back and forth between the US—where their families live—and their place of business in another country. Their wives, in a lighter vein, refer to themselves as 'overseas widows'. According to Erica Lee (2015), there is a term such as 'parachute kids.' It refers to children who live alone in the US with the help of a caretaker while their parents are domiciled in a foreign country, for business or work. Chaney (1979) says that these families come under the category of 'people with feet in two societies.' This kind of arrangement is done not just to secure a better economic future for the families but also to safeguard them against political turmoil in the home nation. Many such families with feet in both nations have the advantage of dual citizenships.

A doctor known to me from Punjab has applied for immigration under EB-5 visa rule in the US. He has a flourishing medical practice in Punjab and wants his two sons to study in the US and settle down in this country. After retirement, my doctor friend himself wishes to settle down in the US for good.

Migration—West to the East

The travels of Marco Polo in the 13th century and the publication of the travels of Sir John Mandeville in 1356 CE describe in detail the incredible wealth and wonders of Asia that had encouraged many to migrate eastward. In the 16th and 17th centuries many from the west went to the east. This included the British, French, Dutch and Portuguese. When the British finally took control of India, more of their countrymen came to the shores of our country. Many died in long ship journeys and others, while in India, died of dysentery, cholera and malaria. Some young people from England were pushed to India by their parents either because of their indolence, dishonesty or extravagance. Some escaped as debtors. Those who lost money due to gambling or failed business came to India to 'shake the Pagoda tree', implying fortune falling in grateful hands (Gilmour). The poems of Rudyard Kipling enticed many young men to venture to India as soldiers or ICS officers.

Those who were not rich enough for fox hunting in Britain could hunt tigers in India.

Migration—East to West

The last century saw the reversal of this movement from less developed east to the developed west. There was a significant increase in the population of Punjab, the Sikh homeland. According to the census, the population of Punjab increased from 3.5 million to 36 million between 1881 to 1901 in spite of cholera, smallpox and periods of starvation. This reduced the per capita land holding. The higher British taxes and the British policy of industrialization favoring

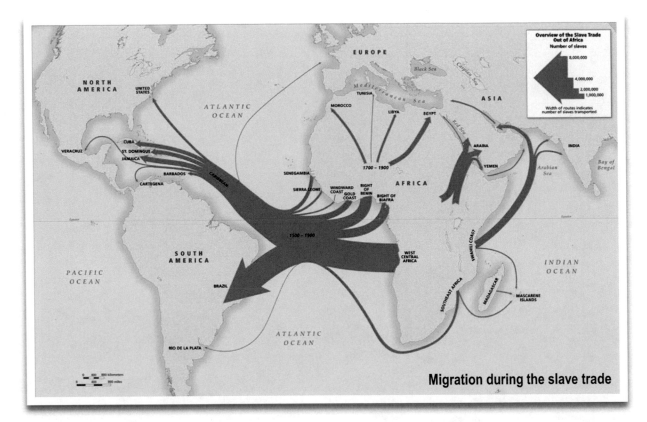

Migration during the slave trade

Great Britain at the cost of their prized colony economically affected the whole of India.

I don't pity Sikh farmers moving west. Sikhs saw more opportunities in the US, Canada as well as other developed countries.

All humans look for greener pastures. Today's green pastures may be tomorrow's desert. Somewhat similar is the direction of migration. Migrants and refugees will always be there. But it will not be one-way traffic. Religious and political persecution as a cause of migration was overtaken by poverty and prospects of a better life in the developed countries.

Most Sikh migrants to North America in the late 19th and early 20th centuries were single and working. They were sending money back home to support their families.

This is also true for other migrants. Large number of Filipinos and some Hispanics work in American households and send money to their home country where their extended families and children live. About ten percent of the Filipino population works abroad and sends money home. They are given the status of heroes in their home country.

Demographic shift and migration

Thomas Malthus, a British clergyman, economist and demographer theorized in 1798 that in future agricultural production will not keep pace with the growth in population, resulting in starvation and famines. Even though such a forecast has not come true to the extent that Malthus envisioned, poverty has led to pull migration to developed and rich countries in modern times.

The opposite trend of negative population growth is of concern in many countries now. To name a few we have Japan, South Korea, Russia and Estonia. Even China has rescinded its one-child policy and wants to have more newborns. The Census reveals that in the last decade the US population did not grow. A Pew Survey of October 2021 shows that 44 percent of childless couples in the 18-49 age group did not wish to have children for any number of reasons.

Such a trend will result in a negative population growth in many developed countries. Humans will still be required in spite of automation, hence the need for young immigrants. I would like to term this as 'beg you' immigration of the future. Little

Migrants moving on bullock carts during Indian partition

wonder then that asylum seekers and other displaced people are generously accepted in many countries as part of a dire need, and not really due to an extreme compassion for refugees.

Recent migrants

After they had started letting go of their colonial territories, Great Britain started accepting people from those very places they had ruled. The US, Canada and Australia are some of the prime examples of nations that have continued accepting immigrants from the rest of the world. European countries, on their part, have accepted a lot of refugees from war-torn countries in the Middle East.

Mental health issues of migrants

Moving to a new country is stressful for all immigrants. Anxiety of the unknown is universal. The migrant anticipates to face challenges such as:

1. Journey: In the early days, migration across the sea by steamship was marred by seasickness, dangers of high seas, malnutrition, diseases and pirates. Illegal migration these days has its own dangers during the journey and is costly.
2. Separation anxiety from kith and kin.
3. The climate, food and housing in the host country was uncertain.
4. The behavior and attitude of the inhabitants of the host society was unpredictable.

disease appeared due to decompensation brought by this displacement. Even in peaceful times Mirsky (2008) reported mental health issues among Russian-speaking Jewish immigrants to Israel.

Other diseases related to migration

In the last few years, there are reports of higher incidence of other migration related diseases such as heart disease, diabetes, hepatitis B, lactose intolerance, cancer of the liver and lung, among Asian-American immigrants.

The migration related diseases associated with the human skin color and ultraviolet light such as skin cancer and vitamin D deficiency have been described later in chapter three.

Migration—brain drain or brain gain?

The word 'brain drain' was coined by the Royal Society of London when a large-scale movement of highly-skilled scientists took place from war-torn Europe to the US, soon after the Second World War. This created a vacuum in Britain that was filled up by the influx of many highly-skilled doctors and engineers from developing countries.

Many educated professionals carry a guilt of betraying the society and nation that nurtured them into becoming successful professionals and later migrating for better prospects to other countries (Cervantes, 2001 and Cherian, 2020).

Migration is not a new phenomenon. Citizens from many developing nations continue to move to the well-developed ones. In the long run, all home countries have benefited from migration. The Jewish state of Israel was created by the Jewish diaspora. In more recent times one has seen the immense contribution of the Chinese diaspora during the rise of China's growth and development.

Some engineers who entered the US with H-1B visas started successful companies in their mother countries. It is a gain for both the home country as well as the host nation. ∎

Migration is stressful. The underlying pre-existing psychiatric condition gets worse, particularly for push migrants. Most of the migrants are strong-willed and optimistic.

Every year during the festivities of thanksgiving in the US there are articles about early Puritan migrants to the US, their prayers, farewells and landings across the sea.

The immigrants these days do not face all those difficulties and land up in known families or land at ethnic and religious enclaves, but nonetheless, it is not a vacation.

Many mental issues were noted when large scale migration of Jewish people occurred after Second World War and holocaust. Over and above anxiety, many cases of Alzheimer's

CHAPTER 2

MIGRATION AND ENTRY TO THE US

The American continent was originally inhabited by indigenous tribes known by different names. These tribes came from Africa and walked across the hypothetical bridge or tunnel at the Bering Strait connecting Chukchi Peninsula, Russia, with Seward Peninsula, Alaska, US.

Migration wasn't easy in the absence of decent navigational tools. Let us not forget that poor navigational aids made a mockery of Christopher Columbus' trip in the latter half of the 15th century. At the directions of the king and queen of Spain, Columbus set out to discover India. Instead he landed in the Caribbean and it came to be known as the West Indies. Later, he discovered major parts of America. Greater modifications to the navigational compass made it easier to discover new lands. Maritime adventures were initiated by Spain when it came to rule the seas. Following suit, other seafaring European nations joined the wanderlust, and showed considerable intemperance when it came to expanding their empires. Britain replaced Spain as the master of the seas.

The first wave of migrants to the US were European explorers who came by sea. Later Puritans landed at various places on the east coast of the US. Jamestown in Virginia became the first colony in 1607 followed by Plymouth in Massachusetts in 1620. They were the Pilgrims and had left Britain due to religious persecutions. It was a classic example of push migration. Subsequent migrations to the US were a result of pull migration that took place from Europe and Asia.

British and Dutch migration to the US was followed by others from different parts of Europe, including Jewish migration before and after the holocaust. Mexico owned a major part of Southwest America before the Europeans arrived. Hispanic migration, mostly illegal, continues till this day. These days immigrants are no longer greeted with open arms and do not get the 'welcome wagon' treatment.

In the past, both the US and Canada needed cheap labor for lumber mills and railroads as new communities were developing. These were the pull factors for Asian migration to North America, specifically the Pacific West. We'll discuss the major migrations and their fallouts in the subsequent paragraphs, mainly the ones concerning the Chinese, Japanese, Filipinos and Koreans. The Sikh migration will be dealt with separately. Migrations from Vietnam,

Cambodia, Laos, Pakistan, Myanmar, Sri Lanka, Bangladesh and other South Asian nations are more recent, and do reflect the social challenges presented at the time of their migration.

ABOVE:
The Statue of Liberty on Ellis Island which was the earliest gateway for immigrants to the US

US entry points
East

The entry to the US in the latter half of the 19ᵗʰ century and the first half of the 20ᵗʰ century was mainly by sea. Ellis Island in New

THE NEW COLOSSUS.
NOT LIKE THE BRAZEN GIANT OF GREEK FAME,
WITH CONQUERING LIMBS ASTRIDE FROM LAND TO LAND;
HERE AT OUR SEA-WASHED, SUNSET GATES SHALL STAND
A MIGHTY WOMAN WITH A TORCH, WHOSE FLAME
IS THE IMPRISONED LIGHTNING, AND HER NAME
MOTHER OF EXILES. FROM HER BEACON-HAND
GLOWS WORLD-WIDE WELCOME; HER MILD EYES COMMAND
THE AIR-BRIDGED HARBOR THAT TWIN CITIES FRAME.
"KEEP ANCIENT LANDS, YOUR STORIED POMP!"
       CRIES SHE
WITH SILENT LIPS. "GIVE ME YOUR TIRED, YOUR
       POOR,
YOUR HUDDLED MASSES YEARNING TO BREATHE FREE,
THE WRETCHED REFUSE OF YOUR TEEMING SHORE.
SEND THESE, THE HOMELESS, TEMPEST-TOST TO ME,
I LIFT MY LAMP BESIDE THE GOLDEN DOOR!"

THIS TABLET, WITH HER SONNET TO THE BARTHOLDI STATUE
OF LIBERTY ENGRAVED UPON IT, IS PLACED UPON THESE WALLS
IN LOVING MEMORY OF
EMMA LAZARUS
BORN IN NEW YORK CITY, JULY 22, 1849
DIED NOVEMBER 19, 1887.

The poem by Emma Lazarus at the Statue of Liberty

York opened an immigration station on January 1, 1892, at a time when most of the emigrants were from Europe. For some years this entry was not welcome for southern and eastern Europeans, but those from northern Europe were accepted with open arms. It belied the wonderful words of Emma Lazarus whose poem is set in a plaque at the Statue of Liberty. One of its lines reads, *"Give me your tired. Your poor. Your huddled masses yearning to breathe free. The wretched refuse of your teeming shore. Send these, the homeless, tempest-tost to me. I lift my lamp beside the golden door."*

Angel Island

West

Organized immigration to the west started on January 21, 1910, at Angel Island near San Francisco, California. While initially this became the entry point for Asians to the US, it is also here that the stringent and harsh provisions of the Asian Exclusion Act were applied to keep the Chinese and others from Asia away.

South

Spain controlled for years what is now the southwest US and ruled over the Navajo Indians. This region had been a part of Spanish-controlled Mexico for centuries, until

Mexico gained its independence from Spain in September 1810. That territory was ceded to the US in 1848 after the Mexican-American War. But the southern border remained porous and had a continuous influx of illegal immigrants from Central and South America. Matters have reached a flash point and the US is seriously considering building a wall on the southern borders.

North

The northern border of the US with Canada is long and has remained porous for a considerably long time. Most of the immigrants used Canada as an entry point to get to the US in order to avoid long formalities at American entry points. The movement of Sikhs across this border, especially during the early parts of the 20th century, remained unhindered. On the western side of this northern border, things remained ambiguous and undefined until the signing of the Oregon Treaty of June 1846. Even though bordered by lakes and woods, the northern border is still not impermeable.

The Great Asian Migration to the Pacific West

Migration powers economic growth, reduces inequalities, and connects diverse societies. Yet it is also a source of political tensions and human tragedies.

—António Guterres, Secretary-General, United Nations

Undeniably, the words of António Guterres provide an accurate picture of human migration over millennia. While opportunities to benefit economically have presented themselves, many of the migrant stories are beset with trials, tribulations, and tragedy. They ring true especially in the US and Canada where the Chinese, followed by the Japanese, Sikhs, Filipinos and Koreans started arriving in ships in the Pacific West Coast well over a hundred to about two hundred years ago.

As they sailed away to a new destiny, leaving their homes and loved ones behind, the early migrants carried with them nothing but a few possessions, and, of course, the dreams of a better tomorrow. Their hopes of flourishing in another part of the world would spring eternal in their hearts. The grass, however, did not always turn out to be greener on the other side. Very little could've prepared the migrants for some of the horrors and hatred they had to encounter in their new, chosen lands.

Both the USA and Canada made serious, sinister efforts to push Asian emigrants back to their home nations. The Asiatic Exclusion League—known initially as the Japanese and Korean Exclusion League—was formed in December 1907. It was entirely mandated, often through the use of stringent measures, to prevent Asians from emigrating to the USA and Canada via the Pacific West. The AEL was not at all averse to using strong-armed tactics, riotous methods, as well as highly intimidating language through newspapers in order to drive fear into the heart of the Asian community. As the Asian presence increased, so did the use of force and violence. Many of the Chinese and Japanese were also summarily deported. There was, to begin with, extremely strict enforcement of the Chinese Exclusion Act of 1882. Soon after when the Japanese and Koreans started moving into the US, according to the *San Francisco Chronicle* and the *Political Science Quarterly*, the League campaigned hard to keep the Asian children out of the public schools. Their bitter and vituperative lobbying succeeded in sowing the seeds of a deep social discord—in 1906 the San Francisco Board of Education ruled that every Japanese and Korean student would join their Chinese counterparts in the segregated Oriental School, established sometime in 1884.

With blinkers firmly in place, the members of the League refused to see any valid reason as to why people of color should be encouraged to populate America in the first place. They made it abundantly clear that the League wanted a White America, nothing less was acceptable. The AEL opened branches along the Pacific West, and turned itself into a menacing cross-border organization that was out to hound out Asians merely on the basis of their darker skin color, and their own ill-perceived superiority. Prejudice ran amuck, and white mobs terrorized Asian settlements with frequent riotous attacks. By every account, racism and its abominable cousin, hatred, had reared their ugly heads in the US and Canada in a major way at the turn of the 20th century. Apart from slavery, this is yet another history that White America is yet to come to terms with.

Within a few months of its renaming, the League in 1908 asked Sikhs from India in no uncertain terms to leave Canada and relocate to the Central American nation of British Honduras, presently known as Belize (see separate story on "No Honduras for us" in chapter six). A Sikh delegation even visited British Honduras to find out the possibilities of sustained means of livelihood. Later on, however, a collective decision was taken by the Sikh community to not leave the shores of Canada. They'd stay back, and struggle for establishing their identity and moorings there. It was no secret that along with other Asian emigrants, Sikhs were sidelined for very savage treatment. This is a subject matter of another chapter in this book.

Chinese migration to the US

"These people were truly, in every sense, aliens. The color of their skins, the repulsiveness of their features, their undersize of figure, their incomprehensible language, strange customs . . . conspired to set them apart."
—Hubert Howe Bancroft, History of California, 1890

According to multiple sources as well as the Journal of the San Francisco-based *Chinese Historical Society of America*, nineteen-year-old Afong Moy was the first Chinese to enter the USA in 1834. Identified as the "Chinese Lady", Moy was brought on a merchant vessel by the Carnes brothers, Nathaniel and Frederick, both traders. The vessel sailed from

Afong Moy, the first Chinese to enter the US in 1834. She was called the "Chinese Lady". Moy made a promotional tour for Chinese goods. While in Washington DC, she even met US President Andrew Jackson

her hometown in Canton, present day Guangzhou, to New York City. In order to promote the sale of Chinese goods, Moy was put in a Chinese saloon with luxurious home furnishings and décor. Her affluence and elegance no doubt piqued the curiosity of New Yorkers as did her little feet, a result of foot binding, a practice not uncommon in China for girls. After leaving New York, Moy visited many of America's largest cities, and while in Washington D.C. even had the occasion to meet with US President Andrew Jackson.

This also more or less coincided with a period when the United States was gaining new economic momentum on the West Coast, thanks to the 49-ers. The 49-ers was a term for immigrants from many parts of the world who first came across gold in California in

1849. It was the year when three hundred and twenty-five Chinese arrived in this Pacific state. As news spread, another one thousand were to reach San Francisco by 1850 and within the next two years as many as thirty thousand Chinese had migrated to the Golden City. All that glittered at the time in California was indeed gold!

In order to cement bilateral ties, the US and China signed the Burlingame Treaty in 1868. On paper, at least, it made it legal and quite uncomplicated for the Chinese to enter the United States. But the reality on the ground was in sharp contrast to the legal provisions. When white men began to lose jobs and employment opportunities to the Chinese, social unrest brewed, and the fires of hatred began to be stoked. Political and labor organizations started to rally against the Chinese immigrants, and the "cheap" labor they offered. Quite obviously they were seen as an inferior race and no bones were made about it. Even newspapers meant for balanced views and opinions threw subtlety out the window, and openly condemned those who had deigned to employ the Chinese. In a land meant to be usurped by whites, the Chinese were seen as an anomaly, an unnecessary burden that needed to be put away somewhere beyond America. Things turned so hostile within merely fourteen years of signing the Burlingame Treaty that the United States Congress rushed to pass the Chinese Exclusion Act in 1882. A complete turnaround had taken place in a short span of time. The mystery around Afong Moy and her ilk had now been replaced with animosity and rancor. The Act prohibited all immigration from China for the next ten years. The Geary Act passed in 1892 further extended this hostile law.

To their clear disadvantage, the Chinese immigrants could neither speak English with any degree of fluency nor understand the lingua franca of America. They were not conversant with the Anglo-Saxon ways of western life and culture. Since they generally came from rural China, they faced great difficulties in finding their feet in large, rapidly growing towns like San Francisco. They faced severe racism and daily humiliation on account of their physical features and their lack of skills in English. They were in certain situations subject to lynching and even hate killings. For their own personal safety, and in order to keep their linguistic identity alive, they steadily retreated into ethnic enclaves that are now popularly known as China Towns, a common phenomenon not just in the US, but in many other parts of the world.

For the Chinese, immigration to the United States had been anything but a walk in the park.

The 'Invasion' that America did not want

Chinese goods were initially brought to Manila, the capital of the Philippines, before they would sail to South America that was also called New Spain by the Spanish colonizers. Spain was at the time ruling much of South America with an iron fist, and had raised its own powerful Pacific empire. According to the *Guampedia*, for about two and a half centuries between 1565 and 1815, the Manila Galleons—the Spanish treasure fleet system—regularly crisscrossed the Pacific between Manila and Acapulco, Mexico. According to the *Asian Journal*, the galleons were built by Filipino craftsmen in shipyards just outside Manila in the port town of Cavite. While Chinese traders funded the business, the galleons were staffed by Filipino sailors with Mexico City officials supervising them.

Gradually, along with Chinese goods, cheap Chinese labor also started making its way into Latin America. The galleons at the time also came to be known as the La Nao de China (China Ships) because of the large number of Chinese labor that they shipped across the Pacific waters. Between 1847 and 1874 around one hundred and twenty-five thousand Chinese workers arrived in Cuba, at the time a Spanish colony. Another ninety-two thousand reached Peru that had ceased to be a colony of Spain. The Chinese were deployed in sugar and cotton plantations, mines, guano pits, railroads, and even as domestic workers. This loose arrangement fell somewhere between free labor and slavery. This was in essence the period of the *La Trata Amarilla*—The "Yellow Trade" and the Middle Passage.

Insofar as the Chinese are concerned, there were three waves of migration. The first one was during the *La Trata Amarilla* when they travelled in the Manila Galleons to Cuba and Peru. The second was when gold seekers came to the Pacific West, mainly California and British Columbia, to strike it rich. They also ended up working as labor in farms and plantations in the Hawaiian Islands, railroads and mines in the US, Canada, western and northern Mexico, and Peru. The third wave occurred when as a result of drastic discriminatory policies in the USA the Chinese retreated to Canada, Mexico and Latin America.

The condition of Chinese coolies inside the Manila Galleons or the La Nao de China was oppressive and dangerous. They were often tied up and herded in like cattle. Not everyone was able to survive seasickness and several did not make it to the other side of the Pacific.

Today the Chinese and Taiwanese are represented in the highest echelons of political governance. Ted W. Lieu was born in Taipei, Taiwan. He has represented California's 33rd Congressional district in the U.S. House of Representatives since 2015. Grace Meng is of Taiwanese descent and is US born. She has represented New York's 6th Congressional district since 2013. Ladda Tammy Duckworth was born in Bangkok, Thailand, to an American father and a Thai-Chinese mother. She has served as a junior US Senator from Illinois since 2017.

Japanese immigration to the USA

"My grandfathers left little behind in Japan; both second sons of peasant farmers, they had no claim to family rice plots. Yet in California they discovered Alien Land laws of 1913 and 1920 that prevented 'Orientals' from land purchases, singling out the immigrants from Asia and condemning a generation to life as laborers. But they stayed, working the fields for strangers. . . They sacrificed so the next generation could have opportunity."

—David Mas Masumoto, 2002

The Japanese had started arriving in the Hawaiian Islands in the 1860s, mainly to work the sugarcane fields. According to the publication *Personal Justice Denied*, the Chinese Exclusion Act of 1882 left a significant vacuum for cheap labor. It immediately had an impact on the migration of the Japanese who were not on the best of terms with China. Japan's population density was on the rise, intensifying pressure on working class citizens. Unemployment was going northward. As news trickled in about better living conditions in the US, the younger sons in Japanese families decided to prospect a brighter future by undertaking the voyage across the Pacific to the Land of Promise. At the time feudal Japan was still in the throes of primogeniture—a practice where the right of succession belonged only to the firstborn child and the entire real estate was passed on to the eldest son.

Between 1901 and 1908, with no restrictions in place following the Chinese Exclusion Act of 1882, around one hundred and twenty-seven thousand Japanese entered the USA. The immigration peaked in 1907, the same year the Asian Exclusion League came into being. The Japanese were economically in a tough place for another reason—the Russo-Japanese War of 1904-05. As they moved into the mainland US, the bulk of the immigrants settled in California while others moved northwards to Oregon and Washington, all in the Pacific West and Northwest. Their main vocation was farming and fishing.

If we look back at history, Oguri Jukichi and his crew were among the first Japanese to reach California after being rescued at sea from a perilous voyage. Their ship, the Tokujomaru, was spotted in distress off the coast of Santa Barbara in March 1815 by the brig Forester, an American vessel flying a British flag. Tokujomaru was bound for Edo (modern day Tokyo) when it was disabled in an oceanic storm. Many lives were lost on board while the ship drifted in the rough Pacific waters for well over a year. At the time Jukichi and a few others were rescued, several corpses were recovered

A resident of Hollywood, California, makes clear her sentiments to any Japanese looking for housing in her neighborhood, around 1923 *Courtesy of National Japanese American Historical Society*

from the ship. The Japanese sailors were later taken on the Forester to Sitka in Alaska. But the Forester's onward journey to Japan was cut short and it had to hastily anchor at the Petropavlovsk harbor in Kamchatka. A Russian ship then helped reach the Japanese survivors, including Oguri Jukichi, home.

According to *Personal Justice Denied*, digital libraries such as JSTOR, and journals such as *Agricultural History*, it becomes evident that it did not take very long before the Japanese became as dispensable as the Chinese before them. Under undue pressure from both the Asian Exclusion League and the San Francisco Board of Education, President Theodore Roosevelt was forced to renegotiate the Gentleman's Agreement of 1907. The immediate fallout was that Japan was asked not to issue valid passports for the US. Only Japanese women who were the wives of US residents were allowed to immigrate. While before 1908, seven in eight Japanese in the US were men, by 1924 this anomaly had been somewhat corrected and the ratio stood at four

women to six men. The year 1924, however, was not something the Japanese, or for that matter any Asian community in the U.S. would like to remember with any degree of fondness. By passing the Immigration Act of 1924, Congress banned the entry of all but a few select Japanese to the US. By then, of course, anti-Japanese sentiments had soared to an all-time high. Just like it was with the Chinese, the Japanese were seen as a community that was seizing away opportunities of livelihood from the white Americans, especially in the lucrative farming sector.

Fears of a "yellow peril" were back. In spite of having passed unilateral legislations such as the California Alien Land Law of 1913 that favored the white Caucasian race, the insecurity just kept snowballing. The reasons were not hard to find. According to the journal on *Agricultural History*, by 1941 Japanese Americans were producing, value-wise, between thirty and thirty-five percent of all commercial truck crops grown in California. They held dominant positions in the distribution system of fruits and vegetables. They were engaged gainfully in railroad, cannery and logging camps, mostly as laborers. There was no questioning their diligence, their unwavering ability to work long hours, and their motivation to return and give back to their motherland. The immigrants also brought with them precious knowledge of soils, fertilizers, irrigation, drainage. They had proven skills in land reclamation, and could successfully cultivate crops on previously marginalized lands. Their deep respect for the soil they worked on, shone through. All this became too much for the average Joe in the US to accept and soak in.

The Japanese Americans who remained in the US after the passing of the Immigration Act of 1924 were essentially the Issei. They constituted those that had immigrated prior to 1924. Since no new immigrants were allowed from Japan into the US after 1924, the Japanese Americans born after this cut-off year came to be known as the Nisei. They were the generation after the Isseis. Among other traits, their spoken-English skills were far superior to the generation before. In general, they became a distinct cohort, linguistically fluent but with "alien" features. Since racism was institutionalized in the US, the Nisei generation was largely restricted to marrying within its own community. The third distinct generation of Japanese Americans that came up after them was called the Sansei.

But the hardships of the Japanese did not abate. Through a draconian executive order signed on February 19, 1942 by Franklin Delano Roosevelt, the 32nd President of the United States, it was decreed that the one hundred and twenty thousand Japanese Americans in the country would be incarcerated. It mattered little that two-thirds of them were US citizens, born and raised in the United States. The order that in one stroke snatched away the freedom of one community remains an epic scar in the history of the Land of Liberty, one that would take many years to be wiped away.

According to a journal of the *American Psychological Association*, the internment was a system of legalized racial oppression, based on race or ancestry, not on the actual activities of the interned. Families with adults and children were interned together. Regardless of its size, each family was given only a single room to live in, and allowed only two suitcases to be brought in as belongings to the internment camps that were spread across ten different centers in the US, mostly in the western states. The camps were heavily patrolled by armed guards, and fenced. From being free citizens who were workers, businessmen, housewives, and school-going children, suddenly the Japanese found themselves being treated as great enemies. In its findings issued in *Personal Justice Denied* in December 1982, the Commission on Wartime Relocation and Internment of Civilians (CWRIC) said that the decision to incarcerate was based on "race prejudice, war hysteria and a failure of political leadership." The families were not allowed until the end of the war to leave the internment camps. The executive order was suspended by Roosevelt after a Supreme Court decision. By then, of course, it was too late. Much had been lost, and an entire community was now forced to rebuild lives from scratch.

On February 19, 1976, President Gerald Ford signed a proclamation that terminated the oppressive executive order 9066 and issued an apology for a national blunder committed thirty-four years ago. "We now know what we should have known then—not only was that evacuation wrong, but Japanese-Americans were and are loyal Americans. On the battlefield and at home, the names of Japanese-Americans have been and continue to be written in history for the sacrifices and contributions they've made to the well-being and to the security of this, our common Nation." In 1980, President Jimmy Carter signed a legislation that created the CWRIC. On August 10, 1988, President Ronald Reagan, based on the CWRIC recommendations, signed what came to be known as the Civil Liberties Act of 1988. On November 21, 1989, President George H.W. Bush signed a bill that authorized payments to the surviving internees. The commission had recommended that each of the internees be paid $20,000, and a letter of apology be issued. The Civil Liberties Act of 1988 covered not just the Japanese Americans, but also the Aleuts of the Aleutian Islands in Alaska who too had been unilaterally interned. February 19, the anniversary of the signing of executive order 9066, is now the Day of Remembrance.

It wasn't until 1952 that the Senate and the House voted on the McCarran Walter Act that finally allowed Japanese immigrants to become naturalized US citizens. But real freedom to immigrate came over a decade later when the Immigration and Nationality Act of 1965 ended over forty years of bans and institutionalized discriminations against Asians. It was only then that the Japanese, like other Asians, began to immigrate to the US in significant numbers once again, much like they had done soon after the passing of the Chinese Exclusion Act of 1882.

Japanese-Americans have been represented in US politics by Kyle Mark Takai, Mark Allan Takano and Mazie Keiko Hirono. Takai served in the Hawaii House of Representatives between 1994 and 2014, and represented Hawaii's 1st Congressional district in the US House of Representatives between 2015 and 2016. Takano has been the US representative for California's 41st Congressional district since 2013. He is a Sansei, the grandson of those born in Japan who immigrated to the US. His family was interned at a war relocation camp during World War II. Hirono was born in the Fukushima Prefecture in Japan to a Japanese-American mother and a Japanese father. She has served as the junior US Senator from Hawaii since 2013. She had earlier been Hawaii's ninth Lieutenant Governor between 1994 and 2002, and had been a member of the Hawaii House of Representatives between 1981 and 1995.

Historically, the United States has tested the Japanese endurance, put them on trial through fire, and stretched their patience to the limit. They deserve every ounce of success that they have today.

Filipino migration to the USA

Towards the end of the 19th century the United States defeated Spain and annexed the Philippine Islands. That is when the Americanization of the Philippines truly commenced. But the Filipinos, euphemistically referred to as "little brown brothers" by William Howard Taft, the first American Governor-General of the Philippines who'd later become the 27th President of the United States, continued to be denied US citizenship. The "little brown brothers", in practice, were never considered equals by the Caucasians.

During Spanish rule of Mexico and the southern US, a few Filipinos arrived in the United States by the Manila Galleons, used also to ferry Chinese across the Pacific to Cuba and Peru (see earlier section on Chinese immigration to the US). According to *The Times-Picayune*, a New Orleans broadsheet, Jacinto Quintin de la Cruz was likely the first Filipino to reach the US. He and other fellow countrymen raised an encampment called the Manila Village, along the northern shore of Barataria Bay, Louisiana. In time, the *Sakadas*—manual agricultural laborers—were imported into Hawaii by the Hawaiian Sugar Planters' Association, mostly between 1906 and 1946.

Filipinos pose before the ruins of their bombed-out clubhouse in Stockton, California in 1930
(Source: Filipino American National Historical Society)

Within the Philippines, the *Sakadas*, mainly from the Ilocos region of the Philippines, worked in provinces outside their own. According to records available in the *Filipino Public Relations Bureau* in the Hawaiian capital city of Honolulu, the *Sakadas* first arrived in December 1906 aboard the S.S. Doric, a British ocean liner that was making its last voyage under that name. That same month the liner was sold to a new company, and renamed Asia.

The *Sakadas* were sturdy in disposition, unflinching while working in harsh conditions, and easily the overwhelming favorites when it came to farm recruitment. The book *The Third Asiatic Invasion* mentions that the Filipinos would be the ones to usually get the backbreaking job of cultivating and harvesting asparagus, celery and lettuce. They were considered more resilient than other Asian ethnic groups and the "lazy" working-class whites.

Apart from the *Sakadas*, the other Filipino immigrants included sailors who'd joined the US Navy and the pensionados—students whose expenses were paid for by the government during studies overseas. In the US, the Filipino agricultural labor moved periodically to varying locations, depending, of course, on the seasonality of the crops. Some even went to the colder climes of Alaska to work in fish salteries and canneries.

Ironically enough, it was their diligence and ability to work harder than most others that proved to be a major disadvantage for the Filipinos. Over time, the tide of opinions within the majority working class white turned sharply against the Filipinos. The harder they worked and produced better results, the more the Filipinos came to be disliked. Like other Asian communities the perception was that they too were snatching away opportunities that were reserved for the Caucasian people. Race tensions seethed, and discrimination became more overt. And when the US economy slipped into a major recession following World War I, racial attacks became the norm. The Filipino influx into the USA was seen as the 'Third Asian Invasion', following the arrivals of the Chinese and the Japanese.

Sociologist Antonio Pido has noted that Filipino immigrants to the US across time have had to face racial discrimination and prejudice in one form or another. The early immigrants, in particular, were at a disadvantage not just because of their low socioeconomic circumstances, but also because racism in the US had turned very bitter and virulent.

There are many recordings of assaults on the Filipino community. According to the *Southern California Quarterly*, Filipinos were shot with rubber bands in October 1930 in Exeter in the San Joaquin Valley, California. Here Filipinos had replaced white labor when it came to harvesting Kadota figs and Emperor grapes. As they became successful at their work, unsurprisingly enough, their female companionship with the white community began to grow. But this kind of social mixing between browns and whites was heavily frowned upon, especially by the white, chauvinistic males. At the time it also amounted to an infraction of the California anti-miscegenation laws that criminalized interracial marriages. Social retribution for such unacceptable behavior was quite swift. The farm belonging to the rancher who'd hired the Filipinos involved with white women was burnt down with the help of the local police.

Things reached a head barely two months later in the town of Watsonville, located in the Pajaro Valley, five miles inland from the shore of Monterey Bay in California. On the midnight of January 18, 1930, a group of about five hundred white men, many of them quite young, came together outside a Filipino dance club in Watsonville's Palm Beach area. The owner, a Filipino, offered dances with the nine white women who lived there. The mob, armed with clubs and other weapons, surrounded the club and ordered the women to leave the place immediately. They also threatened to burn down the club if their orders were not heeded instantly. With their backs firmly against the wall and failing to find any escape route, the owners retaliated by opening fire. The local police somehow brought the tense situation under control with the help of gas bombs. Tensions, though, continued to simmer. A couple of days later a group of Filipino men decided to settle scores with the white men and challenged them to a duel near the Pajaro River Bridge. The ensuing violence deepened the social divide. According to the book *History of Asian Americans—Exploring Diverse Roots*, a group of Hispanic men decided to side with the white men. In no time, riots broke out, and raged uncontrolled over the next five days.

According to authors Erika Lee and Judy Yung, social discontent had reached a flash point as the Filipinos started cornering most of the labor jobs. Many of the white women also favored the more laborious Filipinos, especially since they had regular means of livelihood. In cities like Exeter, Fresno, Stockton and Danuba, the men from the Philippines were frequently attacked, mostly while they were attending street fairs or spending time at pool halls. In no time the riots spilled over into San Francisco and San Jose. No one, it appeared, liked the once-admired Filipinos anymore.

An official apology for the atrocities against the Filipinos in the US came only in September 2011. A resolution authored by Assemblyman Luis Alejo said, "Filipino Americans have a proud history of hard work and perseverance. California, however, does not have as proud a history regarding its treatment of Filipino Americans. For these past injustices, it's time that we recognize the pain and suffering this community has endured."

The Filipinos have been represented in the US political scene by Terrance John Cox who served as representative of California's 21st Congressional district between 2019 and 2021. He is the son of Chinese-American and Filipino-American parents.

Korean migration to the USA

Among the three earliest and more prominent Koreans to arrive in the US were Seo Jae-pil, Ahn Chang Ho and Syngman Rhee. Jae-pil arrived in 1884 after participating in a coup back home, at a time when Korea was a tributary state of China. After becoming an US citizen in 1890 and earning a medical degree in 1892, he petitioned the American Government for independence of his country. His home in Media, Pennsylvania, where he spent over a quarter century, is today a museum that is open to the public. Following the defeat of Japan in World War II in 1945, Jae-pil was invited to take up the presidency of Korea by fellow citizens including the intelligentsia and intellectuals, but he firmly declined.

Like Jae-pil, Ahn Chang Ho came to the US for higher education, arriving in 1902. Like Jae-pil, he also became a political activist, this time during the Japanese occupation of Korea which lasted between 1910 and 1945. A memorial stands in his honor in Riverside, California. There is also the Dosan Ahn Chang Ho Square in the City of Los Angeles in his memory. Also, the University of Southern California restored his family home in Los Angeles, such was his stature within the community.

Two years after Ahn Chang Ho, Syngman Rhee came to the US in 1904 at the age of twenty-nine, soon after being released from an incarceration that began in 1899 for anti-Japanese activities during the Sino-Japan War. In the US he pursued higher education with admirable vigor, graduating with a bachelor's degree from the George Washington University in 1907. He followed it up with a master's degree from Harvard University in 1908 and a PhD from Princeton University in 1910. Upon completion of his studies he immediately left for Korea and returned to being a political activist, like before. He rose in stature and became the founding father of Korea and the nation's first President in 1948, a position he occupied for twelve years until 1960.

According to publications available in the *University of Hawaii Press*, nearly one thousand Koreans came to the mainland US from Hawaii between 1904 and 1907. They followed the first batch of Korean laborers who had arrived in Hawaii on January 13, 1903—now known as the Korean-American Day. As they settled along the Pacific West, the Koreans took up jobs available at farms, as wage laborers in mining firms, and in railroads where they worked as section hands.

But discontent brewed largely about conditions back home in Korea. Between 1905 and 1910 several Korean immigrants to the US formed organizations in support of action against Japanese aggression in Korea. In 1909 two of the largest ones merged to form the Korean National Association. They included the likes of An Chang Ho, Syngman Rhee and Park Yong-man, a Korean nationalist and activist in the US. This umbrella organization played a decisive role during the Korean independence movement that lasted until Japan was defeated in the Second World War.

The Immigration Act of 1924, also referred to as the Oriental Exclusion Act, was a body blow for the Asian community, including the Koreans, when it came to migrating to the US. It would be another twenty-eight years before a window of opportunity for immigration to the US appeared in the form of the Immigration and Nationality Act of 1952. Koreans who were in the US were forced to live in minority enclaves until then. Gradually, 1952 onwards, they could move out to middle-class neighborhoods. When the Immigration and Nationality Act of 1965 was passed, it did away with the restrictive quota system for Asians. It enabled Koreans to move into the USA at a fast pace, surpassed only by one other Asian community, the Filipinos. According to the US Department of Homeland Security, Korea is among the top six countries of origin of immigrants to the US. Besides, data collated from the US Census Bureau and the Ministry of Foreign Affairs in

H.E. Syngman Rhee, founding father of the Republic of Korea and its first President

South Korea shows that Korean-Americans remain the fifth largest Asian-American subgroup after the Chinese, Filipino, Indian and Vietnamese-American communities. The US also remains home to the largest Korean diaspora in the world.

Due to the visible success of Asian Americans, they have often been called the "model minority." But this tag can be quite misleading. According to the Center on the Legal Profession at the Harvard Law School, "despite having the highest median income of any racial group, Asian-Americans also have the largest income gap of any racial group." This holds true for Korean-Americans as well. The *Pew Research Center's* data, for instance, shows that 12.8 percent of all Korean Americans live at or below the poverty line.

Korean-American representation in American politics has not grown at the same pace like some other Asian-American communities. It was only in 1992, over 108 years after Seo Jae-pil made his historic trip to the US, that Jay Kim, a Korean American, was elected to Congress, representing parts of Orange County, California. It took another twenty-six years before the second Korean-American, Andy Kim, was elected to Congress from New Jersey's 3rd Congressional district. Since then three Korean-American women have been elected to Congress.

From exclusion to inclusion, the Korean story in America has indeed come a full circle.

Migration of women

With the feminine movement in full swing, it is time to discuss how migrant women entered the US. Most early settlers who came due to religious persecution were a part of families or clergies who were religious guides. They came via the Atlantic Ocean and entered through the east coast. Subsequent migration of women from western countries was also with families.

Due to unfavorable immigration laws and as a result of adverse economic conditions, the Chinese and Japanese men, unable to return to their native lands, used the unscientific system of picture bridegrooms to pursue a life partner. Many of them would end up doctoring their own images in order to look rich and handsome. In turn women would send their pictures for being selected as brides. When the young brides would eventually land up on US shores to join their bridegrooms, great disappointment awaited them. The men usually looked nothing like the pictures they'd sent out. A number of Japanese men would shift to Hawaii where it was easy to marry and raise a family. Later they would enter mainland US with their families.

After the occupation of Japan by the US following the Second World War, many Japanese women chose to marry American soldiers. Even though subjugated and destroyed by America, somehow the women were drawn to the uniformed GIs and the apparent power they wielded. Many Japanese women married much against the wishes of their patriotic parents who did not like the Americans. Upon marriage to these men from the US Army these women came to be known as war brides. With time, they sponsored other members of the family and chain migration became a norm.

The romantic relationship of American soldiers and Japanese women is the subject of the 1957 movie *Sayonara*. The hero, Marlon Brando, played the role of an American air force fighter pilot who falls in love with a Japanese dancer. Even though the movie dealt with difficult subjects like institutionalized racism and prejudice, Brando mesmerized his audiences to the extent that it managed to win four Academy Awards, including acting honors for co-stars Red Buttons and Miyoshi Umeki.

Before the First World War there were only six Sikh women in the entire US, two of them sisters of one man. Here neither the picture bride nor the war bride system worked. The initial train journey from Punjab to Calcutta, followed by the arduous shipping to the Pacific West via a long layover in Hongkong was not convenient enough for Punjabi women. On the other hand, since the immigration laws were not favorable, the Sikh men could not return to Punjab to find a bride. They were pretty certain that re-entry would be denied to them. The educated among the Sikhs began to marry Anglo-Saxon white women while the labor classes settled for the Hispanic ones. The Luce-Celler Act of 1946 provided a quota for 100 Indians from Asia to immigrate to the US every year. This opened the doors for a few Sikhs to emigrate with their wives and children. The amendments to the Immigration Act in 1965 made things far easier. Many wives were able to join their husbands in the US. It also broke up some of the Hispanic marriages because now the original wives were back.

Post 1965, several Indian professional men came to the US following marriages to spouses who were American citizens. One of my doctor acquaintances commented that this was a kind of a petticoat immigrant visa being granted to such professionals. The days of picture brides and grooms are long over. Now many educated young women enter the US as a student or a professional and settle down by marriage through choice.

In 1946, President Harry S Truman signs into law the Luce-Celler Act. J.J. Singh, standing third from right, was an Indian businessman who had lobbied for the law successfully

Migration to the west did take place in large numbers. But one must not forget that there was a period in history when single western men moved to European colonies, mostly as army or civilian employees. From Great Britain alone, several single men had relations with local women referred to as Bibbies and had progeny who in turn came to be known as Tommy boys or Anglo-Indians. When travel between India and Great Britain became easier, these single men would return to their home country to find brides. It was not uncommon to find young British women waiting at the docks to meet up with well-settled returning men from India with whom they could fancy a chance of tying the nuptial knot.

Migration of children

In most cases, children came to the US along with families. A large group of children were born out of wedlock to American soldiers and local women. There were a sizable number of war orphans as well, brought in to the US from Korea, Vietnam, Cambodia and Laos. From Korea alone, eleven thousand such orphaned children were admitted to the US.

Illegal migrants

Illegal entry to the US began with the onset of exclusionary laws that prevented legal entry. Even though somewhat reduced, they continue till this day. Immigration reforms continue to be a major election agenda in the US. The immigration office reported in 2018 that as on January 1, 2015, there were some 11.9 million illegals staying in the US. Pew research put that figure at 10.5 million in 2017. The Federation of American Immigration Reforms provides figures that are far higher. It is estimated that fifty-five percent of the illegal immigrants are from Mexico alone, they cross over from the southern, porous borders. The other nations that make up the illegals are mainly El Salvador, Guatemala, India, Honduras, Philippines, China, Vietnam, and some more. It has also been recorded that only thirty-eight percent crossed the border illegally while a whopping sixty-two percent overstayed their visitor visas.

Illegal immigration is prolific business for the underworld agents and border security accomplices. The human smugglers from South America, notoriously named coyotes, charge as much as $70,000 to get a single person illegally inside the US. Similar trafficking from Punjab in India is termed *kabootar bazi,* which means flying pigeons. Here the fees are much higher given the greater distances involved, and the unfamiliarity with border language. There have been numerous stories of human cargo being left to rot inside frozen food trucks, boats capsizing in choppy ocean waters and drowning hundreds, the blazing hot deserts in the southwest US claiming lives, and much more. Whenever the border security puts a lock on one door, another one mysteriously opens up, and the illicit emigration of humans continues unabated.

After their work at the Panama Canal construction sites would get over some of the Sikhs used to enter the US through Mexico illegally at the turn of the 20th century. A retired Sikh professor in Alaska once worked as an immigration interpreter for illiterate Sikhs who entered that US state after being flown in by a Chinese airlines company. People go to any extent to get into the US even now. Another racket that has yet to see its end is the saga of fraudulent marriages that has brought notoriety to Punjab. Both expatriate Punjabi men and women get married to spouses in Punjab in exchange for a handsome sum of money. But later when it comes to sponsoring their spouses for immigration, they disappear. It is heartbreaking for the cheated spouses, and does not do the reputation of the state any good. This trend must be arrested at all costs. ∎

POEMS AND LETTERS OF MIGRANTS

Walls at Angel Island have descriptions of harassment of migrants. One says:

"The day I am rid of this prison and attain success
I must remember that this chapter once existed."

—Anonymous

Stay at home and lose opportunity
A hundred considerations lead me to sojourn in Mexico.
Hatred and prejudice against foreigners take away
our property and many lives
Unable to stay on
I sneak across the border to the American side
But bump into an immigration officer,
who sternly throws the book at me
And orders my expulsion back to China.

—Folk song by expelled Chinese-Mexican

"Huge dreams of fortune go with me to foreign lands. Across the oceans."
—Hom, a Japanese poet in Songs of Gold Mountain.

"My beloved wife, it has been several autumns now since your dull husband left you for a far remote alien land. Because I can get no gold, I am detained in this secluded corner of a strange land."
—Husband in the US writes to his wife in China

You have been away from home for years. During that time your second elder brother died. Then your father died, and then your eldest brother died too. I am old and weak and I may die at any moment. You should save some money and should come back at least next year. Come back, don't forget your mother please.
—The pleas of a mother in China to a son in the US.

CHAPTER 3

DISCRIMINATION AGAINST MIGRANTS

Discrimination is universal in all host societies. New immigrants are the first to face job cuts during a recessionary period. This is especially true if they are from the Negroid or Mongoloid races. The attacks come from white supremacists whose latent hatred for other races come to the fore at any such time of economic crisis. Migrants not only have it tough while competing for local jobs, but their culture itself is always under threat. Besides, hybrid marriages are not easy to handle. The quantum of infectious diseases that came in with migrants has subsided, but the entry of terrorists and fanatics, drug dealers and peddlers and other criminals is a new threat.

Many countries have a clear policy of not granting permanent residence or PR to migrants. Only temporary work visas are issued. The economic benefits that migrants bring in are often ignored. For instance, migrants have infused a great sense of enterprise and created numerous businesses, small or large, in nations such as the US, Canada and Australia. Big names such as Google, Tesla, Moderna would not have happened if migrants had not come in.

What causes discrimination

When immigrants reach greener pastures, challenges begin to crop up. They are related to religion, race, identity, color, culture, manners, language and justice systems. They continue to be major challenges for new immigrants even today. In subsequent chapters we'll be dealing with each of these challenges.

God and religion

From the time humans have been around they have deeply understood that there is a Higher Power at work that makes this universe function timelessly with clockwork precision, beyond the comprehension of the ordinary human mind. The galaxies and solar systems play a stellar role over eternity. Unconditionally, the earth goes around the sun, day in and day out, and has been doing so for billions of years. Abundant sunlight is the purest source of life in all forms, and its magic makes everything in nature so joyful. Nature ceaselessly mystifies—the winds blow, rains fall, flowers grow, ice melts, trees shed leaves, seasons change, rivers flow into seas, glaciers sweep down mountain faces and so much more. Man simply has no control over these stupendous, all-powerful phenomena and in spite of the great advances in science, technology and health, he finds himself largely inconsequential and insignificant before the majestic plans of nature. Since this realization dawned early in civilization, man has worshipped the Highest Power—God Almighty—for thousands of years. From the time his consciousness allowed him to grow spiritually, man has worshipped nature. Then religions came up, further bolstering and reaffirming this belief system in the Supreme Power.

Not all religions, though, are organized. For instance, there are no formal holy books and scriptures in many tribal cultures and First Nation people around the world. That doesn't stop them from carrying out their spiritual practices and evolving into higher beings. Organized religions are more orthodox and fundamental in approach. They abide by scriptures and texts and are not easily accepting of other belief systems. In fact, civilizations have clashed for millennia due to this intolerance and non-acceptance. It has been proven time and again that when it comes to religion, one man's belief system has not worked for another. Due to the intolerant and bigoted ones, religion has given rise to militancy, and this is a grave challenge that the world faces. There are also religions which are accepting of multiple belief systems and follow the path of peace and Ahimsa. Overall, my view is that the educated world could be turning more spiritual than religious.

God

The concept of multiple Gods and Goddesses appears in Hindu scriptures dating back to 4000 BCE. The Romans worshiped multiple Gods and Goddesses around the 6th century BCE. The first concept of one God appears in the 8th century BCE. The Jewish prophets spoke of one God in the Old Testament. Let's take a quick look at the central beliefs of different civilizations and religions.

Greek

Plato talked about "a strong belief in a supernatural power that controls human destiny." The Greeks believed in many powerful deities for different functions and determined natural forces.

Egyptian

The Egyptians had many deities. Egyptian Pharaohs had both religious and temporal monarchy.

Judaism

"In the beginning God (Elohim) created the heavens and earth."—Genesis.

Christianity

God is the Eternal Being who created and preserves all things. Christians believe God to be both transcendent (wholly independent of and removed from the material universe) and immanent (involved in the world).

Islam

In Islam, God is the Absolute One, all-powerful and all-knowing ruler and creator of everything in existence. Islam emphasizes that God is strictly singular, unique, inherently one, and also merciful and omnipotent. God exists neither in the realm of the material or the spiritual.

Hinduism

The medieval scripture Rig Veda says God manifested as Creator of the Universe in the beginning, encompassing the collective totality as it is. Like the Pharaohs, Lord Ram hailed from a royal family and is revered by millions of Hindus. Likewise, Prince Siddhartha Gautama became Lord Buddha. Hinduism has many deities.

Sikhs

Sikhism's central message is that there is only one God, and He is Truth. God exists in all of creation, has no fear, nor any hatred, is timeless and universal. The grace of the Guru (Mool Mantar) is the path to God realization.

Deism

This is the belief that God created the universe but has left the responsibility of day-to-day functioning to life on earth. God is not responsible for calamities and famines on earth.

Pantheism

This system of belief says God is present in everything in the universe including humans, plants, other species and nature. This concept is close to the Sikh philosophy.

Humanism

This is the belief in caring for humanity, and this remains the core philosophical objective.

Atheism and agnosticism

Sañjaya Belatti Putra, an Indian ascetic philosopher who lived around the same time as Mahavira and Gautam Buddha about two thousand five hundred years ago, was a proponent of the ajñana school of thought. His teachings have been described as agnostic. Others like the ancient Greek philosopher and mathematician Pythagoras wanted to keep the divine and the human separate. In 1869, Thomas Henry Huxley, a biologist and anthropologist, came up with the term agnosticism. Christopher Hitchens, author and journalist, called himself an anti-theist, finding all religions as false, harmful and authoritarian. Steven Pinker, cognitive psychologist who adopted atheism at the age of thirteen, has remained a cultural Jew.

A Pew survey (2018) has revealed that eighty percent of Americans believe in God. Of the remaining twenty percent, nine percent do believe that a higher power and spiritual force is at work, while the rest ten percent deny that.

Seventeen scholars of religion were present during a discussion on the future of religion that was moderated by Ayesha Khan in 2020. The Sikh religion was represented by Simranjeet Singh. The scholars concluded that the number of believers around the globe may be shrinking while that of non-believers is likely on the rise. The Pew survey had similarly revealed that adherence to religion was on the decline and the atheists were on the rise.

God, religion and my family

I was born into a Sikh family that has a firm belief in God and the Sikh religion. Some traditions in my family flowed through Hinduism, in spite of the Singh Sabha movement. For instance, every year my mother visited the shrine of Sitala Devi, a Hindu deity, for protection against smallpox, chicken pox and measles. She would light up a diya, a small clay lamp, feed it with clarified butter known as ghee, and seek the blessings of the deity. My grandmother, at times of drought, would sing, *"Rabba, Rabba mein wara sadi kothi dane pa."* This means God, please bring us rain so that we may have grains to store.

I prayed for better grades in school. In medical college the going got tough and even though I was praying, my attempts at getting a college degree in the first and second attempts proved futile. My parents insisted that I pray more, and they also prayed for me. When I finally succeeded and cleared my examinations my parents instilled in me the virtues of praying.

After I got married, they prayed for a grandson, also because I had been blessed with a daughter earlier. When my second daughter arrived, they insisted that we pray more for having a son. One weekend I rang them up and announced that they would soon be blessed with a grandson. My parents wished to know how I was so sure? They knew that I did not believe in astrologers and soothsayers. Well, at the time sex determination was possible, and that's how we came to know.

My parents were baffled by the landing on the moon, wireless communication and cloning of Dolly the sheep.

Religion

Various lexicons have described the word religion in different ways. In essence, though, it implies a personal set or institutionalized system of religious attitudes, beliefs and practices in the service and worship of God, and the supernatural. Its origins lie in the Latin religiō which means reverence for God and holiness.

Organized Hinduism and Judaism are around four thousand to four thousand five hundred years old. Sikhism came into being at the start of the 16th century. The religious leader was the one who came to convey the message of God.

Religion, though, came to be associated with the ruler as well. Henry VIII, the King of England in the first half of the 16th century propagated the divine right of kings that was in opposition to Papal supremacy. He had fallen out with Pope Clement VII over the annulment of the first of his six marriages—to Catherine of Aragon.

Clash of the monastery and rulers can be seen during the times of Patriarch Nikon of the Russian Orthodox Church and Tsar Alexis of Russia in the 17th century. For several years Patriarch Nikon overshadowed the Tsar when it came to being a dominant religious and political figure. He was ultimately stripped of his priestly powers by the ruler.

Religious turf wars

Throughout history every religion wanted to control the world, resulting in the use of hard and soft power, that is wars and charity. In the Encyclopedia of Wars, Axelrod and Phillips claim that 121 out of a total 1,763 wars in history were fought over religion. Here is my take on the subject.

1. All new religions will face challenges from existing ones. Religion has turned no less competitive than today's corporate world.

2. For instance, paganism opposed an organized religion like Judaism.

3. Monotheistic religions were opposed by polytheists.

4. Christianity, an offshoot of Judaism, was opposed by Jews and the Romans.

5. Jesus Christ was crucified by the Romans.

6. Multiple denominations of Christianity fought one another. They include Protestants, Catholics, Mormons and others. Resultant atrocities have led to displacement of humanity to safer grounds. The US, to begin with, was a Puritan Christian nation.

7. The Afrikaans of South Africa were a displaced group of French Protestants (Huguenots).

8. The Buddhists were pushed out by Hinduism from India in ancient India. In modern India, however, Nalanda is being restored, while the Dalai Lama who has fled China has his base in Dharamshala, India.

9. The Zoroastrians were persecuted by the Islamic regime in Iran and pushed out. They took refuge in India. Likewise, the Bahais faced discrimination in orthodox Iran. They have a large following in India.

10. Persecuted Jews fled to India and found shelter in the country.

11. Hindus, Muslims and Sikhs were displaced during the painful partition of India.

12. Muslim Rohingyas have been persecuted by Buddhists in Myanmar.

13. The Islamic sects of Shias and Sunnis are constantly at war while the Ahmadis and Sufis are not considered mainstream and, therefore, are declared outcastes.

14. Atheism, agnosticism and humanism are a challenge to all established religions.

15. Minority religious groups are gradually leaving Islamic Middle East.

One is reminded of the famous words of Urdu poet Mohammad Iqbal penned a century ago. They say, *"Mazhab nahi sikhata aapas mein*

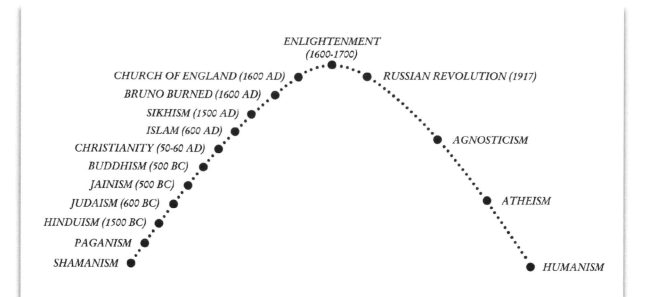

ENLIGHTENMENT
(1600-1700)

CHURCH OF ENGLAND (1600 AD)   RUSSIAN REVOLUTION (1917)
BRUNO BURNED (1600 AD)
SIKHISM (1500 AD)
ISLAM (600 AD)
CHRISTIANITY (50-60 AD)   AGNOSTICISM
BUDDHISM (500 BC)
JAINISM (500 BC)
JUDAISM (600 BC)   ATHEISM
HINDUISM (1500 BC)
PAGANISM
SHAMANISM   HUMANISM

The curve reveals the growth of organized religions till the Enlightenment. The sixteenth and seventeenth-century thinkers in Europe gave credence to reason, individualism, skepticism, and scientific knowledge. This movement further nurtured the growth of agnosticism, atheism, and humanism. The communist movements of the early twentieth century minimized the role of the church and organized religion in some countries. It appears that religion will stay but will not grow. Scientific knowledge, modernity, education, and resistance to social evolutionary changes will further add to the slow demise of religion.

bair rakhna." It means religion never preaches that we divide ourselves through animosity. But the fanaticism in the name of religion being practiced in many parts of the world doesn't quite do justice to his poetic words.

In the US and Canada, both initially Christian Protestant Puritan nations, other religious denominations like Catholics, Jews, non-Christians like the Chinese and Japanese, and Hindus (mostly Sikhs) were not treated at par. While Catholics have found social parity in America, the Jews still face antisemitism.

After the 9/11 bombings of the twin towers at the World Trade Center, hate waves have been unleashed against Sikhs, primarily due to a groundswell of Islamophobia and mistaken-identity. Turbaned Sikhs have been confused for Muslims from the Arab world. Similar had been the situation soon after the Iranian hostage crisis in 1979 when fifty-two American diplomats were held hostage by supporters of the Iranian Revolution for four

hundred and forty-four days. Of late, matters have exacerbated due to a mix of resurgent white nationalism, a toxic political discourse, and xenophobic sentiments.

Future of religion

The future of religion was discussed by seventeen scholars. The opening statement was made by Aysha Khan in 'Religion News Service' (2020). On behalf of the Sikhs, the viewpoints were put forth by Simran Jeet Singh. Professor Ryan Burge stated that there was a slow, continuous increase in NONES (word coined by Barry Kosmin), that of people who were unaffiliated with any religion. By the year 2030, NONES will be the largest group. This increase was at the cost of other religions with maximum impact on Protestants.

Following are the results of a survey suggesting some decline of one organized religion. The figures of other religions are not available. Pew telephone survey (October 17, 2019) of Christianity in the US revealed that in 1990, eighty-five percent believed in religion. The number reduced to eight-one percent and six tenths in 2001, seventy-eight percent in 2012, and sixty-five percent in 2018-2019. In the same period the number of 'nones' (non-believers) increased from sixteen percent to twenty-six percent.

Religion is still a powerful political tool in Southeast Asia. Pakistan, India and Myanmar are current examples. Political Islam is embedded in the Middle East. Educated societies are gradually separating religion from the state as was done during the enlightenment in the west. Half a century down the road these man-made institutions might be considered in dim light and held responsible for many of the afflictions of homo sapiens.

Who needs religion and why?

All human beings need counseling and sharing of pain, physical and emotional. Religion is the one many lean upon during those times. Jesse Ventura, Governor of Minnesota (1999-2003) in an interview went a step further and commented, "Organized religion is a sham and a crutch for weak-minded people who need strength in numbers." In an interview with CNN in October 2010 he said that religion is the "root of all evils."

Humans were not satisfied with God alone and intermediaries appeared in religions of various types. Religious people describe all the virtues of religion, not realizing or denying that during most of the major wars in the past religion was the culprit. "So far we have been fighting the wrong enemy, the real enemy is religion." (Moonzajer).

All humans seek happiness. Does being religious give happiness? Sillick and colleagues (2016) in their study did not find any relationship between religiosity and happiness. The 2018 UN World Happiness report revealed that most atheist (and socially well-off) countries are the happiest while religious countries are poor and unhappy. Finland is the happiest, while Africa and the Middle East are the most unhappy.

Religion and America

The US Supreme Court justice David J Brewer in 1905 said, "The United States is a Christian nation." In Christian west, you are better off as Christian and worse off if you are a Muslim. Sikhs with turban are confused with Muslims and face hate crimes resulting in serious injuries in some cases, and even death (Republica, 2017). Asian religions, including Hinduism, are not spared. The Catholics who once faced discrimination have gradually overcome it. Jewish antisemitism periodically raises its ugly head.

Religious and ethnic identity

Many new immigrants stand out due to their distinct identity and religious symbols as they enter a new country. They may look different from those in the host nation.

Sikh with turbans, Hindu women with sarees and bindi, the burka and hijab of Muslim women, dress of Amish women with long skirts and covered heads, orthodox Jews with black robes, beard and Krupa, the saffron robes of Buddhist monks, are not considered a good fit with Anglo Saxon hosts. It has resulted in discrimination, hate crime, religious and ethnic profiling. Identity has many other components, but appearance is most visible at the first look.

Religious, ethnic and cultural enclaves

These enclaves are a blessing for new immigrants as they face early challenges of religion, color, language, culture, manners and etiquette of host communities. In the US, these are Chinatown, little Italy, little Havana and Korea town. Likewise, there are orthodox Jews in New York, Amish and Mennonites in Pennsylvania and Ohio, and Hutterites in Canada and North Dakota.

Ethnic enclaves are stepping stones and places of acclimatization for newcomers. The dense population of ethnic groups is also politically helpful to them.

Sikhs had enclaves at Yuba City/Marysville in Sacramento Valley and at El Centro in the Imperial Valley of California. Sikhs have ethnic enclaves in Vancouver and Surrey in British Columbia. The ethnic values of original language, culture and manners, reduce as migrants move out of enclaves for better opportunities outside.

Alex Sangha (2012) discussed the pros and cons of ethnic enclaves in Canada. Similar situation prevails in the US. Ethnic density helps in politics, but is an obstacle to acculturation, assimilation and economic opportunities. These enclaves also create some hatred among the host community and breed ethnic criminal gangs.

Race

Since humans from different geographical locations look different physically and in terms of skin color, efforts have been made to divide humans or homo sapiens into different sub-species. Carl Von Linnaeus in 1758 described four distinct subspecies— Native American, West Eurasian, East African and Sub-Saharan African. The color varies in these geographical locations. Red, white, dark and black would go for native Americans, Europeans, Asians and Africans respectively.

Blumenback (1779) later added brown races. Asian Indians fall in the brown category. In 1920, Stoddard defined four colors for the human race. They are black, brown, yellow and white. In the mid-20th century, Carleton Coon, on the basis of color and facial features, divided the human race into Caucasoid, Negroid, Mongoloid, Capoid and Australoid.

This concept of race has been rejected by anthropologists who view humanity as a related genetic continuum. The physical features and colors are evolutionary adjustments. The above classifications became redundant with progress in genomics. Color is the first important marker of one's country of origin and stands up on first sight in America as a determinant of discrimination. Mongoloid facial features follow.

The physical differences have been wrongly used to classify races as superior or inferior, and this has spilled into the national and political arena. The migration of one different looking group into a dominant other group has inevitably led to discrimination.

Asians and blacks are disliked and discriminated against in western white countries. Studies (Posten and Saenz 2019) reveal that by 2050, or even earlier, the whites in the US will become minorities, a humongous worry for those who claim to be the founders of this country. The ownership of the US has moved from natives to white. In coming times, it may shift to brown and black people. This is worrisome to many who claim to be the earlier occupants of America. Hence white supremacist outfits such as the Ku Klux Klan and Proud Boys have come up. These groups advocate the slashing down in immigration numbers, especially from the darker skinned nations. This, however, can have adverse economic consequences, as warned by experts.

Color

In his book *The Rising Tide of Color—The Threat Against White World Supremacy* (T Lathrop Stoddard 1920), the author defined four colors for the human race. They are black, brown, yellow and white. America was inhabited by natives, and white migrants eliminated them. Later, black people were brought as slaves, and brown-skinned humans came from southeast Asia, neighboring South America and southern Europe. 'Yellow peril' was a term used to describe the threat posed by Japanese and Chinese migrants to America. The white Protestant remained in the saddle.

Skin color is a result of the natural selection theory of Darwin. In equatorial regions the dark skin is a protection against intense sun and ultraviolet light. Light skin in such conditions would result in folate depletion, damage to DNA and neural tubes, and defects in embryos. It can also cause skin cancer. Dark skin in low UV light environments of the US, away from the equator, can cause Vitamin D

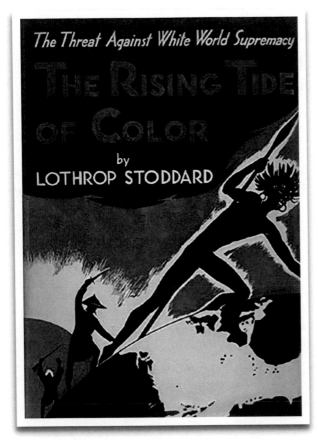

At the bottom of the cover is a Sikh with a white turban

deficiency, and even rickets. The evolutionary change in skin color is a long process, but population mix and amalgamation moves faster to bring about its change.

Nature, the mother of evolution, did not anticipate that the equatorial people with melanosis—those with the excess skin pigment, melanin—would move north and be considered a lower race, while ironically enough, the melanin-deficient white skinned people would be considered superior when it came to race. Nature, perhaps, is aware of this timeless black and white conflict and, therefore, did not include either while designing the beautiful rainbow in the skies!

Dislike for black color has been a part of human history and probably began with darkness at night when artificial light sources were non-existent. Who or what is to blame? The rotation of the earth around the sun that causes darkness at night, or the shield of melanin created against UV in the skin of equatorial humans?

Dark has become symbolic for bad. Crimes are committed in darkness. White flags are raised for peace and surrender, black flags as protest. Black is worn on funerals. When we feel that we've been slighted, we say, it is unfair, or not fair, implying once again that what is not fair cannot be right.

Philosophically, one says, I was kept in the dark about an issue. Dark clouds on the horizon spell bad outcomes. There is black market and the stock market has 'dark pool' trading. In Punjab "*tera muh kala*" (you have a dark face) implies you've been shamed. One punishment for crime in Punjab, India, was to put the offender on a donkey, color his face black, and circulate him in town to shame him. Recent (2020) anti-farmer laws in India are called *kala kanun* (black laws).

Daisy Grewal (2017) did a psychological study of black and wrote "Bad is Black" in the Scientific American. There was an ingrained ugly bias in western countries against black even before slavery. The Oxford English dictionary describes black as something that is "deeply stained with dirt, soiled, dirty, foul, has a dark or deadly purpose, is malignant, pertains to or involves death, is deadly, baneful, disastrous, sinistrous, foul, iniquitous, atrocious, horribly wicked, and indicating disgrace, censure, and liability for punishment.

Bias against the color black became more pronounced during the times of slavery. Similar bias to a lesser degree is directed at people with brown color of Hispanic and South Asian descent as well as the yellow Mongoloid races. This bias against yellow, brown and black color has been the subject of books and news media.

Stoddard (1920) provides a historical narrative about the achievements of various races that have conquered various landmasses on earth. The Nordic race dominated with the colonization and subjugation of the yellow Mongoloid races of China and Japan and other Pacific Rim nations. Also, the black and brown races of Africa and southeast Asia were conquered. This began with Alexander the Great and was followed by colonization by the western white race. The author also goes on to describe the attack on the white race by the Mongolian hordes of Genghis Khan, and the brown conquerors of the Ottoman Empire. The defeat of Russia by Japan in the Russo-Japanese War in 1904 was termed the yellow victory.

All the points mentioned above by Stoddard are in the context of migration of Asiatic races to North America. They include the yellow race of China and Japan, brown and black races of South and Southeast Asia, such as the Hindoos (mainly Sikhs). He alerts white America of the perils of the invasion of yellow, brown and black races who were begging to enter the continent in the early 20th century, but whose presence and multiplication over time could put in danger an entire culture, civilization, prosperity and even religious identity. At the time he wrote his book, Stoddard failed to mention the red and brown races of South America, largely Hispanic. They are today a dominant non-white population segment, at least in the US.

Stoddard did predict, with some amount of accuracy, that whites would be expelled from black and brown colonies and even expressed fear that collectively the black, brown, yellow and red (Spanish and native Americans) races would outnumber white Americans in the future. The cover of the book shows a Sikh with a white turban below black and yellow colored individuals.

According to the Naturalization Act of 1790 only the free white people of good character could become naturalized citizens in the U.S. This excluded native Americans, indentured servants, slaves, free blacks and Asians. Early Sikh migrants along with other colored people were subjected to anti-citizenship laws. To the color bias were added religion, language, dress and culture.

Web DuBois wrote that the 'color line' still persists. Currently, color bias reduces as one moves upwards' from the shade of black to brown, and yellow to white. This bias may turn favorable for the darker skinned by 2050, when black and brown will outnumber white in the US (Posten and Saenz). The reducing birth rate among the white population further makes the outcome favorable for non-whites. According to William Frey (2014), the US will become a white minority nation by 2045. What will America look like in millions of years? The dark color will disappear and will not be needed for protection as colored people will move away from the ultraviolet light of the equator. Will racial bias then disappear? Color does matter. It is quite evident that white Sikhs of 3HO, an offshoot Sikh organization, are far less prone to hate crimes in spite of wearing the turban as part of their identity.

If black or brown is bad, what can be done to treat or cover it? The late American entertainer Michael Jackson gradually developed light skin on the face, and it became a subject of intense media speculation on what he was inflicting on himself. His dermatologist revealed that he had developed an autoimmune disorder of the skin called vitiligo that was causing a loss of melanocytes that produce the dark pigment called melanin. It was resulting in white patches of skin and progressively affecting his entire body.

In many Asian and African countries medicines like Konica Acid, Hydroquinone, Alpha hydroxy acid and Glutathione are used to lighten skin. Mercury compounds used in the past are now illegal due to side effects. Darwinian reduction in dark color will take millions of years after man moves away from the equator. Should one wait that long for human bias to wither away?

In the midst of all the negativity around the color black, there are some positives. A Punjabi singer in order to boost the morale of the dark-skinned people of India wrote, "*Kala sha, kala mera, kala hey sardar, goreyan nu daffa karo.*" (Black is beautiful, get rid of the white). Many want to dye their hair black in order to look younger and to hide their white hair which is a result of aging. Also, those suffering from vitiligo—the condition that Michael Jackson had—are desperate to darken the white.

Continuing with the positives, the recent

'Black Lives Matter' movement in the US following the killing of George Floyd brought focus back on African-American heritage. Beyoncé released the visual ode *Black is King*.

We've seen how blacks are at the receiving end in a white society. Now let's take a look at what is happening to the white race in Negroid societies. Since most African and Caribbean nations are now free from their colonizers, the whites who ruled them have mostly left. The few that are there have a minority status. In South Africa we've become accustomed to the term "reverse racism." White Afrikaners of Dutch ancestry who once ruled over the native black population through the oppressive and inhuman apartheid policy are today in a minority. There is a backlash because of the historical wrong inflicted on the blacks. As a result, businesses and farms belonging to Afrikaners have been taken over, causing a major exodus of the white population to nations in Europe, America and significantly to Australia which itself officially practiced a White Policy until 1973. This is unfortunate, for the great liberator of South Africa, the legendary Nelson Mandela, had pleaded with the black race that in the interest of sustainable economic growth of the rainbow nation the white population should not be impacted adversely. This, however, has not been the case.

Albinism has created an artificial white group among blacks in Africa. This is a genetic disorder causing lack of melanin. These people, though, are looked down upon in spite of their whiter skins. Clearly, what is sauce for the goose is not sauce for the gander.

Manners, language, new culture and civility

Immigrants from developing nations are often hated for their manners, mannerisms and conduct. People from the developing world speak quite loudly in public places, something that the local Americans quite dislike. Abrasive behavior also does not go down too well with the Americans. For instance, while "thank you" and "sorry" are used very frequently by Americans, the Asian population is not very adept at using these terms. They are not quick to apologize, nor prolific in the usage of the word "thank you." Americans are also likely to wave out to strangers while walking in a park, while Asians maintain an unsmiling countenance, a result of the way they are brought up. Most Sikhs who came to America at the turn of the 20th century had little education and were largely unlettered. Their personal habits, including the sense of hygiene, had nothing much to cheer about.

Many of them used to spit in public without a thought in India and found that the same action brought ridicule, taunt and derision in America. Some of them were shouted at for violating social norms. The Indian habit of answering nature's call on the roadside has been frowned upon. The same, abominable habit often made them social misfits in North America. Another loathsome inclination among Indian men has been to stare at women. In white America, Indians ogled at skirt-clad women, often staring disconcertingly long at their legs. This was looked down upon as outrightly uncivilized and perverted by the white population and earned the men from Punjab no brownie points from the white population. I can only shudder to think what would be going through their minds in today's world of mini-skirts, bikinis, scrub suits with hanging drawstrings in front.

In general, Indian men were also rather thrifty when it came to offering tips after service. They spoke half-baked English at work but when it came to demeaning the locals they would turn to the Punjabi dialect. Needless to say, it did not win them too many friends in the local society.

There were other reasons for hatred, but these were the white man's making. Sikhs were ridiculed for wearing turbans. The white people looked at them as rags and towels. American colloquialism for new immigrants can be both embarrassing and unpleasant. I take this opportunity to share some of my own experiences when I landed in the US in 1967, completely unaware of the local lingo and daily conversational style. My host parents once invited me over and asked me, "Do you want a cookie?" It was as though someone had thrown a curve ball at me. Flummoxed, I was at a loss for words. In my college if someone was called a cookie, it wasn't very charitable. It implied that the person wasn't the brightest going around. Here in America, cookie means biscuit. The new culture was slowly seeping into my consciousness, but I wasn't always ready for the new words. Over the years there are many more words which have now become part of my lexicon. In America we say gas, instead of petrol, hood instead of bonnet, fall instead of autumn, subway instead of metro, vacation instead of holiday, apartment instead of flats. The list is long.

On a funnier note, my senior physician at Drake Memorial Hospital in Cincinnati, Ohio, asked me about the disposition of a particular patient. I promptly responded that the patient was happy and in a good mood. He rephrased his query: "Where is he going after being discharged?" Another good friend of mine from India patiently waited for over an hour after his medical residency interview was over, all because the director interviewing him had said, "see you later." The director, of course, had not wanted my friend to wait outside, but that is what American English initially did to people like us.

I personally felt handicapped when in resident physicians' gatherings most of the conversation centered around American football, baseball, and, of course, politics. I would definitely feel like a rank outsider during those moments. It's the plight of every new immigrant. Until, of course, you've learnt that the American way is about baseball, apple pie, hot dog and Chevrolet. Once you've adapted to that, you can start working on Americanizing your accent. But that is something that is not so easy. After all, the accent is imprinted and impaled in the speech center in the brain.

Justice system

The justice system and law enforcement have a bias against color and not against the new immigrants as such. White immigrants new to America are treated far better than the African Americans who have been in the US for generations. Who can forget the case of Rodney King? America has had its darker moments—the Greenwood, Tulsa massacre of 1921, for instance. It has also had its Rosa Parks moment, and much more. It's not a history the country can be proud of. The common thread in all these incidents was the way law enforcement failed the black citizens of this country.

One cannot sweep things under the carpet. Law enforcement has a linear relationship with the shade of skin. In descending order, the treatment seems to get unfairer. At the top of the pecking order are the white Anglo Saxons, followed by the brown, yellow and black populations. But what is admirable in this great nation is that the justice system becomes fairer at the level of appeals court and the higher courts.

When it comes to the Sikh population in America, I cannot say with any degree of certainty that they are unfairly treated by the law enforcement. But when I see that turbaned Sikhs are targets of violent attacks and racial taunts, I can only say that somewhere law enforcement has its work cut out. They need to step up when it comes to protecting the fundamental rights of every citizen in this country, including Sikhs and other minorities. People like Bhagat Singh Thind and Pakher Singh Gill went through humiliation in US courtrooms. In 1968 I was given a ticket by a traffic policeman for a minor fender-bender automobile incident. There was no fact finding and it was a one-sided, unilateral decision, which still rankles me. But those were times when America was a nation that was meant for whites. Things need to change for the better now. ∎

Discrimination is universal in all host societies. New immigrants are the first to face job cuts during a recessionary period. This is especially true if they are from the Negroid or Mongoloid races. The attacks come from white supremacists whose latent hatred for other races come to the fore at any such time of economic crisis

❀

The word 'brain drain' was coined by the Royal Society of London when a large-scale movement of highly-skilled scientists took place from war-torn Europe to the US, soon after the Second World War. This created a vacuum in Britain that was filled up by the influx of many highly-skilled doctors and engineers from developing countries

CHAPTER 4

ADAPTATION, ACCULTURATION, ASSIMILATION, MELTING POT

When Europeans discovered the 'New World' as they called the Americas, it was already inhabited by people whom they had identified as Indians. Over time, in North America, the Indians were described as Red Indians because of the burnt tone of their skin. Since the connotation 'Red' prefixed to Indian had an element of derisiveness attached to it, they came to be known as Native Indians. Today, those terms have been replaced by First Nation, indicating the original settlers who came to occupy the soils of the Americas thousands and thousands of years ago.

The First Nation tribes had their own domains, primarily headed by chieftains. They had a clan mentality and preferred to live in isolated habitats, without assimilating with others. The First Nation people refused to be a part of the culture that the Europeans brought with them. Unsurprisingly, the Europeans looked at them as enemies in an alien land. Clashes began over territorial occupation, and soon, due to their superior arms and ammunition, the Europeans decided to do what is commonly known as ethnic cleansing. They wiped out large swathes of the First Nation populations settled all over the Americas. In South America such ethnic cleansing was carried out by the Spaniards and the Portuguese, and to a lesser extent by the Dutch, French and British. In North America, Spaniards, Nordics, Anglo-Saxons, French and Germanic races competed for territorial supremacy. The sufferers were the natives.

The majority of the Founding Fathers of the United States were of English (Anglo-Saxon) ancestry. Thus, an Anglo-Saxon Protestant culture was created and the prevalent language became English in the US, and English and French in Canada. All the other migrants from western and southern Europe had to fit in with this imposing culture, and had to speak English. The progeny of African slaves born in the US began to speak English as well. Even the Hispanics who remained after the Spanish territories went to the Anglo-Saxons are English speaking. There is, however, a large group of illegal immigrants from Central and South America that is deficient in English and can hardly speak the language.

The "Asiatic hordes" as the white man would describe the immigrants from Asia began to come to the Americas in the late 19th and early 20th centuries. The first lot came from China. They were followed by the Japanese, Hindus (mostly Sikhs), Filipinos and Koreans mostly (see separate chapter on Human Migration). Following the First and Second World Wars, migration from southern and eastern Europe increased. The holocaust and its aftermath saw Jews fleeing Europe and landing up in the US in large numbers.

Today, the modern-day US has people from practically every nation on earth. Similarly, people of all religions live here. The French-American writer J. Hector St. John de Crèvecœur in 1784 published a two-volume version of *Letters from an American Farmer*. In that he described through the eyes of the fictional narrator James, an American farmer, this: "I can relate to a family, where the grandfather was English, wife Dutch and the four sons were married to wives from four different nations." This typifies what modern America is, an assimilation and amalgamation of different cultures.

In his 1964 book *Assimilation in American Life: The role of race, religion, and national origins,* Milton M Gordon has spoken about seven types of assimilation. He has also elaborated on the concepts of acculturation, amalgamation and melting pot. He pointed out two kinds of cultural traits—the intrinsic, consisting of religion, music, language, literature, entertainment and a sense of the past, and the extrinsic comprising dress, manners, accent and emotional expression. While the extrinsic is relatively easy to assimilate, the intrinsic takes much time and effort. For Sikhs, turban is not an extrinsic cultural trait, rather it is an intrinsic part of

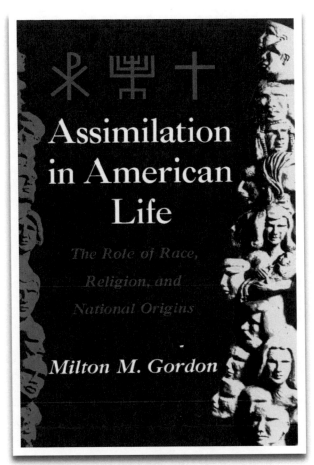

their religion. Amalgamation, the crossing of different religions and cultures, accentuates the process of assimilation.

Let's take a look at the modes of assimilation of new immigrants.

Anglo conformity

This would mean dissociating oneself from the home culture completely and becoming a part of the western, host country culture. Anglo conformity has been diluted gradually with continued immigration from different countries and cultures. The colored and brown will gradually outnumber the white, as we've discussed separately earlier in the book. America, therefore, will not have pure Anglo conformity, going forward.

Cultural pluralism

Most of the early immigrants to America were Protestant Christians who dominated the demography of a young nation. The Catholic Irish and Jews were discriminated against. There were also sharp cultural differences as

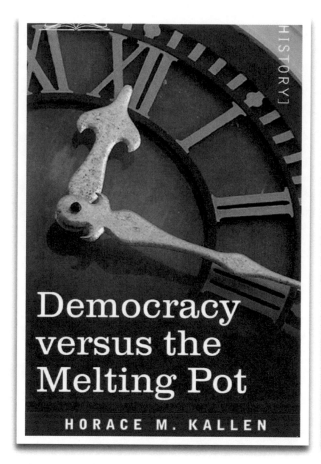

migrants came from far and wide. The original settlers, of course, wanted a quick Americanization with Anglo conformity. In order to counteract this idea and movement, Horace M Kallen, a Harvard-educated philosopher, came up with a book in 1915 titled *Democracy Versus the Melting-Pot—A Study of American Nationality* in which he promoted the idea of cultural pluralism. In this concept, immigrants of the same culture or nation could live as isolated, local communities with less mixing and amalgamation. That way they could retain their language and religion, and yet remain part of a larger democracy. Kallen used the term 'orchestration', akin to many different musical instruments producing the desired music. This experiment that was tried by Scandinavian and German immigrants failed, largely due to urbanization and mobility.

But smaller communities continue to exist in America. We have already discussed the Amish before. In my small town of Weirton in West Virginia where I lived and practiced there are small Serbian and Polish communities. There is a Serbian picnic ground

and an old Kosciuszko hall.

Enclaves have their own distinct advantages. They reduce the trauma of change, and slow down the process of Americanization. At the same time, they can slow down the process of prosperity and economic upliftment. Sooner or later, all immigrants take the next steps—that of adaptation, assimilation and becoming a part of the melting pot.

Multiculturalism

Both Canada and Great Britain deserve credit for the way they treat minority and immigrant groups. After all, different cultures, religions, races, ethnicities—particularly of minority groups, require special nurturing and acknowledgement within a dominant social group. Terms such as salad bowl, kaleidoscope, cultural mosaic, rainbow nations have been used to describe such vibrant states. For long, social scientists have debated the pros and cons of multiculturalism for immigrants. Immigrants typically integrate into multicultural societies but pay a price for

doing so by way of slower economic growth and facing hatred from the host society.

Adaptation and transnationalism

In her 1998 book titled *Forever Foreigners or Honorary Whites? The Asian Ethnic Experience Today*, Mia Tuan describes the lives of Chinese and Japanese Americans who have been denigrated as "foreigners." Tuan specifically takes a look at the ridiculing style of New York Senator Alfonse D'Amato who while appearing as a guest on a radio show adopted a mock Japanese accent while speaking about Judge Lance Ito who had presided over the high-profile O.J. Simpson case. Ironically, like Ito, D'Amato also is a third-generation American whose grandparents had immigrated to the US. While Ito's grandparents had come from Japan, D'Amato's had come from Italy. D'Amato's 'singsong pidgin' showed how even a judge of the standing of Ito did not escape ridicule as a result of his ethnicity. Tuan says that families of Chinese and Japanese immigrants have traditionally preferred adaptation over

assimilation, and that has perhaps made them less acceptable in American society right from the time they started arriving at US and Canadian shores.

Adaptation without assimilation is possible in a shrinking world, made more global by modern means of communication and greater mobility. There are immigrants whose wives and children are in the US while they themselves spend a considerable amount of time in their home country doing business. In such cases, the families are stereotyped as having an astronaut husband, widowed wife and parachuted children.

Acculturation and assimilation eventually lead to the melting pot, a term that even though in vogue since 1780 gained much popularity in 1908 based on an eponymous play directed by Israel Zangwill, a British author who was at the forefront of cultural Zionism. *Melting Pot* portrayed the life of David Quixano, a Russian Jew who survived the pogrom that killed his mother and sister. Quixano not only wishes to forget this traumatic event in his life, but he also wants to see a society free of ethnic divisions and hatred.

Melting pot is the cultural integration of immigrants into American culture. The end result is not necessarily Anglo conformity, but rather a mix of differing cultures. This is in contrast to the concepts of cultural mosaics, salad bowls, kaleidoscope or multiculturalism seen in Canada and Great Britain.

Stages of Americanization

Personally, I prefer the term Americanization over acculturation, assimilation and melting pot. Over time, I've zeroed in on the following stages:

Isolation phase: An immigrant new to a host country more often than not lands up with a relative or a friend. He remains isolated, and is anxious to move on. This anxiety may drive him into taking up a poorly-paying job with the help of a relative or friend. But this also gives him a chance to make the next move that will take him to a better place. The isolation phase does not last very long.

Sandwich phase: The immigrant finds a job and straightaway plunges into the whirlpool of ethnicities at his workplace. He is trapped somewhere between his own culture and that of the host nation, all amid a sea of other varying cultures. This is a phase that can last much longer than the one in isolation.

Salad phase: After a while the immigrant starts a family, has his home, and is part of a neighborhood where his children attend school. There is a circle of friends and interaction with other cultures is forced. In spite of the mixing and mingling, the immigrant continues to identify with his own culture. In ethnic enclaves there is adaptation, and no assimilation, at least for a while.

Amalgamation phase: This is biological crossing through interfaith and intercultural marriages. It is the fastest route to assimilation, especially if the partner happens to be a local Anglo-Saxon whose ancestors immigrated generations back.

Assimilation phase: This is usually a third-generation phenomenon and, therefore, is time taking. The prime reasons for reaching this phase include the role of educational institutions, intermarriages and detraditionalization. Christmas, Thanksgiving and Valentine's Day become part of the cultural milieu, but ethnic festivals are also celebrated, perhaps with diminishing enthusiasm.

Melting pot: This is the final stage created by a melting of all cultures. The end product may be better than the sum of separate cultures. It is not in keeping with Anglo-Saxon Protestant conformity.

Pace of Americanization

This process moves with different speeds. It depends on color, religion, culture, education, length of stay, external symbols, geographical location, and, of course, amalgamation. The role of these factors is explained below.

Color: The speed of assimilation reduces as one descends on the stairway of contrasting colors. It starts with white and is followed by black, brown (South and Southeast Asians, Hispanics), yellow (Mongoloids) who've been termed 'foreigners forever.' White people from various cultures assimilate well in the US, as do the African-Americans. The Asian brown community has difficulties in assimilating with both the local white and black communities, and even the brown Hispanic and southern European ones. The Japanese and Chinese communities, in particular, stayed isolated for long.

Religion: The assimilation process is best for Christians and worse for Muslims. Those who fall in between include the Hindus, Buddhists, Jains, Bahais, Sikhs.

Education: Picking up English language skills and professional qualification promotes assimilation.

Identity: The turban, Krupa, hijab are handicaps to assimilation.

Amalgamation: Marriage with a spouse from the host society is the fastest route to assimilation.

Geographical location: The pace of Americanization is fast in smaller cities and slower in ethnic and religious enclaves.

Assimilation begins with the first generation, progresses through the second, and is completed in the third one. Amalgamation is the biggest promoter of assimilation. Religion, its symbols, ethnic and religious enclaves, are the biggest roadblocks to assimilation. Depending on nationality or religious group, assimilation varies and becomes a multigenerational process. Most of the third generation eastern and southern Europeans have assimilated well in the US. In contrast, the Chinese and Japanese have not been able to do so. About the assimilation of Sikhs there has been no study, but it is likely to be slow like other Asian communities. It is far easier for white Christians who are well educated and have an adequate working knowledge of English to assimilate in American society. The black community whose forbears were slaves have integrated and assimilated well. Other African-Americans who have immigrated from the

> **Due to the several reasons mentioned earlier, human migration will continue unabated. In the initial period, new migrants may face many difficulties, including discrimination. Once they take a decision to stay permanently, the process of adaptation, acculturation and assimilation in the host society begins**

Caribbean have likewise assimilated better than brown and yellow races. The Orthodox Jews, Amish, Jehovah's Witnesses and some Mormons are still not a part of the melting point in spite of having spent generations in the US. Sikhs, Muslims and Hindus who are first generation are in the salad phase, while those from the second and third generations have slowly moved to adaptation, assimilation and to the melting pot stage.

Immigrants and American values

The Founding Fathers of the US declared "that all men...are endowed...with certain Inalienable Rights, that among these are Life, Liberty and the pursuit of Happiness. That to secure these rights Governments are instituted among Men, deriving their just powers from the consent of the governed..."

Which brings me to this question that has bothered me now for fifty-five years of my stay in the US: "Were these Inalienable Rights meant for the white race only? What about the massacre of the native Americans and the early settlers, and the gross injustice and slavery perpetuated for centuries against the African Americans?"

Humanity wants answers, before we salute Lady Liberty.

Summary

Due to the several reasons mentioned earlier, human migration will continue unabated. In the initial period, new migrants may face many difficulties, including discrimination. Once they take a decision to stay permanently, the process of adaptation, acculturation and assimilation in the host society begins. These processes start with the first-generation immigrants and are completed by the third generation. Their pace depends on a variety of factors such as color, race, religion, ethnicity, technical skills, and command over the English language. Ethnic and religious enclaves slow down the processes of adaptation, acculturation and assimilation.

When one takes a look at the long history of migration, it becomes evident that there has been a gradual improvement in the relationship of migrants and the people of the host nation. Due credit for this must be given to globalization and what we call a Shrinking World. This is further expedited through education, science, improved transportation and communication. It leads to alleviation of poverty, more beneficial social programs, better job opportunities, and lesser competition in the labor market.

Religiosity has reduced in the west, the concept of race has been repudiated by anthropologists, and color bias is on the decline. Movements such as Black Lives Matter have had a positive impact. As discussed before, the US will become a white minority nation in a few decades. Reduced birth rate will serve as a pull factor for increased immigration. This, in turn, will reduce discrimination. Insofar as Sikhs are concerned, there will be greater acceptance of the turban.

At times of economic recession, however, discrimination could go up. Occasionally, then, the white supremacists, Proud Boys, Ku Klux Klan, antisemitism and other divisive forces will rear their ugly head. Overall, though, we can see a change for the better coming into North America. ∎

CHAPTER 5

SIKH MIGRATION
SIKH ORIGIN, HOME AND SIKHISM

Before discussing Sikh migration, it is important to know about Sikhs, their home, religion, culture and heritage. Who were the ancestors of Sikhs? Possibly, migrants known as Indo-Scythians from central Eurasia, later called Aryans, who came millions of years ago and settled in the North and Northwest of India.

This part of India had flat land with plenty of agricultural potential and was, therefore, attractive for early human migrants. It was known as Sapta Sindhu—the Land of Seven Rivers—in the Vedic period. The Ramayana and Mahabharata speak of this region as the Panchanada—Land of Five Rivers. The Persian name Punjab, also meaning Land of Five Rivers, was later adopted to name the region. Punjab is the birthplace of Sikhism and has remained a home to millions of Sikhs, Hindus and Muslims. These people call themselves Punjabis.

In the past, India could be reached only by land routes. There existed a favorable entry point in the Northwest mountainous region known as Khyber Pass. Punjab was connected to the Middle East and Central Asia through the Silk Route. The Sindhis, as well as the

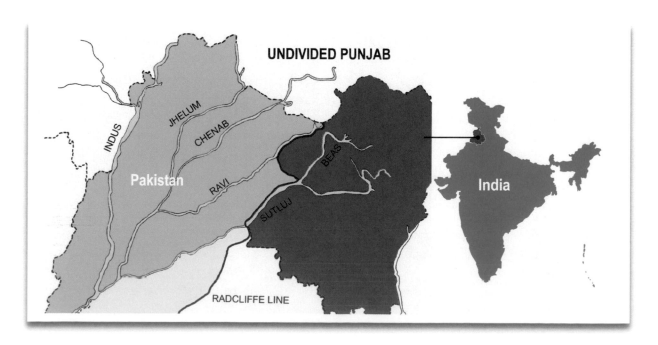

Bhatia Khatries, were actively trading with far-off nations.

According to scholars of human migration, the Aryans are considered as the descendants of a mixture of eastern Scythians and Greeks who were the first to enter India from central Eurasia through the Khyber Pass. Subsequently, the Greeks and Mughals invaded North India. The Aryans, the Muslim Lodhi and Mughal dynasties found a permanent base in India. Alexander, the Ghaznavids, Ahmed Shah Abdali, Nadir Shah Afshar, the British and other Europeans were sojourn migrants. Sikhs, therefore, had an ancestry of various cultures and have a hybrid population with superior eugenic transformation with a spirit of adventure, mobility, exploration and entrepreneurship.

Before the annexation of their homeland by the British in 1848, the Sikhs were well-established in India. The British remained in Punjab for just about a century and unlike earlier invaders did not permanently settle down in India to create any genetic hybrid. Few Anglo-Indians of mixed marriages migrated to Great Britain after Indian independence in 1947.

Indian independence, itself, was a watershed moment in the modern history of Sikhs. Their homeland Punjab split into the eastern and western parts, post-partition. The latter became a part of Pakistan and Sikhs migrated to east Punjab. The traumatic upheaval of partition left Sikhs homeless, without property and businesses. Even Nankana Sahib, the birthplace of Sikhism, was left behind in Pakistan.

Sikhism and Sikh Gurus

Sikhism had its birth in the 15th century in the North Indian region of Punjab. There are approximately 25 million Sikhs spread all over the world. Most of them live in east Punjab which split from greater Punjab at the time of Indian independence in 1947. Within India, Sikhs are settled across various provinces, with a major chunk residing in the capital city of New Delhi.

Sikhism's first appearance coincided with the Bhakti movement. The founding father of

Guru Nanak Ji   Guru Arjan Dev Ji   Guru Gobind Singh Ji

the Sikh religion, Guru Nanak Ji, was revered by the leadership of all other religions, including Islam. There was no opposition to the Sikh community during the early years of the inception of Sikhism. Guru Nanak Ji was followed by nine more living Gurus. Then the Guru Granth Sahib, the holy book, became the future Guru.

Guru Nanak Ji preached *Naam Japo* (prayer), *Kirit Karo* (hard work), *Wund Shako* (sharing). He also preached *Sewa* (service), *Sarbat da Bhala* (doing good for all) and *Langar* (free kitchen). He preached equality of humanity, and laid emphasis on removing gender and income inequality. He was liked both by the leaders, as well as the masses, of all the prevailing religions in India.

Guru Angad Ji, the second Guru, created the Gurmukhi script for the Punjabi language.

Guru Amardas Ji, the third Guru, started the concept of *Manjis* and *Peedis*. A *peedi* is a small wooden cot. The Sikh Piris—female Sikh preachers and holders of religious authority—would teach Sikhism to other women. The *manji* also means a wooden cot, and it stood for preaching Sikhism to men by holders of similar religious authority.

He was also against the wearing of veils by women. He propped up widows, and encouraged inter-caste marriages. He condemned the inhuman practices of *Sati* where a wife burnt alive when her husband died, and that of female infanticide. He recommended that Sikhs meet twice every year at Goindwal, on the banks of the river Beas. He wrote and compiled the first Sikh religious text known as the *Goindwal Pothies*.

Guru Ram Das Ji, the fourth Sikh Guru, established the town of Ramdaspur. It later came to be known as Amritsar. He also designed Harmandir Sahib, the holiest Sikh Temple. He formalized the Sikh system of marriage, *Anand Karaj*—the ceremony of joy inside a Sikh Gurdwara, and *Lavaan*—the pheras in a Sikh wedding whose count is to be four. He further strengthened the system of the *Manjis* and *Peedis*.

By the time the leadership of the Sikh religion passed on to Guru Arjan Dev Ji, the fifth Guru, the Mughals who were ruling large parts of northern India, were alarmed. They saw it as a direct challenge to the mass conversion into Islam that was going on at their behest. Sikhism had become a distinct religion from Hinduism, and was attracting a large number of followers. Guru Arjan Dev Ji refused to comply with the orders of Mughal Emperor Jahangir to remove all references to Islam in the first official edition of the Sikh faith—*Adi Granth*—that he had created.

He started the system of *Dasvandh* that involves one-tenth part or ten percent of one's income as a charitable giving in the Sikh community. Charity had been a part of Sikh tenets since the days of Guru Nanak Ji. Guru

Guru Granth Sahib Ji

Arjan formalized it. He was tortured and executed in 1606 and his martyrdom is a watershed moment in the history of Sikhism and the Sikhs at large.

Saddened and angered by the cruelty with which his father was martyred, Guru Hargobind decided that the Sikh community needed to protect itself. He introduced the process of militarization in Sikhism. He introduced the concept of saint soldier through mīrī and pīrī (temporal power and spiritual power). These were symbolized by the wearing of two swords. He had the Akal Takht (the throne of the timeless one) raised in front of the Harmandir Sahib in Amritsar. The Akal Takht represents the highest seat of temporal, political and spiritual authority for all Sikhs.

The challenges to the growing Sikh community were to continue in the Mughal era. Guru Har Rai Ji extended his protection to Prince Dara Shikoh, the eldest son of Emperor Shah Jahan who was influenced by the moderate Sufi stream and was also the heir apparent to the Mughal throne. This incensed Aurangzeb, Shiko's younger brother, who was a conservative Sunni. After he succeeded Shah Jahan to the Mughal throne, Aurangzeb summoned Guru Har Rai Ji. But instead of going himself, the seventh Nanak sent his elder son Ram Rai to represent him. Aurangzeb questioned Ram Rai about a verse in the Adi Granth—the holy text of Sikhs at

the time—which the Mughal ruler had found disparaging for Muslims. Ram Rai changed the verse in order not to create a conflict with Aurangzeb. But that did not go down well with his father, Guru Har Rai Ji, who excommunicated Ram Rai. Instead Guru Har Rai Ji nominated his younger son Har Krishan to succeed him as the eighth Sikh Guru. But Guru Har Krishan Ji was only seven when he passed away.

Guru Tegh Bahadur Ji, the ninth Sikh Guru was the son of Guru Hargobind Ji. He was saintly and had no army. At the same time, he was gallant and very brave when it came to the protection of human rights. He saved Kashmiri Pandits from persecution by the Mughals and raised the city of Anandpur Sahib on the banks of River Sutlej. Guru Tegh Bahadur Ji chose to give up his life for he refused to embrace Islam. He was martyred for he wanted his countrymen to have the freedom of religious practice. He wanted Sikhs, Hindus and other non-Muslims in India to follow and practice their belief systems. He sacrificed his life along with Bhai Mati Dass, Bhai Sati Das and Bhai Dayala. His execution furthered hardened the resolve of the Sikhs to fight tooth and nail against Muslim atrocities and persecution. The protection of human rights became central to Sikh identity.

In the Indian capital city of Delhi, the Gurudwara Sis Ganj Sahib in Chandni Chowk was built at the place where Guru Tegh Bahadur Ji was executed by a fanatical Aurangzeb for refusing to embrace Islam. Not very far away, the Gurudwara Rakab Ganj Sahib came up where one of Guru Tegh Bahadur Ji's disciples burnt down his own house in order to cremate his master's body.

Guru Gobind Singh Ji, son of Guru Tegh Bahadur Ji, succeeded him as the tenth Sikh Guru after the martyrdom. He founded the warrior community of Khalsa in 1699 for the defense of Sikhism and Hinduism against the bigoted Mughals. The creation of the Khalsa was the most seminal political event in Sikh history. A small population of Khalsa Sikhs was able to eventually carve out a large kingdom in North India.

He also introduced the five Ks—the five articles of faith that Khalsa Sikhs have at all times. They are *Kesh* (uncut hair), *Kara* (a steel bracelet), *Kanga* (a wooden comb), *Kachh* (cotton underwear) and *Kirpan* (steel word).

Guru Gobind Singh Ji's four sons died during his own lifetime. The two elder sons, Baba Ajit Singh, 17, and Baba Jujhar Singh, 14, fought extremely bravely on the battlefield at Chamkaur against all odds with only forty warriors for company. They were pitted against a Mughal army of a hundred thousand men. Eventually, after wreaking havoc in the Mughal army with their awe-inspiring skills, speed, craft and determination, they lost their lives. The younger of the four sons, Baba Zorawar Singh, 9, and Baba Fateh Singh, 7, along with their grandmother Mata Gujri were captured by the Mughal governor Wazir Khan at Sirhind. When they were taken to his court, they said, "*Wahe Guru Ji da Khalsa, Wahe Guru Ji di Fateh.*"

Wazir Khan offered to spare their lives if they converted to Islam. If not, they would be killed. According to *Sikh Dharma International*, Baba Zorawar Singh said loudly, "My father is Guru Gobind Singh Ji, my grandfather Guru Teg Bahadur Ji and my great grandfather is Guru Hargobind Ji. Death means nothing to me. Our death will fan the flames that will drive all the tyrants from this land."

The *Sikh Dharma International* further mentions that when Guru Gobind Singh Ji was informed about the death of his young sons, he listened with an emotionless face but a weeping heart. He took an arrow and thrust it into the ground, pulling out a bush. He said, "Such a tragedy will not go unnoticed in God's Court. Like this weed, the Mughal Raj will be uprooted."

Guru Gobind Singh Ji wrote a beautiful letter to Aurangzeb, known as the "Zafarnama" which means the "Letter of Victory." He chastises the Emperor for his cruelty, his falsehood and his deceit; explaining the Sikh code of warfare and exposing Aurangzeb for his corrupt morality.

In the Zafarnama, Guru Gobind Singh Ji wrote, "When you swore an oath on Mohammed and called the Word of God to witness, you should have kept that promise. If the Prophet himself were present here, I would make it my special duty to inform him of your treachery. Even though my four beautiful sons were killed, the Khalsa remains behind like a coiled snake. What brave deed is it to quench these few sparks of life? You are merely stoking a raging fire."

When Aurangzeb received the Zafarnama, he was aghast with the bare truth of the evil he had done. Fearing God's judgment, he pledged to meet with Guru Gobind Singh Ji. That was, however, not to be. Aurangzeb died before that came to pass.

Before he left his body, Guru Gobind Singh Ji declared to the Sikh community that the future Guruship was vested in the holy book Guru Granth Sahib Ji. His sacred words were, "*Sab Sikhan Ko Hukam Hai Guru Maneyo Granth.*" In other words, the holy book was to be the eternal Guru.

ATROCITIES AGAINST SIKHS OVER CENTURIES

Every new religion faces challenges from existing religions and there are battles and wars among religions. The followers face atrocities and challenges. Sikhism is no exception. This began with the Mughal invasion of India and continues to a lesser degree even today.

Mughal period

Sikhism was in its infancy when Babar invaded India. Guru Nanak Ji first hand witnessed the torture and misery which he aptly described in Babar Vani.

As Sikhism grew, the subsequent Mughal rulers committed atrocities to curb its popularity. The 5th and 9th Sikh Gurus were tortured to death. The 10th Guru fought battles to save Sikhism and sacrificed his four sons.

Subsequent years were not kind to Sikhs and are painfully described below:

The question that burns even today is, "Was the sacrifice of Guru Teg Bahadur Ji and his four young grandsons in vain?" After all, as enumerated in the chapter on Sikh Gurus, they became martyrs so that Sikhs and Hindus would have freedom of religion.

The years following the martyrdoms heightened the challenges faced by the Sikhs even though the Order of Khalsa continued to draw more and more followers. In the late 17th century and almost throughout the 18th century, wearing a turban in the Aurangzeb era and beyond was akin to inviting a death warrant for the Sikhs. They were systematically targeted, and their population was wiped out in large numbers. You may call it whatever you like—ethnic cleansing, pogrom, genocide—it does not take away from the inhumanity unleashed upon the Sikhs by the ruling Mughal and Muslims rulers.

From publications like the *Defense of Europe by Sikh Soldiers in the World Wars* and *A History of the Sikhs from Nadir Shah's Invasion to the Rise of Ranjit Singh* it becomes evident that anyone who managed to cut off the distinctive head of a Sikh or Khalsa was offered a blanket in appreciation. While in general monetary rewards were on offer for information on the whereabouts of Sikhs, a large sum was always on offer for the delivery of a Sikh head. Such a macabre and hostile scenario created great fear and panic among Sikhs who fled away to mountainous regions. Many did away with their hairs and other symbols in order to save themselves. But armies were set up to especially hunt them down, bring them back, and execute them in full public view. It became lawful to plunder the home of a Sikh. Anyone found withholding information on Sikhs was liable for execution.

The man whose despotic reign of terror first struck the Sikhs was the Lahore governor Zakariya Khan Bahadur. His policemen combed down villages and brought back Sikhs by the hundreds, all fettered in chains. They were publicly executed at the horse market in Lahore, a place termed Shaheed Ganj—the place of martyrs—by the Sikhs.

The Mughals clearly saw the Sikhs as a threat. According to the *Encyclopedia Britannica* and the *Institute of Sikh Studies* in 1746 the Mughal army killed an estimated seven thousand Sikhs in and around Lahore. An additional three thousand Sikhs were taken captive in what has come to be known as the Chhōtā Ghallūghārā, or the small massacre. Sixteen years later it was to be followed by the Vadda Ghalughara, the great massacre, in which up to twenty thousand Sikhs may have lost their lives. Women and children were not spared either.

Many other despots and tyrants order their killings. The names of Yahiya Khan and Mir Mannu, both of whom were governors of Lahore during the mid-18th century, especially come to the fore. Lakhpat Rai, a diwan—revenue minister—in Lahore was another merchant of terror who was avenging the killing of his brother. The *Encyclopedia of Sikhism* says he ordered the genocide of "infidel" Sikhs who were rounded up daily and executed. According to a publication of District Gurdaspur in Punjab, he went as far as filling the holy sarovar at the Golden Temple with sand.

According to publications by the *McGill-Queen's Press*, *Minerva Book Shop* and the *Punjabi University*, the reign of terror unleashed by Mir Mannu is simply horrifying. He organized new artillery and a unit of nine hundred men that was especially tasked to hunt down the "infidels." These mercenaries of death chased down Sikhs for miles at a stretch every single day so that they may receive their reward of ten rupees for every head of a Sikh they brought back. According to the publication *Sikh History*, Sikh men were captured alive and as a rule beaten up and put to death by the savage strokes of wooden mallets and hammers. Mir Mannu sent out bone chilling orders to not only kill any Sikh man in sight, but also to round up Sikh women from homes along with their children. The women were forced to relentlessly grind

Banda Singh Bahadur

Maharaja Ranjit Singh

grain in prisons, until parched and starving they'd fall down and lose their consciousness. What the Mughals unleashed against the Sikhs was carnage at its very worst.

The torture and sacrilege were ceaseless. According to the *Historical Dictionary of Sikhism* by Rowman and Littlefield, a Mughal military officer Massa Ranghar not only prevented Sikhs from accessing the Golden Temple, but also caroused with dancing girls and consumed meat and alcohol in the Sanctum Sanctorum in the midst of the sacred pool. The other great oppressor was Ahmad Shah Abdali whose forces made a devastating assault on the Sikhs on behalf of the Durrani Empire. Given this background of massacre and genocide, the very survival of the Sikh community had become extremely difficult. Their immense sacrifices and martyrdoms to preserve the religion at all costs must, therefore, be understood in view of the enormity of what they went through.

With the gradual demise of the Mughal kingdom, the Khalsa (Sikhs) took over and created the Sikh kingdom with consolidation of Sikh misls (Sikh principalities). This was a glorious and peaceful period lasting over one century when Sikhism grew. The Mughal empire started going on a decline during the latter part of the 18th century and the brave Sikhs began to regroup themselves. In Maharaja Ranjit Singh they found a towering leader who helped establish the Sikh Empire, also called the Sarkār-ē-Khālsā, in 1799 after the capture of Lahore. According to the *Encyclopedia Britannica* and publications of the *Cambridge University Press*, the empire was built from a collection of Sikh misls—twelve sovereign states—and at its peak in the 19th century it extended from Khyber Pass in the west to the western region of Tibet in the east, and from Mithankot in the south to Kashmir in the north.

According to the *Encyclopedia of Sikhism*, Ranjit Singh's rise was meteoric. He was the leader of a single misl but managed to unify the separate Sikh misls, finally succeeding in capturing Lahore from its Afghan ruler Zaman Shah Durrani. He was crowned Maharaja of the Punjab in 1801 and his coronation was carried out by Sahib Singh

> Indian independence, itself, was a watershed moment in the modern history of Sikhs. Their homeland Punjab split into the eastern and western parts, post-partition. The latter became a part of Pakistan and Sikhs migrated to east Punjab. The traumatic upheaval of partition left Sikhs homeless, without property and businesses. Even Nankana Sahib, the birthplace of Sikhism, was left behind in Pakistan

Bedi, a descendant of Guru Nanak Ji. The Sikh Empire had Lahore as its capital city. Its four provinces included Multan, Peshawar, Kashmir and, of course, Lahore. Maharaja Ranjit Singh ruled his empire with an iron hand but his demise in 1839 caused a leadership crisis. The British sniffed an opportunity to move in and take advantage of the weakening empire. The First Anglo-Sikh War fought between the Sikh Empire and the British East India Company in 1845 and 1846 resulted in the annexation of Kashmir. But the Sikhs did not give up without a huge fight with every single member of the Governor General's staff either killed or wounded. According to the publication *Maharaja Ranjit Singh, the last to lay arms,* the British General of the day Sir James Grant said, "Never in the annals of warfare has a British army on such a large scale been nearer to defeat, which would have involved annihilation."

The Second Anglo-Sikh War was the final nail in the coffin of the Sikh Empire. Punjab itself was annexed by the East India Company along with the region around Peshawar that subsequently became a part of the North-West Frontier Province. That also led to the formation of a lieutenant governorship in Lahore that was a direct representative of the British Crown.

British Raj

A small number of British and other Europeans took control of India. The British finally prevailed in the whole of India while the French and the Portuguese had smaller enclaves.

To run India, the British used the divide-and-rule and carrot-and-stick policies. To please the Sikhs, they gave them the status of a martial race and recruited them in large numbers in the Imperial army. This did not please the other freedom seekers and the British used the stick of atrocity disdainfully to contain them. This began with two Anglo-Sikh wars, Namdhari massacre, Komagata Maru tragedy, Ghadar movement and the associated death sentences and life imprisonments, the Jallianwala Bagh massacre and deaths related to the struggle for the control of Gurdwaras. The last atrocity was huge, and the loss of human lives and property led to the partition of Punjab in 1947.

Indian Independence

Sikhs were just recovering from the atrocities of partition when the separatist movement of Khalistan brought about another painful chapter in their history. It resulted in the Congress government's attack on the Golden Temple (Operation Blue Star). There was the subsequent killing of Mrs Indira Gandhi, then prime minister of India, by her own Sikh bodyguards. Her death unleashed an unprecedented genocide against Sikhs all over India. Recently more than five hundred Sikh farmers died taking part in a peaceful and prolonged agitation around the nation's capital with utter disregard from the ruling elite.

These atrocities and deaths remind us of the American Civil War when Abraham Lincoln said at Gettysburg in 1863: "...These dead shall not have died in vain."

SIKH CHALLENGES SINCE ITS INCEPTION

I have discussed atrocities against Sikhs over centuries. Like other religions, Sikhs faced many other challenges as well. It is clear from history that religions feel safe and are able to progress when they have the blessings of the ruling classes. Guru Gobind Singh Ji was quite right when he'd commented, *"Raj bin dharm nahi"* (religion cannot flourish without political blessings). Sikhism was able to grow during the Sikh kingdom. Later on, it faced challenges yet again.

1. Sikhism as a separate religious entity faced a challenge by the dominant religion Hinduism. Buddhism, Jainism and Zoroastrianism are on the fringes. A small Jewish population has returned to Israel. Sikhism was also on a decline and got a lifeline through the Singh Sabha movement. Amritdhari and Keshdhari Sikhs are already on a decline in the west. Islam and Christianity are not giving up in spite of state oppression.

2. Sikh identity crisis, Sikh turban and other religious symbols, particularly in the US, have caused hate crimes and job discriminations.

3. Punjabi language and Gurmukhi script, the media of Sikh theology, faces decline. Sikhs struggled to carve Punjabi Suba but were deprived of many adjoining Punjabi speaking areas and the Punjab capital city of Chandigarh.

4. Punjab, the home of Sikhs, has seen depletion of underground water and is losing the claim to river waters in spite of their riparian rights to river waters.

5. Sikh institutions like Akal Takht, SGPC and Akali Dal are on a downhill path. The Sikh Gurdwara continues to play an important role but attendance is falling in the case of second and third-generation children, both in India and in the west.

6. Detraditionalization, though universal to all religions, is a matter of concern for Sikhs.

7. Sikh marriage is facing challenge from interfaith and same-sex marriages.

8. Agriculture economy that has been the mainstay of rural Punjab is facing challenges in terms of high cost of production, and low selling prices. This primarily resulted in the year-long agitation by the farmers, Sikh and others.

9. Atheism, agnosticism and humanism are on a rise in the west and pose the toughest challenges to all established religions.

SIKH THEOLOGY

The basic theology of Sikhism, the identity of Sikhs, their institutions and way of life is described below:

1. **Religion:**

A. Basic theology.

1. *Nam Jap* (prayer) of one God.

2. *Kirit Kar* (work hard).

3. *Wund Shako* (sharing).

B. Complimentary.

❖ Equality of humanity and gender.

❖ Down with ego, pride, lust, greed, anger.

❖ Take part in fellowship and congregation—Sangat.

❖ Take part in eating together on the floor—Pangat.

C. Baptized Sikh (Khalsa).

1. Baptized Sikhs have five Ks—*Kanga* (comb), *Kirpan* (sword), *Kachha* (shorts), *Karra* (steel bangle), *Kesh* (uncut hair), along with a turban as a symbol of Sikh religious identity.

2. Males were given the name Singh, meaning lion, and females were given the name Kaur, meaning princess.

3. Their disciplined way of living means they are to remain free of intoxicants, halal meat (sacrificial meat), adultery, and are required to pray five times a day.

D. Offshoots of Sikhism.

E. Religious symbols.

❖ Turban and 5Ks for all Sikhs, and a must for Khalsa Singhs.

F. Customs include *Nam Karan* (naming ceremony of a newborn), *Dastar Bandi* (turban initiation), and cremation.

G. Other beliefs—After life, reincarnation, heaven and hell.

2. Sikh Institutions
A. Gurdwara.
B. Akal Takht.
C. Shiromani Gurdwara Parbandhak Committee (SGPC).
D. Akali Dal (Sikh political party).
E. Langar.
F. Educational institutions such as Khalsa schools and colleges, and Sikh education chairs in universities.

3. Family Structure.
A. Filial piety.
B. Marriage.
C. Assimilation.

4. New social issues.
A. LGBTQ.
B. Same-sex marriage.
C. Global warming.
D. Environmental degradation.
E. Pollution.

The three pillars of Sikh theology are *Nam Jap, Kirit Kar* and *Wund Shako.*

Nam Jap
(Prayer to God)

All organized religions believe in the existence of God. The opening page of the Sikh scripture, Japji Sahib, begins with Mool Mantar, the

This Mool Mantar is copy from old text of Guru Granth Sahib Ji and is handwritten by Guru Arjan Dev Ji in Gurmukhi script

description of God, Akhal Purkh or Wahe Guru (the Sikh name for God). In Mool Mantar, Wahe Guru is omnipresent, the Creator, with no physical shape or form, with no birth or death, no reincarnation, no fear or malice. The existence of one God is fundamental to Sikh theology.

Kirit Kar
(Work hard)

Sikhism is the only religion that emphasizes the value of hard work in everyday life.

Das Naun Di Kamai

Guru Nanak Ji, while on a visit to Eminabad, Pakistan, declined an invitation from the royal family of Malik Bhago. Instead he preferred to stay with Bhai Lalo, a person who worked hard each day with his hands, and earned a livelihood. Given this outstanding philosophy, it does not come as a surprise to find that the hard-working Indian Sikhs have a higher per capita income than most other communities. One can rarely notice a Sikh begging, or subsisting on public assistance.

Wund Shako
(Sharing)

Sikhism believes in sharing resources for those in need. Charitable giving is a part of basic Sikh theology. The founding father of Sikhism, Guru Nanak Ji, said, *"Ghal Khaye Kichh Haathon De Nanak Rah Pacchane Se."* It means work hard and give some charity from your earnings. Later, Sikh Maryada, or code of conduct, recommended 10 percent (*daswund*) of one's income to be given as charity. This was a time when there was no formal income tax system.

Complimentary

Gender and income equality were emphasized in Sikhism, much before it became a subject of discussion in modern times. Sangat, or congregation, was empowered with the message of democratic decision-making. Pangat conveyed the message of equality and humility when everyone ate langar (free meals) while sitting

THE SIKH 5 K's

Kesh uncut hair | Sikh men cover their uncut hair with a turban.

Kara a steel bracelet

Kanga a wooden comb

Kaccha cotton underwear

Kirpan a dagger

given the name of Singh (lion) for men, and Kaur (princess) for women.

The Panj Piaras constituted the supreme cabinet of the Khalsa. Not only did Guru Gobind Singh Ji get baptized by them, but he obeyed their command and left the battle fort of Chamkaur Sahib, much against his inner wish to fight.

The explicit purpose of the Khalsa has been self-defense, as well as the defense of the helpless. They believe in justice for all. Khalsa's code of conduct includes, at all times, to adhere to the 5Ks. The turban for the protection of the head, and uncut hair, became the most important symbols of Sikh identity. Khalsa was the need of the time when Sikhism itself was under threat from the ruling Mughals. Khalsa was Akal Purakh Ki Fauj—The Army of God. Khalsa fought for the cause of Sikhs, and others.

The different offshoots of Sikhism

Sikhs do not constitute a homogenous society. Keshdhari Sikhs (with unshorn hair and turban) and Amritdhari Sikhs are considered mainstream Sikhs. Over time, with slight differences, various offshoots have come up. Some of these offshoots believe in a living Guru. Some of the Sikhs have been converted from the lower castes of Hindu society. Sikhs have lived in isolated enclaves at different places in India. They have adopted Sikhism during the time of the travel of the Sikh Gurus.

Let us take a look at the offshoots.

1. **Older offshoots.**
   ❖ Nihang Singhs
   ❖ Sehajdhari
   ❖ Namdhari
   ❖ Nirankari
   ❖ Radha Saomi
   ❖ Ravidasis
   ❖ Valmikis
   ❖ Udasi
   ❖ Nirmala Sikhs
   ❖ Ranghreta Sikhs
   ❖ Mazhabi Sikhs
   ❖ Sikligar Sikhs

2. **Newer offshoots**
   ❖ Sikh Dharma of Western Hemisphere

on the floor. Sitting on chairs and eating on tables is new for Sikhs in the west. The description of Sikh Rehat Maryada traditions and customs (Sikh code of conduct) appear in a later section (future of Sikhism).

Khalsa (baptism)

The Khalsa was created by tenth Sikh Guru Gobind Singh Ji at a baptizing ceremony in the city of Anandpur during a Baisakhi function in 1699. Guru Gobind Singh Ji empowered five of his followers from different regions and belonging to different castes of Hindu society during the baptizing ceremony. To them was given the name of Panj Piaras, the Five Loved Ones. The tenth Guru, in all humility, then asked the Panj Piaras to baptize him into the Khalsa Order. The baptized were

3HO (Sikhism+yoga)

❖ Atheists and Agnostics.

❖ Cultural Sikhs

3. **Other Sikhs** (isolated in different geographical locations of India in the past)

❖ Sikhs of Odisha

❖ Sikhs of Bangladesh

❖ Agrahari Sikhs of West Bengal, Bihar, UP, Jharkhand

❖ Dakhni Sikhs of South India

❖ Assam or Axomiya Sikhs

Offshoots

Contrary to popular belief, the Sikhs are not a homogenous set of people. The Keshdhari Sikhs, ones with unshorn hair and turbans, and the Amritdhari Sikhs, the ones that are baptized, are considered a part of the mainstream in Sikh society.

May I add, though, that irrespective of what kind of Sikhism one practices, it does not have any bearing on American society which is based on meritocracy. There is no caste system among Sikhs in America, and they've found success without any such equations coming into play in their day-to-day lives. And this has been the case for over a hundred years. Let me give you the classic example of Jawala Singh who became a Ghadar revolutionary. He was a low-caste Sikh from the village of Thathian near Amritsar in Punjab. But in America it did not stop him from becoming the undisputed potato king from his base in Holtsville, California. His financial success enabled him to adequately fund the Ghadar movement, the Stockton Gurdwara, and Indian students who had come to study at the University of California at its Berkeley campus. He even endowed students with scholarships until such time the Ghadar movement ran into rough weather.

Over the years, though, several offshoots of Sikhism have come up, and passing references have been made to them in other chapters in this book. Some of these offshoots believe in a living Guru, others are based on converts from lower-caste Hindu society. Also,

Nihang Singhs

Gatka

there are Sikhs within India who are now located in different enclaves outside their native Punjab. They adopted Sikhism during the travels of Sikh Gurus, or are migrant Sikhs.

Typically, an offshoot refers to a branch of a plant, or something that develops itself from the original. The offshoots of Sikhism are somewhat similar. Let's take a look at them.

Nihang Singhs

Nihang Singhs are not to be found in America and, by and large, are not relevant to the Sikh community. They are also called Akalis who were originally armed Sikh warriors. In the past, Nihang Singhs were respected armed guards of the Sikhs. So honorable were they that women would open doors for them even at night without any fear. In Punjabi they would say, "*Aye Nihang Booha Khol de Nishang.*"

Over time, the Nihang Singhs may have lost their raison d'être, a proper direction in their lives. Many of them have strayed with little education. Homelessness and lack of education has come to mark their wayward existence. A few of them practice a hippy culture, where enjoying rounds of Shaheedi Degh, a concoction of almond, milk, cardamom and cannabis has become the primary focus of life.

Aggression and violence have been noted in this community. One group of Nihang Singhs chopped off the hand of a police officer in Patiala, Punjab. He was enforcing curfew norms at the height of the coronavirus pandemic. Another group went against the verdict of the Akal Takht—the highest authority that addresses spiritual and temporal concerns of Sikhs—and baptized a man whose Sikh credentials had been annulled. On October 15, 2021, Nihang Singhs lynched one Lakhbir Singh for desecrating a Sikh holy scripture at the Singhu border where farmers were agitating against Indian farm laws, since repealed.

Besides, as an armed wing they have lost their relevance. The days of foot soldiers with swords are gone. Modern armies rely more on heavy artillery and advanced remote weapons. The Nihang Singhs, therefore, contribute little to Sikhism and remain largely marginalized. With better education and greater employment opportunities showing up, the ranks of this clan will shrink further. Gone are the days of seeing them as armed soldiers on horsebacks. But they sometimes appear in Sikh parades in the US and manage to roll back the years by demonstrating versatile skills of war in the days gone by, known as the Gatka. They also mimic other events of the past on horseback.

Sehajdhari Sikhs

The Sehajdhari Sikhs have been an integral part of Sikhism since its inception. According to the *Sikh Missionary Society of UK* and others, the Sehajdhari Sikh has chosen the path of Sikhism but has not yet become an Amritdhari or a Khalsa. In fact, the Khalsa and Amritdhari are interchangeable expressions referring to those initiated into the Order of the Khalsa established by tenth Guru Gobind Singh Ji. It was in a famous ceremony well over three hundred years ago during Vaisakhi of 1699 that the Amrit—the sacrament of the double-edged sword—was administered and that created the first group of Amritdhari Sikhs.

The Sehajdhari Sikh, on the other hand, believe in the tenets of Sikhism and the teachings of the Sikh Gurus but are not inclined to adorn the five symbols of the Sikh faith. Since they were slowly progressing towards becoming Khalsa their name became Sehajdhari. At a time when turban-wearing Sikhs were savagely hunted down by the Mughal governors and their armies, then captured, executed and beheaded, Sehajdhari, Nirmala and Udasi Sikhs were brave enough to be caretakers of Sikh shrines. It is a testimony to their sacrifice in the most oppressive period for Sikhs in history. They have been deprived of voting in the Shiromani Gurdwara Parbandhak Committee (SGPC) elections for not keeping the symbols of Sikh faith. They have felt isolated and are unhappy. Their ranks are shriveling.

Radha Soami Satsang Beas (RSSB)

The RSSB, founded in 1891, has a presence in about ninety nations today. It is guided by the fundamental spiritual beliefs that are at the very core of most religions under the tutelage of a living spiritual master. He is seen as a manifestation of God. Headquartered on the banks of the River Beas in Punjab, RSSB members can often be seen wearing the turban and following the Guru Granth Sahib.

In RSSB, Radha Soami translates to Lord of the Soul, satsang stands for a group of truth-seekers, while Beas refers to the town on the banks of the eponymous river. It is a non-profit organization and has no affiliations to any political or commercial entity.

At the heart of the RSSB teachings is a belief that there is a spiritual purpose to human life, and that is to experience the divinity of God who resides in all of us. There is only one God and we are all expressions of His love.

The current Guru of RSSB is Guru Gurinder Singh Dhillon.

Nirankari Sikhs

This sect was founded by Baba Dyal, a Sehajdhari Sikh, in northwest Punjab in 1851. According to the *Encyclopedia of Sikhism Volume III, Punjabi University, Patiala* and others, Baba Dyal wanted to restore the practices and beliefs of Sikhs prevalent when first Guru Nanak Ji was alive. According to publications of *Routledge* and *Infobase*, the movement came up after the collapse of the Sikh Empire following the passing away of Maharaja Ranjit Singh.

Settled across the country, Nirankari Sikhs are to be found all the way from Srinagar to Kolkata. They follow many of the practices of Sikhism, believe strongly in the formless God without any image, preach *nam simaran,* that is remembrance and repetition of God's name. They, however, believe in the continuation of the living Guru after Guru Gobind Singh Ji. In their lineage, the current leadership is with Satguru Sister Sudiksha.

Namdhari Sikhs

The Namdharis appear like all devout Sikhs, keep their hair, but like the Nirankari Sikhs believe in a living Guru. They have a distinguished, horizontal and boat-shaped style of wearing their turbans. Also, due to the special chanting of hymns that they do, and the voice that emanates when they greet one another, they are identified as Kukas. They are headquartered at Bhaini Sahib, Ludhiana, in

Satguru Ram Singh

Punjab and Udai Singh is their current Guru. Of all the offshoots of Sikhism, the Namdharis made the maximum sacrifices during the freedom struggle in India, especially during the non-cooperation and Ahimsa (non-violent) movements to bring down the British Empire, according to the *Encyclopedia Britannica.*

On April 12, 1857, the Namdhari Sikhs under Satguru Ram Singh peacefully declared independence from British rule by raising a white flag and boycotting British-made goods, endorsing Swadeshi (local) items instead. This happened less than a month before the start of the first war of Indian independence—the Sepoy Mutiny—that commenced on May 10, 1857.

According to the *Department of NRI Affairs* in the Punjab Government, in 1871, the

Namdhari Sikhs

Namdhari Sikhs had been hanged without trial in Amritsar, Ludhiana and Raikot following violence that had erupted after attempts were made to desecrate the Golden Temple in Amritsar. In early January 1872, Gurmukh Singh, a Namdhari Sikh, had requested a vegetable vendor in Malerkotla to show mercy on an ox that was overburdened and on the verge of collapse. This led to an argument that was settled in a court by a fanatical Muslim judge who ordered that the ox be slaughtered before the very eyes of Gurmukh Singh. This cruel judgment deeply hurt the sentiments of the Sikh community. On January 13, 1872, a group of one hundred and fifty Namdhari Sikhs went to Malerkotla to avenge the injustice. In the fighting that ensued several lives were lost, including those of British officials.

The despotic L Cowan, the deputy commissioner of Ludhiana, was ordered to take retaliatory measures. He took over charge from the minor ruler of Malerkotla and ordered that the Namdhari Sikhs be brought before him and "blown to bits." Over two days between January 17 and 18, 1872, sixty-six Namdhari Sikhs were executed by being blown away by cannon balls. That indeed brought about a grisly death.

Among those who were murdered was Bishen Singh, a twelve-year-old boy. Cowan's wife begged him to be merciful and spare the minor's life to which the deputy commissioner acceded on the condition that the boy would henceforth distance himself from the Sikh faith practiced by Satguru Ram Singh. Incensed by this outrageous suggestion

Namdhari Shahidi Smarg in Malerkotla

Bishen Singh grabbed hold of Cowen's beard fiercely and did not let go until his body was shred to bits.

In the memory of the martyred stands the *Namdhari Shahidi Smarg* at Malerkotla in Punjab, a sixty-six feet tall memorial called the Khanda. It has sixty holes, the larger ones represent the adults and the smaller ones the minors who were barbarically decimated by the British over those two days in 1872. In his book, *Indian Home Memories*, Henry Cotton says that, "for my part I can recall nothing during my service in India, more revolting and shocking than those executions…"

Satguru Ram Singh was arrested and exiled to Rangoon, Burma, in 1872, where he breathed his last. The head at present is Guru Shri Uday Singh.

Mazhbi Sikhs and others

Mazhabi Sikhs are to be found mainly in the northern Indian states of Punjab, Rajasthan and Haryana. Mazhab is an Arabian word that means religion. The Mazhabi Sikhs follow mainstream Sikhism. They made up the Imperial Army unit known as the Sikh Light Infantry. Indeed, their bravery is known in every corner as the British made them fight in hostile terrains across the world.

They were mainly converted into Sikhism from the backward Hindu castes. According to a publication by *Sage,* a low caste Hindu, Bhai Jaita Ranghreta, carried the decapitated head of Guru Tegh Bahadur Ji from Delhi and brought it to his son Guru Gobind Singh Ji. In recognition of their devotion, these low-caste Hindus were admitted to the Khalsa and were called Mazhabi. According to the publications of the *Dunedin Academic Press* and the *Scarecrow Press,* one group within the Mazhabi community calls itself the Ranghreta and claims a higher status because of what Bhai Jaita Ji did. It is said that Guru Gobind Singh Ji had uttered "Ranghreta Guru ka beta", implying that Bhai Jaita Ranghreta was the son of the Guru.

Other similar groups exist. According to publications of the *Anthropological Survey of India,* the Sikligar Sikhs, for instance, are found in Punjab and Haryana. *Sikli* is a Persian word for one who shines metals. Sikligarh Sikhs made weapons for the sixth Guru and the tenth Guru. Their dire economic condition has forced them today to do odd labor jobs, some of them make utensils for households. The Sikligars are also Hindus. According to publications of *Ashgate Publishing,* the Chuhras or the Balmikis whose traditional occupation is sweeping and are, therefore, considered untouchable by Hindus, converted to Sikhism and adopted many of its practices during the colonial period. Likewise, the lower-caste Hindus who were leather tanners and referred to as Chamars converted to Sikhism. They

came to be known as Ramdasia Sikhs.

The Ravidassia sect came up during the early 20th century in colonial India. Their movement based itself on the teachings of Satguru Ravidass.

Sikh Dharma International and 3HO

The founder of Sikh Dharma International Yogi Bhajan was born Harbhajan Singh Puri in 1929 at Kot Harkarn in the Gujranwala district of undivided India. His family which was landed and owned sizable property in the Himalayan foothills was uprooted during the violent turbulence of partition, losing all the wealth it had acquired within a matter of days. Harbhajan Singh and his loved ones had to subsequently endure the hardship and penury of refugee camps along with hundreds of thousands who'd fled to the Indian side of the divide. In 1953, two years after obtaining a master's degree in economics, he joined the Indian Government's revenue service. Following postings in various parts of the country, he eventually landed up in Delhi as a customs inspector.

He began to spend more and more time with spiritual teachers. One such, Dhirendra Brahmachari in New Delhi, taught him yoga therapy, something that would serve him well later in life. In 1968 he moved to Toronto, Canada where he started teaching yoga. Within months, though, he moved to Los Angeles where he'd base himself for the rest of his life.

It is in Los Angeles that he started 3HO (Healthy, Happy, Holy Organization) Foundation. It had a meteoric rise, expanding

Yogi Bhajan

Sikh Dharma International

to thirty nations with over three hundred centers and thousands of followers. At 3HO, vegetarianism, meditation and Kundalini Yoga were practiced. Both genders wore the signature white turbans, kept unshorn hair and would sing rhymes from the Guru Granth Sahib. Yogi Bhajan was a deeply committed Sikh who believed in Guru Nanak Ji. While some puritanical Sikhs have not easily come to terms with the liberal mix of Sikhism and yoga, he's been hailed for spreading Sikhism in the west. Time magazine in 1977 called him a womanizer. His previous follower Premka, now Sahara Dyson, in her 2020 book *White Bird in a Golden Cage 2020* described him as a rapist and a child abuser. Handicapped by a leadership crisis, the organization has never been the same since the passing away of Yogi Bhajan in 2004.

Other Sikhs

During the travels of Sikh Gurus there was conversion to Sikhism in Bengal, Bihar, UP, Odisha and Jharkhand (Agrahari Sikhs), Assam (Axomiya Sikhs) and Southern India (Dakhni Sikhs). They have steadfastly held on to the scripture and the Guru Granth Sahib Ji but are not Khalsa or Keshdari Sikhs.

Cultural Sikhs or newer Sikhs

As a people, Sikhs are born into a particular religion, in our case Sikhism. Later, they may convert to another religion or turn atheist and agnostic. This has happened in the past, and will continue in the future. Like I've mentioned in another chapter, the liberation martyr Bhagat Singh was an atheist while the celebrated writer Khushwant Singh was agnostic. Recently, Bhakhtaur Singh Gill, a Sikh in Punjab, made headlines for promoting atheism. Many non-believers, however, are proud of their Sikh heritage, customs and traditions. They wear turbans, visit Gurdwaras primarily for non-religious activities such as langar. They even carry out a far bit of community socializing there.

Non-believers as a group are well recognized among the Jewish people. They have come to be known as cultural Jews. Some of them visit synagogues to follow Judaist customs and traditions. According to novelist Stephen E. Tabachnick, they do not practice the faith, however, and also do not follow the scripture. They, therefore, differ markedly from orthodox, reformed and Zionist Jews.

In my quest to find out about cultural Sikhs, I sent out questionnaires to about a hundred adults comprising twenty first-generation Sikh families and their children. Unsurprisingly, my questionnaire was not welcome and in some cases the respondents were considerably vexed. One respondent made his views clear to me in no uncertain terms, stating my questionnaire was certainly going to stir up trouble. The respondent said that Sikhs have enough problems on their hands and categorically asked me to not start a new one. "Do something productive…" was the respondent's terse advice to me. Well, I'm writing a book.

SURVEY OF SIKH FAITH

There has been a recent surge in agnosticism and atheism in the western countries. This is a brief survey in this regard among Sikhs.

The survey questionnaire was sent to one hundred adults from Sikh families who are above the age of eighteen. In all thirty-two responded. Twenty-four of these believed in God and the Sikh religion while another eight had differing views, given below:

An eighty-year-old who had a doctorate degree and retired from a senior corporate entity commented: "God is essentially a concept developed due to human insecurity, fear, lack of knowledge and many other factors. Everybody's God is different. I believe in Guru Nanak Ji's God but am unable to perceive clearly his realization of God. My God is quite a bit different than Nanak's God."

One forty-nine-year-old with a master's degree believes in God. He says religion is a manmade concept. "I do not practice the traditional component of Sikhism. I, however, respect Sikhism immensely and feel proud to be a Sikh."

A college student commented, "I have no strong belief in the existence or non-existence of God. I am still trying to figure it out. I encourage the belief and practice of religion because it

Name (Optional): ....

Place of birth: ....

Age: .... Male: .... Female: ....

Single: .... Married: .... Children: ....

Education: ....

Do you wear a turban? Yes: .... No: ....

Visit to the Gurdwara. Yes: .... How often: .... No: ....

Did you visit Harmandir Sahib? Yes: .... No: ....

Do you believe in the existence of God? Yes: .... Not sure: .... No: ....

Do you believe in religion? Yes: .... Not sure: .... No: ....

Give brief comment about your thinking on:

God: ....

....

....

Religion: ....

....

....

allows people to come together and have faith and unity, especially in times of hardship."

A seventy-year-old physician had this to say, "Old axioms may have validity. God made man, or did man make God. "I believe in religion and reincarnation where your deeds on earth will determine your fate in the afterlife."

A seventy-five-year-old physician had this to say, "Manmade beliefs are extremely abused and exploited for financial, political and selfish motives."

A twenty-nine-year-old graduate student commented, "I don't believe in God or religion."

A forty-eight-year-old MBA commented, "I do not believe in things I cannot see or that which is not scientifically proven. The primitive societies believed in God to explain mysteries of the world. Egyptian Sun God or Greek God Zeus, are examples. Religion is a manmade way to control society with rules and norms."

A forty-six-year-old put it this way, "God is perfect, but I don't believe in religion created by society."

This is not a credible survey due to apostate fear and has no input from less educated Sikhs. But it provides an inkling to the changing concepts of God and religion among Sikh families. What would be their status in Sikhism? Would Akal Takht declare them non-Sikhs? Or accept them as cultural Sikhs?

Sikh identity and religious symbols
The turban and the 5Ks

The turban and the 5Ks—*Kesh, Kirpan, Karra, Kanga* and *Kachha*—are the most visible symbols of the Sikh faith. They are a part of the baptism into Khalsa, and are also carried by mainstream Sikhs. Some may raise the question, are these symbols relevant for Sikhism today? My take is that the symbols may be considered outdated at this time, but they carry an emotional value beyond the material. In 1980, Henry Corbin, the French philosopher-theologian, said, "They symbol is not an artificially constructed sign. It flowers in the soul spontaneously to announce something that cannot be expressed otherwise. Its unique expression of the thing symbolized as of reality is that it becomes transparent to the soul, but it transcends all expressions to penetrate the meaning of a symbol which in no sense is equivalent to making it superfluous or abolishing it, for it always remain the soul expression of the signified thing with which it symbolizes." This summation explains the role these symbols play in the life of a contemporary Sikh.

SIKH IDENTITY

Sikhs are unique when it comes to their identity. They have a religious identity as well as an individual identity.

Religious and community identity

The religious identity is portrayed as a high-flying kesari (yellow) flag called the NISHAN SAHIB with the Khanda emblem that adorns all Sikh Gurdwaras. A smaller version of the Khanda is seen on Turbans, armored vehicles of the Sikh regiments, car windows and the headgear of political leaders.

The Turban is an important religious symbol and is unique to the Sikh religion. Complimenting these visual symbols is the loud slogan, BOLE SO NIHAL, SAT SRI AKAL, the clarion call of the Sikhs. There is also CHARDI KALA, a greeting of optimism.

The NISHAN SAHIB is a cotton or a silk triangular emblem of Sikh identity that is

Nishan Sahib

Sant Teja Singh

hoisted on a tall pole. It changed from white at the time of Guru Amar Das to the current kesari, or yellow color. It is hoisted at all Sikh Gurdwaras, the insignia represents Sikh regiment of the Indian Army. In the US, the Pacific Coast Khalsa Diwan Society bought a residential lot at 1930 South Grant Street at Stockton, California to build a Sikh temple or Gurdwara. When the NISHAN SAHIB was hoisted on it on October 24, 1912, on an existing frame building, people in that neighborhood protested. But Sant Teja Singh—widely known as the First Ambassador of Sikhism to the Western World—intervened and explained the religious importance of the NISHAN SAHIB. Then peace prevailed in Stockton, and all was well.

The hoisting of the NISHAN SAHIB on Indian Republic Day on January 26, 2021 at the Red Fort in New Delhi at the time of the farmers' agitations brewed up a nationwide storm. A NISHAN SAHIB-bearing head cover was used by Prime Minister Modi while canvassing for election in Punjab. The Sikh Regiment still carries the emblem on the Pakistan and China borders.

Turban

Sikhs are now the only religious community that has a turban both as a community and a religious symbol.

Chardi Kala greeting of optimism along with *Sat Siri Akal* (Timeless Being, God) are Sikh words for greeting each other.

The annual parades of multicolor, turban-wearing Sikhs led by the Panj Piaras (Five Beloved) in big cities are a spectacle of Sikh identity.

Individual identity

The Sikh male identity is unique with visible, uncut hair (*kesh*), turban and bangle (*karra*). Most Sikh women, though, look no different from other migrant or local women that have brown or darker skin tones. Other features of nationality such as profession, membership to organizations, do not come into play in the day-to-day life of a Sikh.

Male identity

The Sikh male identity in the US has three components:
1. Personal.
2. Religious symbols.
   A. Visible: Turban, uncut hair, sword (only in India).
   B. Invisible: *Kachha* (shorts), *Kanga* (comb).
3. Social Identity.

Personal
Color and facial features

Sikhs in the US are recognized by their skin color and their religious symbols. Most Sikhs in the US are either brown, or dark brown in skin tone, and are of medium height. In the past, they've been referred as brown-black Caucasians in a bid to differentiate them from Negroid and Mongoloid physiognomy. A small number of Sikhs who live in Pakistan, Afghanistan and Kashmir have fairer skin tones. A group of converts to Sikhism who are a part of Sikh Dharma International (3HO), an offshoot organization, are white, and are to be mostly found in the western states of the US, and in the larger cities. They are disciples of Yogi Bhajan.

Religious symbols

Sikh religious symbols consist of the 5Ks and the turban. These could be visible as well as non-visible. The visible ones are turban, uncut hair and the bangle. Swords are not visible in the US. The *kachha* (shorts) and the *kanga* (comb) are invisible.

A. Visible religion symbols
Sikh turban

In a recent book titled the *The Sikh Turban in North America* in 2020, I've described at length the social, political and economic issues related to the Sikh turban world over. Special emphasis has been laid on the situation in North America. Sikh turbans have been the subject of ridicule, ever since the time the first Sikh stepped on the shores of North America in 1899. According to the *Khalsa Samachar,* back in 1907 two hundred Sikh factory workers were asked to remove their turban in British Columbia, Canada. In 1913, principal William Gourie of the central school in Vancouver demanded that Hindoo boys (Sikhs) remove their turbans in order to conform to local norms, archived information in the *Khalsa Samachar* of that year reveals. While the situation has improved in Canada, in the US school bullying, job discrimination and hate crimes are still rampant.

Sikhs can easily be identified from a distance because of their turbans. Few non-Sikhs wear turbans, but again, the style and configuration invariably are in variance. Muslims from Iran, certain African nations and Mullahs (Muslim priests) wear turbans. Some African-American women, in the past, wore pre-made headdresses. At a recent fashion show, female models of Gucci were seen sporting turban-like head gears.

With Sikh migration abroad, turban has a huge impact on how Sikhs function, and above all make a living. Sikhs with turban face discrimination at employment. The economic well-being of the community defines its future in the global world. Can the Sikh community progress and still abide by its most important symbol, the turban? Dawkins in 2008 spoke about atheism and agnosticism. Add to that what Darwin calls redundancy—they are modernity, detraditionalization, and lack of utility.

The turban carries dire consequences of mistaken identity in the US, especially in times of Islamophobia in the US. In 1979, following the Iranian hostage crisis, Sikhs, mistaken as Middle-easterners, were attacked. Likewise, following the 9/11 attacks on the twin trade towers in the heart of New York, Sikhs have had a horrid time. The turban-wearing Sikhs have been confused with Muslims and have been singled out for hate crimes and harrowing discrimination.

Identity is not a big issue in countries where Sikhs are settled for a long time. Most of these are in neighboring nations like Pakistan, Myanmar, Afghanistan, Thailand and British colonies of the past such as East Africa, Hong Kong, Singapore, and Malaysia. Sikhs also have been around in large numbers in the UK and Canada where mistaken identity does not get translated into hate crime. It is to be noted that small Sikh populations in Argentina and more recent migrants to Italy, Norway and some other Scandinavian nations are coexisting peacefully.

If humanity can coexist peacefully in educated western societies that have greater tolerance for a multi-religious, multiracial and multicultural society, I'm confident that the turban will be accepted as well. Self-employed Sikhs can function fairly well with the turban, compared with those working for others in the industrial labor force. There are examples of some Sikhs who decided to wear the turban after retirement. Today's world, dominated by the internet and online communications, interfaith marriages, and a plethora of social media, can go one way or the other when it comes to the turban. Sikhs hope the world moves in favor of the turban.

The survival of religion and traditions in the west are directly related to the political and financial muscle of a community, as well as the state policy of multiculturalism versus the melting pot. In multicultural Canada things are in sharp contrast to other western countries where the melting pot will draw into its fold other religious and cultural values of new immigrants.

Immigration to the west remains a bittersweet experience. The quality of life has definitely improved for immigrants. But the price one has had to pay insofar as religious freedom, retention of cultural values and identities are concerned is also heavy.

5Ks

Kesh, Karra, Kanga, Kachha, Kirpan
(Uncut hair, Bangle, Comb, Shorts and Sword)

The turban, unshorn hair, and the *karra* remain the only visible symbols for Sikhs in the US. *Karra* is a less specific symbol of Sikh identity since many non-Sikhs wear it as a fashion or as jewelry. *Karra*, along with skin color and turban, further compliments the Sikh identity. I recall a shaved relative of mine, not wearing a turban but just a *karra*, went to a winery for wine tasting. The young bartender who was a shaved Sikh looked at the *karra* and realized his client was a Sikh. It started an immediate friendship which was to last for long. But there are times when merely wearing a *karra* does not give away the Sikh identity. On the other hand, the *kirpan*, visible abundantly in India and a few other countries, is not to be seen in the US.

B. Invisible religion symbols

The other components of Sikh identity—the *kirpan* (sword), *kanga* (comb) and the *kachha* (shorts) are not to be seen in the US. A small hidden *kirpan* too is a rarity. Even though invisible, they can be used for religious and racial profiling.

On the rare occasion a tattoo on the hand that says '*Ek Um Kar*' from the Sikh scripture signifies one omnipotent God. It does give out the Sikh identity.

C. Social identity

The Sikhs are to be found across all walks of life in the US. Without any class profiling, one can see that they are doctors, professors, engineers, businessmen, farmers, owners of gas stations and fast-food outlets, and are taxi drivers. They are members of various professional bodies, including the Rotary Club and other public service organizations. A few are in politics. One was the head of the taxi owners' association in New York city. Two very tall young Sikhs are basketball players, while a couple of them are wrestlers. They've built a reputation for themselves in the US.

Female identity

The components are

1. Personal
2. Religious
3. Social

Personal

Well educated Sikh women do not have any distinct personal identity. Those born in the US are usually dressed like mainstream females in this country. Many of them wear the *karra* and have the middle name Kaur. Like their male counterparts, many of them resemble brown Caucasians. Educated Sikh women do not face any kind of discrimination. Many of them earn more than their spouses and, therefore, qualify as 'better' bread winners than their turban-wearing husbands who then tend to become stay-at-home fathers.

Religious identity

Most educated Sikh women in the US do not have any religious identity. Most of them wear the *karra*. The bangle is not religion-specific, and is worn as an ornament by many non-Sikhs. Members of Sikh Dharma International or 3HO including men and women wear white clothes and white turbans. The turban, *kirpan* and other 5Ks are not uncommon among baptized Sikh women in India. But higher education and the constant striving to move up the social ladder are not something that devout Sikh women look up to.

Social identity

There is no real distinction here when compared to the rest of the host society. Sikh women are in local politics and a part of the parent group in school. Some are in commissions and county boards. Some like Nikki Haley have become governors.

In India many women are used to kitty parties. The American Sikh women, though, remain far too busy for such parties, and they do not exist for them. The highly religious among Sikh women form Kirtan and Gurbani recitation groups (reading of Sikh scripture in groups) and meet at individual homes, by rotation. They all look forward to big weddings, quite in contrast to women in the host community.

Identity, turban and skin tone

In Islamophobic America, Sikhs have become victims of mistaken identities ever since 9/11 shook the foundations of secularism in the US. The situation in neighboring Canada is far better, given the larger percentage of Sikhs in the total population.

In the US, discrimination against Sikhs begins from the time boys wearing turbans start getting bullied in schools. Job discriminations have been rampant, just like multiple hate crimes.

Baptized or turban-clad Sikhs are handicapped when it comes to social mobility. Sikh women are reluctant to date or marry turbaned Sikhs.

Turban-wearing Sikhs in the top echelons of our society are not that visible. There are, however, exceptions to the rule. Ajay Banga who has retired from Mastercard wears a turban. So do Ravi Bhalla, Mayor of Hoboken, New Jersey, Aman Bhutani, CEO of GoDaddy.com, and Gurbir Singh Grewal who is in a senior position with the Securities and Exchange Commission in the USA. Few turban-wearing Sikhs are to be found in small town school boards and as county commissioners. All this is somewhat surprising given that the turban is the most visible sign of recognition of a person from the Indian subcontinent. After all, turban-wearing Sikhs are well known all over the world and easily stand out.

Harassment, discrimination and racial profiling are quite prevalent. A survey by the *Sikh Coalition* in 2010 revealed that sixty-nine percent of turban-wearing Sikhs in the Bay Area of San Francisco have suffered bullying while thirty percent have been physically hit and twelve percent have reported employment discrimination.

We need to look objectively as to why this is happening, and how the Darwinian theory is seemingly at play. When the tenth Sikh Guru created the Khalsa, religious symbols were the need of those dire times. The Sikhs desperately needed to protect their identity which the Mughals were trying to erase. The Khalsa came together as a united entity to withstand the plundering of wealth and forced conversions into Islam by the Mughal rulers and their slew of ruthless commanders. Khalsa was also called Akal Purkh Di Fauj (Army of God). Now, with modernization, there are several impediments to being a baptized Sikh. Uncut hair, wearing a turban, carrying a sword are all losing relevance as Sikhs strive to make a mark in the business, corporate and social spheres. In fact, there are studies and surveys that show that there is a considerable reduction in the numbers of baptized Sikhs in the UK. Similar must be the case in the US as well.

The question before us, therefore, is what is likely to replace the Khalsa, going forward. Necessity, as they say, is the mother of invention. Sikhs will invent and implement what is the need of the hour—higher education, wealth creation, charity, unity and greater political involvement in North America. This will be the future Khalsa that will promote and protect all religious, cultural and complimentary ethics of Sikh society. This is not going to come about through any mandate or ordinance. Once again, the Darwinian principle of achieving one's goals with the least amount of expenses, or resources, will come into play. It does appear that in North America, at least, with time the 5Ks will not be practiced so rigidly among Sikhs, given the reasons furnished above. This will be the case even though the number of Sikhs is likely to increase. I'd, of course, be delighted to be proven wrong. Overall, as of now, Sikh enclaves in the US and Canada have a number of turban-wearing populations. It will be a challenge to see this continue.

There are some distinctive communities and ethnic groups in the US that have symbols and customs that do not resonate with main street America. Orthodox Jews, Amish of Pennsylvania, Jehovah's Witnesses come to mind straightaway. These groups, however, differ from Sikhs in that they live in enclaves and have restrictive choices when it comes to vocation and customs. But Sikhs, by nature, cannot be constrained. Author G.S. Aurora, talking about Sikhs who had migrated from India to Great Britain had aptly titled his 1967 book *The New Frontiersmen,* a commentary on how the community survives abroad with its identity intact.

My own view is that Sikhs will continue to fight for the survival of turbans, and at the same time continue to change. According to the *British Sikh Report* of 2018, half of the Sikhs in Britain are *keshdhari* (unshorn hair) with turban. My earlier book, *The Sikh Turban in North America,* did publish an encouraging survey in which the majority of the participants have expressed optimism about the future of the turban.

When it comes to color, the general brown skin tone of the Sikhs will become more acceptable over time. On the positive side, the brown pigmentation is less prone to the dangers of ultraviolet radiation when contrasted with the equatorial black and Nordic white skin tones. There will be less discrimination as societies will become more cosmopolitanized. According to the US Census report, by the year 2050 whites are quite likely to become a minority in the country. Some others say that colored races will outnumber whites by 2035. This could then prove to be a dramatic shift from the days of the bloody Civil War in the 19th century and the White America that the majority in the US and Canada wanted in the first half of the 20th century.

Sikh family structure

Mankind in primordial times were primarily hunters and gatherers. They did not have organized families until they started settling in villages and towns. For very long periods man lived as a part of an extended family in which food and lodging was shared. Extended families had their advantages, they offered multiple mothering, interaction and socializing with other family members that would provide man the skill sets required to deal with the world at large.

The extended families remained a feature until the onset of the industrial revolution and its new cousin, urbanization. That immediately had a disruptive effect, and the concept of nuclear families was born. This phenomenon became prevalent in the west, and began, over time, to gradually catch up in the east. Most of the societies of the old civilization were patriarchal in nature, and Indians and Sikhs were no exception.

The Sikh marriage ceremony was formalized by the Fourth Sikh Guru Ram Dass Ji. Oftentimes, it was brokered in Punjab by the Raja (*Nahii*) and his wife (*Nain*). Gender selection and female infanticide has been criticized in Sikhism. The newborn had name ceremonies as per guidance received from the Guru Granth Sahib. Adolescent Sikh boys have a turban-tying ceremony.

Sikh families are mostly bio-nuclear, that is husband and wife are in a marital relationship with less divorces. Domestic violence and extramarital affairs are, however, universal. Sati—the abominable practice of burning a widow, usually a very young girl, at the funeral pyre of her husband (usually much older to her) was a curse in Hindu society until Raja Ram Mohan Roy raised his voice against it. Sikhism was very much against such an abhorrent and inhuman practice and preached the marrying of widows.

Guru Nanak Ji spoke about gender equality much before it became a fashionable term in the West. By the way, even after screaming about gender equality from the rooftops, the US as a nation is yet to find its first woman President. In Britain, by contrast, the Queen rules and there have been lady Prime Ministers.

Brothers are caretakers of sisters in the Sikh community, both before and after the marriage of the female sibling. This is indeed unique and has no parallel in western society. The bonding has sweetly blossomed over the ages. When one of the earliest Sikh immigrants arrived in the US, he brought with him his two younger unmarried sisters. He was their protector.

In turn Sikh sisters tie a thread called the rakhi around the wrist of a brother once a year and pray for their long life. In earlier times, the sister would hold the reins of a horse before the brother went to war, praying for his safety. In Punjab, paeans have been sung on this sacred relationship and many a poem and song has been penned in its honor. This is a distinctive aspect of Punjabi and Sikh literature.

Filial piety is a common feature in Sikh society. Immigrant Sikhs from Punjab hold on steadfastly to family, cultural and religious values as long as they can. There is deep respect for parents and the elderly. Unlike in the western societies, the word Ji is an honorific that is used to address seniors. So, uncle ji, aunty ji and *behen* ji are common terms used to address an uncle, aunt or another lady. Sikh people would mostly bend down to touch the knees of the elderly as a sign of respect. Teachers are held in very high esteem, and favorite ones even worshipped like Gurus. At times of need, Sikh families reach out to help each other out in the best possible way.

The Punjabi dictionary has specific nomenclatures to address relatives. *Bapu* is an address for a paternal grandfather, likewise *Bebe, Dadi* or *Maanji* are terms for a paternal grandmother. On the maternal side are terms like *Nana* and *Nani*. Similarly, *Massi* and *Masser, Bhua* and *Phuper* stand for mother's sister and her husband, and father's sister and her husband respectively. An unrelated elderly can be referred to as *Bapu* Ji or *Babba* Ji.

There has been a shift tough. The younger generations do not touch the knees or the feet, like we would. The American way is winning and the Sikh youth, caught in its fold, are no longer prone to express themselves uninhibitedly. The honorific Ji is slowly fading away, and not everyone is deferential to seniority and age. When a relative who'd retired as a brigadier in the Indian Army was visiting us for a few days, my son, six-years-old at the time, described his driving as "lousy" in his own American accent. The brigadier had an international driving license, had driven armored vehicles in his youth, and here he was digesting this from a little boy who had his American expressions!

The descendants of the Sikh pioneers who started arriving in America nearly one hundred and twenty-three years ago have not, unhappily enough, held on to tradition. Like the tagline in a liquor advertisement that ran for years in India used to say, "Tradition is what it used to be." Only surnames like Pannu, Thind and Saund survive. The values the forebears brought along are no longer visible.

Extended families are turning nuclear as mobility increases and greater opportunities beckon in faraway places. Dating and cohabitation is on the rise, and the age-old tried and tested system of arranged marriages is on the wane. Traditional marriage customs such as *mangni* or engagement are rapidly being replaced by the ring ceremony, a direct fallout of the fast-food, instant gratification culture. Same-sex marriage, divorce, intrauterine insemination, in vitro fertilization, surrogate motherhood have become commonplace. These issues are confounding for the first-generation immigrant Sikhs. Newer immigrants, on the other hand, are unable to easily come to terms with the LGBTQ communities and those who have same-sex marriages. Absorbing this culture shock remains a challenge.

There is a growing proclivity for interfaith marriage in the US. For Sikhs this phenomenon is more prevalent in small communities but very less in coastal cities and Sikh enclaves. Since there is a mismatch in numbers of young, marriageable Sikhs, interfaith marriage is the only option left when it comes to finding a life partner.

Sikh charity is less directed to public causes and more to Gurdwaras and religious occasions. This may be due to a lack of financial stability. Most Sikhs, however, do *Nitnem* (daily prayer and *Japji*) and pray to succeed when starting a new venture, business or before travelling. I'm of the firm belief that these shortcomings are not going to last forever. They will blow over once there is greater adaptation and more assimilation.

Filial piety and Sikhism

In the Orient, filial piety, or love and respect for one's parents, elders and ancestors, is an ancient practice. East Asian cultures, particularly those that are Chinese Buddhist and Taoist, have followed the Confucian tenet of filial piety. Confucian, named after the great philosopher Confucius (479 BCE), focuses on the virtues of personal ethics and morality and extends to the practice of good conduct not just at home, but outside it as well. This cultural philosophy was majorly adopted in Japan and Korea. In Punjab, filial piety was a well-known practice, particularly among Sikhs.

For instance, an elderly male in the family was given high respect and privacy. His bedroom was away from those of younger family members. As a physician, I was once making a home consultation visit to check a comatose man. His son, a judge of a High Court, removed his shoes while entering his sick father's room. When I inquired if his father lived with him, the judge replied politely, "No, I live in their service." The judge, of course, lived in his allotted official bungalow, but did not fail in his duty to look after his elderly father.

In Singapore, Taiwan and India it is an offense if one does not look after elderly parents. Hong Kong provides tax allowances to citizens willing to live with elderly parents.

The story of Shravana Kumar, distantly related to King Dasharatha, is mentioned in the Ramayana, the ancient Hindu text. Shravana's parents, Shantanu and Gyanvati were hermits, but both of them were blind. Shravana took them to the four most sacred places of Hindu pilgrimage to purify their souls. As affording transport for them was beyond his means, he put each parent inside a basket tied to either end of a bamboo pole. He then put the bamboo pole on his shoulders and went on the pilgrimage.

Sikh customs and traditions

Like any other religious and cultural group, Sikhs have ceremonies and customs during important events in their life cycle. The important ones include *nam karan*—the naming ceremony of a newborn, *dastar bandi*—the turban-tying ceremony of adolescent males, marriage ceremony, *rasam pagri*—offering of the turban to the eldest son at the death of the father, and cremation.

Nam Karan and Dastar Bandi

The naming ceremony of a newborn and the *dastar bandi*, or turban initiation at an adolescent age, are done by very few Sikh families in the US. They take place in the presence of Guru Granth Sahib Ji.

As a Gyani or clergy randomly opens the holy book, the newborn Sikh gets a name that starts with the first letter of the left page.

The Sikh boy wears a *Jurra* for the protection of uncut hair. It is collected on the top of the head in a rounded ball and is secured by a handkerchief and rubber band. At about age eight or nine, the hair is protected by a *Patka*, a square piece of cloth that covers the entire head secured with a knot. At the *dastar bandi* ceremony, a young adolescent Sikh youth is given a lesson on tying a Turban. Thus, flows the tradition of starting with a *Jurra*, moving on to a *Patka*, and then a Turban.

Sikh marriage

According to the *Stanford Encyclopedia of Philosophy* (2016), Greek philosopher Plato was the first proponent of eugenics in his influential work *Republic* (375 BC) that was essentially a Socratic dialogue with Socrates as the protagonist. Plato believed that in order for a predictable improvement of the human race, sexual reproduction ought to be monitored and controlled by the state. Temporary marriages, he averred, should be arranged on festivals when reproduction could take place. This would orchestrate eugenic breeding. The raising of children should then become the responsibility of the state. Aristotle, his student for twenty years at the Academy of Athens and another renowned philosopher of the times, differed from his master, stating that marriage should be individualized with the state having no role to play. Other Greek philosophers considered marriage good for procreation, but sinful if lust was involved. Marriage remains an institution for regulating sex, reproduction and family life.

American political philosophers John Rawls and Michael Sandel, and German philosopher Georg Hegel had their own definitive views on marriage, and had varying opinions on the subject. Women had little or no views on the subject as they were considered the weaker sex. Things began to change, however, when women suffrage became a reality and the 19th amendment legally guaranteed them the right to vote. Since then, the institution of marriage has not remained male-dominated, at least in the US.

Over the last half-a-century, or so, volatility has crept into the institution and its stability is no longer assured. Some of the factors for this have been the women's lib movements, a more permissive society, the rampant usage of birth control pills, and the economic independence of women. Almost half of American marriages end in divorce. Which begs the question—if marriage is not for sex, companionship and economic togetherness, then what is it for? Back in the day children were a shelter for one's aging parents, and they ran the family farm. Things have changed now.

According to an article in 2009 by Mark Kantrowitz who quotes the *US Department of Agriculture*, it costs $234,000 to raise a child from birth through age seventeen. Several studies and surveys do indicate that people without children are in fact happier. So, is marriage merely a tradition then? Traditions, we know, change all the time. The wave against marriage is prevalent in all western societies, and the east will follow suit.

It was the third Guru Amar Dass Ji who formulated the Sikh marriage ceremony called *Anand Karaj*. It was further formalized by fourth Guru Ram Dass Ji. The groom leads the bride in four rounds (*laavan*) around the Guru Granth Sahib. At a recent wedding ceremony, the bride expressed her desire to lead in two of the rounds, emphasizing gender equality.

Tradition was that in the past Sikh marriages would be arranged by a professional team of Raja and his wife (*Nai* and *Nain*). The consequences of many such marriages are well known. Highly-educated, devout Sikh families have become victims of failed marriages of their children. Some of them had interfaith remarriages that have enabled them to settle down better. In my view, it is almost impossible to find a *Puran* Sikh (complete Sikh) spouse in the US, it is akin to going on a wild goose chase.

Historically, Sikh and Punjabi communities had the following reasons to venture into marriage:

1. The Punjabi farmer worked on a farm and needed somebody, a wife in charge of the household and kitchen.
2. Sexual fulfillment in a conservative society with no sexual freedom.
3. Raising children to help in the family business and for safety and care in old age.
4. Definite economic benefits if the in-laws happen to be well-to-do.
5. In a society with less females as a result of the horrific practice of infanticide, marriages somehow improve social status within the community.
6. Sikh Maharaja Ranjit Singh took Moran Sarkar, a Punjabi Muslim woman, as his wife. This was in order to create religious harmony. The Maharaja of Patiala had about three hundred wives. This was to develop deeper relationships with the subjects and not for sex, or procreation.

   Queen Victoria had many grandchildren who married into royal families all over Europe. That kept the blue-blood lineage alive, but more than that the marriages built friendly relations with other countries and they helped avoid wars in Europe.

The early Sikh settlers in North America could not return to Punjab to find a bride as their re-entry was uncertain given the racist, anti-Asiatic laws in place. Many of them married locally, if the opportunity arose. Most married Hispanic women, especially in California, due to a similarity brought about by skin tone, family values, occupation and the most common denominator—discrimination by the white American society. In modern times, Sikhs in North America are better off. They have a choice of a partner in marriage. Sikhs value the institution and have lesser incidence of divorce. Live-in relationships, common law and same-sex marriages are frowned upon, but not for very long. Old ceremonies of *Chhuara* or *Mangni* (engagement) are replaced by the ring offering. *Muklawa* or permanent residence with the family of the in-laws and the *Kund* (veil over the face) ceremony are no longer to be seen.

In my view, the newer Sikh immigrants to North America will make a serious effort to hold on to traditional values. They'll also continue to thrive in the Sikh enclaves.

Sikhs and interfaith marriage

Since there is a mismatch in numbers of young, marriageable Sikhs, interfaith marriage is the only option left when it comes to finding a life partner. In some places due to hybrid interfaith marriages, a melting pot has taken place. Children from such marriages are well respected, though, and constitute the mainstream. Exogamy itself is on the rise in the US.

Interfaith marriages are, no doubt, painful for the current generation of Sikhs. Cohabitation and premarital sex are becoming common in Sikh families now. This phenomenon, in the long run, does not bode well for the Sikh community. But similar is the situation with other religions as well.

Subsequent generations will be no different than the society at large in the US. They will have interfaith marriages of their free choice, and not due to any limitation or compulsion. Things were not the same for the early Sikh settlers at the turn of the last century who were compelled to marry Hispanic women. One of the reasons was that in case the Sikhs returned to Punjab to find a bride, the anti-Asiatic laws in place in the US and Canada could easily prevent their re-entry. The children of such mixed marriages, at the time, were not respected. They were seen as neither Sikh, nor Hispanic.

LGBTQ
(Lesbian, gay, bisexual, transgender and queer or questioning)

Of late, the LGBTQ community has garnered a lot of social attention. Educated societies have accepted them and have given them the respect that is due. Every religion is debating the issue of same-sex marriage, new modes of fertilization, aberrations of sexual differentiation. The issue has been discussed at length by Sikhs in Great Britain.

Same-sex marriage

The older generation and the Akal Takht have criticized same-sex marriage as it is against Sikh Maryada (Paul 2021). For example, a recent same-sex marriage between two individuals—Sarbjeet Singh Neel and Leela (wife)—in the presence of the Guru Granth Sahib Ji has not met with the approval of Jathedar Giani Harpreet Singh of Akal Takht. The couple was reprimanded for going against Sikh Maryada and the local Gurdwara was advised to take away the saroop or holy book from them, as reported in *The Tribune* in 2020.

Pope Frances recently talked favorably about same-sex marriage (X Frances and Rocco, 2020). This turned out to be a landmark and bold declaration from the Vatican after the subject had been discussed for years in the Catholic Church. Recently, German Catholic leaders supported gay couples.

The Sikh scripture is neutral about same-sex marriage. I'm sure Sikh Gurus will gladly accept this new social challenge.

Manas ki Jaat Sabhe Ekay Pehchanbo
(Human species has the same genes)
Guru Gobind Singh Ji

Cremation

According to studies undertaken in 1997-98 by R Gillespie in the Willandra Lakes region of Australia—a UNESCO World Heritage Center in New South Wales—archaeological records of cremation date back to at least 17,000 years. Here the partly cremated body of a Mungo lady was found at

Lake Mungo—located in the center of the Willandra Lakes system. Alternative death rituals that emphasize one method of disposal such as burial, cremation or exposure, have gone through periods of preference in history.

The Romans practiced cremation. The Abrahamic religions were, however, opposed to this. At one time it was punishable by law in the Christian world, but now cremation is becoming prevalent in it. The administration in London built a crematorium in the heart of this metropolis in the middle of the nineteenth century. For some, the decomposition of the human body that is buried is quite nauseating, hence cremation is preferred. It is also cheaper and environmentally-friendly, with alkaline hydrolysis being the latest trend.

Sikhs have cremation as a final rite for the disposal of the dead, a practice that was adopted from Hinduism. Cremation is carried out with prayer (*kirtan Sohila*) for the departed soul with recitations from the Holy Granth.

Sikhism, afterlife and reincarnation

Certain religions like Hinduism consider the idea of life as a continuous, uninterrupted process where the body dies but the soul continues its journey. The concept is that the soul is imperishable, it was neither born, nor does it die. It is also believed that a single soul goes through eighty-four human forms before merging with the greater soul of the universe. Upon death, there is transmigration where the soul passes from one body to another. Reincarnation itself is the philosophical and religious belief that the soul, or the non-physical essence of the body, is reborn upon death in a different physical form.

Sikhism drew from this idea. The tenth Sikh Guru Gobind Singh Ji is said to have meditated in his previous life at the high Himalayan place of Hemkund Sahib. This, though, has been a subject of much debate among Sikh scholars.

The movement of the soul depends on its karma. Good deeds are rewarded to souls when they appear in better species among the living beings. The cycle of life and death concludes with Mukti or Moksha, oneness with God.

No surveys have been done on the afterlife. But there are quite a few world-renowned practitioners of past life regression. Some humans while being regressed have been able to speak a language completely different or alien to the ones they've spoken or been exposed to in the present lifetime. The believers of past lives say the alien language has been there in the subconscious from a previous birth.

In ancient Egypt, when the ruling Pharaohs died, they were laid to rest along with their favorite food items, jewelry and even models of pets. The belief system was clear that the deceased was moving on to another journey of life. Greek philosopher Socrates accepted death cheerfully in the belief that his soul would continue to fulfill his wishes and ideas in the afterlife.

The idea of heaven and hell has been promoted by Islam. It says if you do good deeds in this life, you go to heaven. If you commit bad ones, you go to hell. There is no in between place, so either you've done good, or evil, and, therefore, passed or failed. In heaven you receive the company of beautiful women (hoors), at the other side of the spectrum one burns in hellfire and starves. Political Islam has exploited this and encouraged violence against *kafirs* (non-believers or infidels, as they are derogatorily termed) and have often tasked *fidayeen* squads to carryout suicide bombings with the objective of mass killings.

The movement of a soul depends on karma and it continues its journey through the cycle of life and death. In the prevailing religious thinking, if good deeds have been done, this cycle of life and death ends with *Mukti*, oneness with God.

SIKH INSTITUTIONS

Sikhs have four important religious organizations.

Sikh Gurdwara Sahib

This is the most important Sikh institution and plays a highly significant role in the daily life of all Sikhs. The first religious meeting place for Sikhs was constructed by Guru Nanak Ji at Kartarpur, Punjab in 1521. This institution was called Dharamshala. The fifth Sikh Guru Arjan Dev Ji compiled the holy Guru Granth Sahib and requested a Muslim holy man, Mian Mir, to lay the foundation stone for the building where the Guru Granth Sahib was placed. It had openings on all four sides, implying the place was welcome for people of all religions and social status.

The sixth Guru Hargobind Rai Ji gave the current name Gurudwara, meaning abode or place of the Guru. There are hundreds of Sikh Gurdwaras all over the world. Harmandir Sahib is the most important, and the first among them. The Gurdwara is the very first institution that is set up when Sikhs migrate to a new place or country.

Many Gurdwaras are splendid buildings but in the words of the Sikh scholar Bhai Gurdas, they can be humble places too. *Jithai jaae behai maeraa satgur so thaan Suhaavaa Ram rajee*—wherever there is the Guru Granth Sahib Ji, that place is rendered sacred.

In North America, the first Guru Granth Sahib Ji was brought to Canada by Bhai Arjan Singh in 1904. The first Sikh congregation for *path* (prayer) in the US took place on November 1, 1911, at the Nand Singh camp near Stockton, California. Jawala Singh and Wisakha Singh were partners in a potato farm and prayers were held in the barn of their farm.

The first Sikh Gurdwaras in North America were established at Vancouver, Canada in 1908 and at Stockton, California, US in 1912. A few years ago, the Sikhs of Dubai built a large institution, where many Muslim royalties broke their religious fast in the month of Ramadan in 2018.

The Sikh Gurdwara is a multipurpose facility and differs from single purpose worship places of other religions. Compared to other religions, there is no monthly fee.

Sikh Gurdwara at Hong Kong

Hundle family stranded in Hong Kong Gurdwara, on their way to Canada in 1912. Left to right Atma, Iqbal, grandmother Bishen Kaur, Teja and Jermeja

The organization is run by voluntary contributions, without any membership. It is open to everybody, without any restrictions being set on caste, creed or religious affiliations. Some of the main functions of the Gurdwara are outlined below:

- ❖ Spiritual and religious teaching.
- ❖ Equality.
- ❖ *Pangat,* which is a congregation that takes part in *Langar* (free kitchen) after a religious function. Here the rich and the poor, young and old, male and female, sit and share their meal together, conveying the universal message of equality and brotherhood among all.
- ❖ *Sangat* is a congregation for thinking in a group. Contemporary issues, including those that are social and political in nature and have a bearing on society, are discussed within the confines of a democratic setting. The *sangat* also acts as

Sikh Gurdwara in Vancouver Canada

Sikh Gurdwara at Stockton California

a platform for psychological ventilation of one's feelings and needs.

* Social club: There is a weekly *Dewan* or prayer at the Gurdwara. This is also a time for meeting and enjoying a community *langar*. A Gurdwara caters to the needs of everyone in the community, especially the newer immigrants.

* Serai (inn): These were meant for overnight stays at a time when hotels, motels and modern-day facilities like AirBnB did not exist. Some of these are still operational and many people avail of their free facilities. One can cite the example of the Sikh Gurdwara in Hongkong which became a transit point for early Sikh immigrants who were emigrating from Calcutta port to the Pacific West. Many families stayed at this place for weeks, before boarding ships for North America.

* Weddings: Most Sikh weddings are formalized in the presence of the holy Granth and conducted by a Sikh Granthi or priest. Wedding reception halls are part of many Gurdwaras. The newlyweds receive their sacred blessings here and the entire ceremony is inexpensive.

* Sikh Gurdwaras in many cases offer free healthcare services.

* The concept of service or *sewa* in the *langar* and kitchen are early lessons in leadership and egalitarianism in young Sikhs. A Gurdwara in Myanmar even organized funerals for the poor, irrespective of their religion.

* Blind persons are trained as *Ragis* or *Kirtinias*, spiritual singers. They are the Sikh Stevie Wonders of the world.

* In the past the Gurdwara was the place for education of girls until such time schools were established for them. They were taught in the Punjabi language and they picked up the Gurmukhi script.

Like in any other institution, the Sikh Gurdwara is not immune to conflicts and confrontations. This is the way the world works whenever power, privilege and money come into play. When matters are not amicably sorted, it is not uncommon to hear that a conflict has led to the setting up of a parallel Gurdwara.

Interestingly, while studies and surveys indicate that attendance in churches and synagogues may be falling in the US, the same cannot be said of Gurdwaras. This is because it remains a multipurpose facility, as mentioned a while earlier. It is a place of spirituality, political discourse, free food and lodging, social meets, quite unlike other places of worship.

The most challenging part, however, is that

Sikh temple at El Centro California

Akal Takht

only about three to four percent of the second and third-generation Sikhs attend Gurdwaras. This decline is made up by newcomers and the retired elders, the first-generation immigrants. If the Sikh population grows, so will the attendance in Gurdwaras. The unification of all offshoots of Sikhs will help grow visitors to the Gurdwaras. Let us hope that things will change for the better.

Akal Takht

Akal Takht is one of five Takhts, but is the one that has the supreme authority over the others. It was started at the Harmandir Sahib complex in Amritsar by Guru Hargobind Rai Ji after the assassination of his father, Fifth Guru Arjan Dev Ji, by the ruling Mughals of Lahore. He was convinced that Sikhism needed to be militarized if it had to survive. On June 15, 1606, he raised a nine-foot cement slab and called it the *Akal Bunga*. It was to receive the shape of a formal structure by the Khalsa general Jassa Singh Ahluwalia and was further decorated by the Sikh general Hari Singh Nalwa. The name was formalized subsequently as Akal Takht, meaning the Throne of the Timeless One.

Sixth Guru Hargobind Rai Ji put two swords—one for *Piri,* and the other for *Miri,* thereby delegating both spiritual and temporal authority to the Akal Takht. Sikh leaders have, over the years, passed *Gurmattas*, or resolutions, for matters that concern the Sikh community. Prominent Sikhs have also been conferred the *Saropa* (yellow cloth worn around the neck as a robe of honor) for doing good for the community. Those who failed to follow the Sikh code of conduct and committed ill deeds have been punished by a process called the *Thankhia.*

Bhai Gurdas was the first caretaker or Jathedar of the Akal Takht. Giani Harpreet Singh is the current spiritual head or Jathedar of the Akal Takht. It had been destroyed and damaged in the eighteenth century by Ahmed Shah Abdali, a barbaric invader from Afghanistan, and by Indian Prime Minister Mrs Indira Gandhi on June 4, 1984. It was rebuilt into its current form through voluntary service, known as *kar sewa.* There are four more regional takhts.

Akal Takht has the following responsibilities and authority:

1. It promotes the concept of *Piri* and *Miri* (Saint Soldier).
2. Declares *Hukamnama* (order) and *Matta* (resolution) regarding community affairs.
3. Safeguards Sikh Maryada with reward (*Saropa*) and punishment (*Thankhia*).
4. To conduct itself as an independent body.

Akal Takht is the seat of religious and political discourse. It also remains the authority to honor and punish leaders within the Sikh community, depending on their conduct. The institution functions under the overall command of the Jathedar of Akal Takht and the Panj Piaras (Beloved Five).

The twin concepts of *Miri* and *Piri* were the need of the hour at the time they were adopted by Sixth Guru Hargobind Rai Ji. While the concept of *Piri* or spirituality will always be welcomed, the concept of *Miri* undergoes changes in democratic setups. The *Miri* is a temporal authority for the protection of the self and others. In a democratic set up in India, the Sikhs cannot have their own army, but they do have alternate means of protection for themselves and others. Sikhs can draw their power from their unity, education, enfranchisement and wealth. The Jewish community has proven this as true in the US. The Akal Takht's *Hukamnamas*—resolutions and messages—should shape the new *Miri* and *Piri*.

The Akal Takht also has to be in step with modernity and the changes it brings about. For instance, the head Jathedar has recently sought an explanation from a Gurdwara Sahib in Canada where a marriage ceremony was conducted while the bride and groom were seated on chairs before the Guru Granth Sahib Ji. This is not an acceptable practice in India.

While there is absolutely no question of treating the Guru Granth Sahib Ji with anything less than the utmost respect, in the case of a disabled person an exception may be made and it can be kept on an elevated platform. The use of chairs inside the Gurdwara Sahib has been challenged in the past, but due to increasing demand from senior citizens with knee and leg problems, relaxations are being made. Rala Singh of RalaMelons about whom I've described in a separate chapter on *Sikh Pioneers and Trailblazers* was not very amused by the orthodox approach of the priests at the Gurdwara. He went back to his episcopal church. The Gurdwara Sahib management failed to provide him with a chair following a knee surgery. With longevity should come

adjustments, and there ought to be flexibility in these minor issues of Sikh Maryada.

Like the case in Canada about the seating issue, the Akal Takht has also recently challenged a same-sex wedding at Sacramento, California. The Sikh holy scripture remains non-committal on the issue of same-sex marriage. The LGBTQ community that has remained long ignored by Sikh institutions deserve respect, and same-sex marriage should be permitted

When it was set up, the Akal Takht was an independent body. The Sarbat Khalsa and later the Shiromani Gurdwara Parbandhak Committee (SGPC) used to appoint educated, independent, responsible and devout Sikhs as the Jathedar, and this can be substantiated by the list of names who've headed the Akal Takht over the years. But with time, this august institution has lost some of its spiritual and temporal authority. The primary reason is the way it has been run by the SGPC for their narrow political ends. The SGPC, itself, remains a tainted political entity and, no doubt, it has brought the Akal Takht's credibility down along with its own. The Jathedar, therefore, is constantly politically manipulated. A credible alternative to a Jathedar would be a board of trustees comprising non-political heads of Sikh education chairs in India and overseas.

The Akal Takht can even look to seek out and emulate the model of the Vatican and the coronation of the Pope. This can reinvigorate this once hallowed institution and restore its authority and responsibilities. The decentralization of Sikhism and vesting all authority in the local *sangat* (congregation) is even better.

Shiromani Gurdwara Parbandhak Committee

The SGPC is the most important Sikh religious body that manages Sikh Gurdwaras in Punjab, Haryana and Himachal Pradesh. It also, through its organizational cadres, controls Sikh politics. The SGPC was established around 1920 for managing Sikh Gurdwaras.

Dating back to the times of the Khalsa Raj that began with Guru Gobind Singh Ji in 1699 and up to the early 20th century when the British ruled India, Sikh Gurdwaras were managed by mahants, descendants of Nirmala and Udasi Sehajdhari Sikhs. Over time, they began to misuse the financial resources of the Gurdwaras and desecrated their religious sanctity. Gurdwaras became hereditary property and mahants became British agents. When the Singh Sabha, the Sikh intelligentsia and devout Sikhs were made aware of this, a movement under the banner of the Shiromani Gurdwara Parbandhak Committee (SGPC or the Committee of Shrine Management) began to take control of the Sikh shrines. The British who perpetrated the loathsome divide-and-rule policy sided with the corrupt mahants. But as the Singh Sabha movement gained momentum, the British felt it could eventually grow to threaten their empire in Punjab and in India. They passed the Gurdwara Act in 1925 in the legislative assembly. The Sikhs later changed the name to Shiromani Gurdwara Parbandhak Committee. The current budget of the SGPC is a staggering $130 million.

The SGPC took over the enforcement of the Gurdwara Act in November 1925 but not before a bitter war raged. The sidelined mahants hired goons and criminals and murdered two hundred devout Sikhs. During this tumultuous transition among those who led the SGPC included the likes of Teja Singh Bhuchar, Kartar Singh Jhabbar and Bhai Lachman Singh, the last named becoming a martyr for the cause. The British regime also tried to throw a spanner in the works by trying to disrupt the organizational efforts of the SGPC by setting up a committee of thirty-six Sikhs two days before a general assembly of the Akali leadership was called. But another committee of one hundred and seventy-five members took over the management, formally establishing the SGPC.

The committee began to take over the management of Gurdwaras one by one, and at places faced resistance from the incumbent mahants. Overall, though, the transition took place peacefully, especially in the Gurdwaras whose sources of revenue were few. Since its inception, the SGPC has had very large financial resources at its disposal. These resources have been developed from the lease money received against land given to various Gurdwaras. In addition, there is the donation received from the devotees. The donations are used for missionary purposes and running educational institutions and free kitchens or *langars*.

Since the beginning the SGPC did remarkable charity work but over the last few years things have fallen into disarray. Funds have been misused for personal purposes by one political family. The committee also debarred Mona and Sehajdhari Sikhs from its membership largely as an election ploy which is detrimental to Sikhi at large, promoting visits to Gurdwaras, and for getting more donations. The last general secretary, the late respected business leader Harcharan Singh, had pointed fingers at the SGPC's poor management and misuse of funds. Elected members have received undue favors which are now coming out in the open. As a result of this muddying of the waters, today Gurdwaras in other states want their own independent bodies that are not answerable to the SGPC. The SGPC in New Delhi already has its own managing committee.

In March 2022, *The Tribune* from Chandigarh, Punjab, reported how at least twelve SGPC members have demanded that a panel of retired High Court judges probe the "large scale corruption" going on in the committee that is tasked to manage hundreds of Gurdwaras across India. Allegations range from undervaluing lease prices causing losses to the SGPC to the raising of excessive funds from directly managed Gurdwaras, in violation of norms. This is just the tip of the iceberg, and the allegations run quite deep including the way the trusts control engineering and medical colleges run by the SGPC. These institutions are receiving the equivalent of millions of dollars in Indian rupees from the SGPC, but they have very little accountability. There are allegations of embezzlement of funds in the corridor scheme set up around the Harmandir Sahib. Even financial resources utilized for procurement of langar commodities that are used on a daily basis such as ghee, pulses and sugar are being siphoned off, according to several of the SGPC members who have come out in the open and revolted against the managing body.

There is, of course, no smoke without fire. So much noise cannot be made for nothing. My take is that in view of the large-scale allegations that are being leveled on the financial management practices of the SGPC and the divide it is causing within the Sikh community, an independent, privately managed company that is not run by Sikhs will do a better job in handling the huge endowments and resources. The Sikh auditing body has not quite been able to keep itself away from the quagmire of corruption. A Sikh committee not related to SGPC membership should approve the annual budget. The elected members are grossly ill-equipped and poorly trained for doing so and must give way to a professional outfit in this climate of nepotism and corruption. This would also benefit not just Sikhs in India but the Sikh diaspora spread across all continents.

Akali Dal

The Shiromani Akali Dal is a center-right Sikh political party for the protection of rights of the Sikh community. It was conceived as the youth wing of the Shiromani Gurdwara Parbandhak Committee (SGPC) before being commissioned as an independent political party on December 14, 1920 by Sarmukh Singh Chubbal. The Akali Dal became famous when Master Tara Singh became its president. It remains the oldest political party in India after the Indian National Congress.

The Akali Dal was created to safeguard the rights of the Sikh community. Prior to the partition of India and Punjab, it formed a coalition with the Congress and the United Party of Malik Khizar Hayat Tiwana. Post-partition, it fought for the creation of a Punjabi Suba, the riparian rights of the river waters of Punjab, and for Chandigarh as the sole capital. The Akali Dal was at the forefront of agitation when Indira Gandhi declared emergency in India. Following the Anandpur Sahib Resolution of 1973, the Akali Dal demanded a federal structure insofar as center-state relations are concerned. At the Moga conference in 1996 it somewhat relaxed its position on Sikh issues and passed a resolution with a definitive leaning towards being a Punjabi party.

The Shiromani Akali Dal as a political entity has become largely redundant. In the elections held in Punjab in March 2022, the hundred-year-old political party was all but wiped out, its presence reduced to a mere three seats in the 117-member state assembly. In the earlier state elections in 2017 it had only fifteen seats, and clearly its relevance for the people of Punjab has been going down dramatically. By aligning with the Bharatiya Janata Party (BJP), the Akali Dal neutralized its pro-Sikh agenda. By the time the Akali Dal broke this alliance during the protracted farmers' agitations near the Delhi border recently, politically its stock had gone down dramatically. The Sikh rural farmer, the main vote bank of the Akali Dal, deserted the party in the March 2022 elections and instead chose to put his weight behind the Aam Aadmi Party.

Not only has the Akali Dal abandoned its Sikh agenda, it has lost the respect of the Sikh masses. It turned into a dynastic party before splitting up into various factions such as the Shiromani Akali Dal headed by Sukhbir Badal, the Akali Dal Amritsar headed by Simranjit Singh Mann, the Akali Dal Taksali headed by Ranjit Singh Brahmpura, and the Akali Dal Democratic led by Sukhdev Singh Dhindsa.

The Akali leadership's cosy relationship with Gurmeet Ram Rahim Singh Insan, the self-proclaimed Guru, was the root cause behind the desecration of the holy Granth, and the killing of two agitating Sikhs. Of late, over 300 Saroops (Guru Granth Sahib holy

books) have been found missing, raising serious questions over whether they have been stolen, or sold. This kind of sacrilege was unheard of in earlier times, and frankly quite unthinkable.

Langar

The langar is a free kitchen for all, irrespective of caste, creed, social status or religion. It is a part of Sikh tradition in every Sikh Gurdwara. The largest free kitchen in the world is at Harmandir Sahib. At this holy place a free, simple meal is provided to anywhere between forty and eighty thousand visitors every day. It is equivalent to a soup kitchen in the US but is not restricted to only the poorer sections of society.

Over the centuries several world personalities have sat in *pangat* (on the floor) for *langar* at the Harmandir Sahib. The Mughal ruler Akbar sat at a *langar* at the Khadur Sahib in the presence of Guru Amar Das Ji. When Dr Paul Michael Taylor, PhD, from the Smithsonian visited Punjab, he was served a *langar* meal at both the Khadur Sahib and the Harmandir Sahib. Members of the UAE's royal family broke their Ramadan fast at the Dubai Gurdwara.

According to available sources, the *langar* was started by Guru Nanak Ji at Kartarpur, a place that is today a part of the Punjab province in Pakistan. This is where he retired after his extended travels. When Guru Nanak Ji started the *langar*, it wasn't for food alone. He created a sense of service and equality for all in the setting of the *pangat* (eating while sitting on the floor). Third Guru Amar Dass Ji insisted that his followers first eat at the langar before meeting him.

Volunteers get an opportunity to cook, serve, and clean up the utensils. It is by far one of the most important gifts he gave to his community of followers and to the world at large.

Approximately two centuries later Europe and North America created houses and farm houses for the poor. But the destitute were looked down upon to an extent that the vendue system prevailed. Those unable to support themselves were auctioned off to the lowest bidder. Today, in America, we have soup kitchens. They are the American version of the Guru's *langar*.

This august tradition continues in every corner of the globe where Sikhs live. When the *langar* kitchens opened up at the height of the coronavirus pandemic, they were recommended by the local authorities for smaller, economically affected communities living in California. The pandemic, though, galvanized the Sikh community into playing a larger role. Not just langar, but free oxygen cylinders were provided to the needy at various places.

Sikh women in farmers agitation 2020-2021

Sikh schools, colleges and chairs

Maharaja Ranjit Singh distributed quida, a small education booklet. He did not, however, start a school system. The British started a school system for boys. Later the Singh Sabha movement promoted schools for Sikh boys and girls. Singh Sabha leaders approached Sikh princely states and raised the first Sikh college on a three hundred-acre sprawling campus in 1892. MGV Cole was the first principal of Khalsa College, Amritsar.

Punjab has many Khalsa schools and colleges. Khalsa schools also function in few western countries including the US and Canada. Sikh study chairs exist in many universities across the US and Canada.

Sikhism and gender equality
"Charde Mirze Khan nu Jat Wangel denda mutt, Chhud ranna di dosti khurien jina di matt"
(Do not have friendship with women because their wisdom or intelligence is in their heels, not in their brain).

The above poem is from the tragic love epic of Mirza Sahiban. It was set in Punjab, India and written in the latter half of the 17th century by Hafiz Barkhudar and poet Pillo. The above lines are an embarrassing testimony to the kind of disrespect women had to face in Punjab about four hundred years back. Worse must have been the case prior to that.

Gender inequality has been an intrinsic part of human society around the world. Medieval Hindu society objectified women and reduced them to fodder that men could enjoy, and control. Some of the customs and practices that prevailed in parts of India were highly objectionable and not very flattering for women.

Manu the lawgiver is remembered more for the curse of the caste system and less for positive views on women's role in the progress of the family. He wrote, "Where women are not revered, all rites are fruitless, since where the women of the family are miserable, the family is soon destroyed, but it always thrives where women are not miserable." (Doniger, 1991). His writings were lost in the tumult of time.

Some improvement occurred during the Vedic period but the custom of sati—the forced or voluntary life sacrifice of a woman on the burning pyre of the deceased husband—continued till the British along with Raja Ram Mohan Roy banned it. The Hindu temple Sabarimala in the state of Kerala did not allow entry of menstruating women till the Indian Supreme Court declared it illegal. The widows were outcast and could not remarry.

Hinduism has many women Goddesses such as Durga, Lakshmi, Kali and Saraswati, but women still majorly remain at the fringes of society. Some women in royal families asserted their opinion, as mentioned in the epic text Mahabharata written in the 2nd century BCE. Women have been victims of early marriage, denial of education, and property rights. The Arya Samaj movement in North India in the latter part of the nineteenth century did try to remove many flaws in Hinduism, including sati and the subservient status of women.

Buddhism which appeared around 6 BCE gave equal rights to women in all walks of life, including education, the choice to marry, and even to become monks. Buddhism was the lone voice among organized religions of the time. This did not last long after Hinduism took over India again.

Muslim invasion of India was a further blow to the rights of women. Polygyny and triple *talak* (divorce by calling the word *talak* three times) is still prevalent in some Islamic countries. The practice is clearly not in conformity with modern times and is now banned in India.

Christian west did not promote women's rights till Christine de Pizan talked about it in her masterpiece, *The Book of the City of Ladies.* Although written in 1405, this work did not receive recognition until the eighteenth century. In 1700, Mary Astell, considered the first English feminist, anonymously wrote the book *Some Reflections Upon Marriage.* Her famous line was "If all men are born free, how is it that all women are born slaves." In 1774, The Shakers, an evangelical Christian group, spoke about women's rights. America only allowed women's suffrage as late as in 1920, buttressing further the argument that women have been historically wronged and sidelined. It took another eighty-six years before the *MeToo* movement gained currency in the social media in 2006.

In 1792, the British pro-feminist Mary Wollstonecraft wrote *A Vindication of the Rights of Woman: with Strictures on Political and Moral Subjects.* The collaborative work of English philosopher John Stuart Mill and his wife Harriet titled *On Liberty* was published in 1859, one year after Harriet had passed away. In 1869, Mill continued work on an unfinished book and finally managed to publish *The Subjection of Women* in 1861. At the time, raising the subject of gender equality easily offended European sensibilities. Men were, of course, unquestioningly seen as the superior species.

Sikhism's Founding Father Guru Nanak Ji whose thinking was way ahead of the times has left us with powerful words to dwell upon—*So kyon manda akhiay jit jamme rajan.* It means, "why should we denigrate the one who gave birth to kings?" Guru Nanak Ji used the power of the pen to promote gender equality.

Likewise, third Guru Amar Dass Ji spoke strongly against the practice of child marriage. He also advocated remarriage for widows. He appointed many women as missionaries of the Sikh faith, and to conduct themselves as clergy.

Ninth Sikh Guru Tej Bahadur Ji on a visit to Amritsar was given the cold shoulder by those in charge of the Harmandir Sahib. A group of women, however, extended greetings to him. He commented, "*Myian Rab Rajian.*" It means women have the blessing of God.

In his Rehatnama, Bhai Prahlad Singh wrote against the detestable practice of female infanticide. "*Meena aur Masandia, Mona Kuri jo Mar,*" were his words. They meant that the killing of girls should be boycotted by society. Taking inspiration from the words of infinite wisdom spoken by the Sikh Gurus, the Singh Sabha movement in Punjab, India, began earnestly to promote education for girls, remarriage of widows, and the discontinuation of the practice of dowry.

Two ceremonies conducted during Sikh marriage require attention. During the *Lavaan* ceremony—when the bride and groom circle around the holy Guru Granth Sahib Ji—the bride should be given the choice to lead, with mutual consent. Traditionally, it is the groom that leads. Besides, the singing of *pallia taiddae laagee* (subservience to the groom) does not do justice to gender equality.

Particularly in rural communities, Sikhs devised their own system of widow remarriage. The widow of a deceased brother would usually be remarried to his younger male sibling, the custom being called *chhader pauni* (keeping family honor). It subtly promoted the practice of polyandry within a household. If in vogue today, such issues would be considered as evil.

Punjabi language and Gurmukhi script

Punjabi language is one of the Indo-Aryan languages with roots in Sanskrit. It is the language of the northwest Indian state of Punjab. Sheikh Farid (1173-1266 AD) was the first to give it literary status. Later Guru Nanak Ji gave it a poetic shape. Second Guru Angad Dev Ji followed up by implementing the Gurmukhi script. Fifth Guru Arjan Dev Ji compiled the Guru Granth Sahib Ji, most of it in Punjabi.

Waris Shah, in 1766, wrote *Heer Ranjha,* one of the tragic romances of Punjab. The other famous Punjabi love stories include *Mirza Sahiban, Sassi Punnhun* and *Sohni Mahiwal.* During the time of the Sikh Empire, Maharaja Ranjit Singh distributed *Qaida*, a Punjabi language primer for the public. He, however, did not promote Punjabi as an official language.

Following the partition of India, major Punjabi speaking parts became a part of Pakistan. But Punjabi was not developed as a mother tongue in Punjab, Pakistan. In India, the Punjabi Suba was established on the basis of language. This, of course, came as a breath of fresh air for the language. But due to a lack of any concerted effort by the state to promote it, the usage of the language began to decline. There were rumors in the Indian media that in its report on world languages, UNESCO had expressed concerns about the slow demise of the Punjabi language. This piece of floating rumor was later to be contradicted by Jagmohan Singh, editor of the *World Sikh News* who came up with a thorough research in 2019. Overall, there are one hundred and ninety-one regional and vernacular languages in India that are on a decline. One must remember that religion flourishes on the basis of its native language and script.

The Guru Granth Sahib Ji, the Sikh religious holy book, has been written in Punjabi and follows the Gurmukhi script. The generation of Sikh immigrants to the US who arrived post-1965 is able to speak and understand the Punjabi language. Many of them are able to read and write Gurmukhi as well. The second and third-generation Sikhs, however, have neither picked up the language, nor the script, and are unable to read and understand the Guru Granth Sahib Ji through direct reading. They are dependent on its English translations that are now readily available in several Gurdwaras across the US and Canada. But as is evident, the translations are usually a poor substitute for the original text.

The Punjabi language in Gurmukhi script is the medium of Sikh theology and is, therefore, important to all Sikhs. It seems that today both the language and the script are under attack. Most of the blame must go to the Sikh community for this decline. Punjab too is complicit when it comes to this regressive state of affairs. After all, it is the state's responsibility also to create syllabi in schools that mandatorily encourage the use of the mother tongue of Punjabi as a medium of instruction and communication, along with other languages like English and Hindi. Such a practice of promoting the mother tongue through a scientifically designed school curriculum is prevalent in many non-Hindi speaking states in India.

The first blow to the Punjabi language was dealt after the partition of India in 1947. Even though Punjabi is the mother tongue of Punjabis on the Pakistani side, the nation ignored the language in its school syllabi and official correspondence. Pakistan chose to lean towards Urdu which was the medium of communication before partition. Its symbiotic relationship with the Middle Eastern states further encouraged the use of Urdu. The Gurmukhi (literally meaning from the Guru's lips) script was despised in the Islamic Republic of Pakistan on religious grounds.

To exacerbate matters, on the Indian side the pro-Hindi Jan Sangh (which became the BJP) ignored Punjabi. Hindi had the status of a national language but unlike in other non-Hindi speaking states (like Gujarat, Maharashtra, Bengal, Tamil Nadu, Assam, Kerala to name a few) where the mother languages flourished, Punjabis had to officially speak and correspond in Hindi, the lingua franca.

But the entire blame cannot be shifted to the political party alone. Punjab, created on the basis of the Punjabi language, itself failed as a state to promote its own mother tongue, jeopardizing its future. The elite and educated Sikh families have long felt that speaking in Punjabi is infra dig and beneath their dignity. They are more at ease while conversing in English and Hindi. In their scheme of communication those who speak in Punjabi are considered anachronistic, less sophisticated, and lacking class. The lamentation of Punjabi poet Surjit Patter is, therefore, not quite out of place: "My language is on the verge of death. Each word and each sentence gasps for breath…" Clearly, the Punjabi language and the Gurmuki script are in danger of being wiped out, as each succeeding generation stops reading, writing and speaking its mother tongue.

Overall, older languages are going through a tough phase. For instance, at Hindu weddings Sanskrit shlokas (verses) are recited. Unless the priest makes an effort to explain their significance and import, their meaning is lost on most. Likewise, Buddhist scriptures were written in Pali. But in practice their translated versions are now used at monasteries across Japan, Korea and Thailand. In both cases, the original finer content of the Hindu and Buddhist scriptures have made way for translated versions. It is never a good idea to dilute your culture. Short cuts are never going to work out in the long term.

As a young writer, Balwant Gargi, the famous Punjabi dramatist and playwright, met with Nobel Laureate Rabindranath Tagore and sought his advice on improving his presentation style. Tagore who had returned his knighthood to the British over the reprehensible April 1919 Jallianwala Bagh massacre asked the young man in no uncertain terms to pursue his writing skills in Punjabi, his native tongue. Tagore's advice was given in spite of the fact that Gargi had done his advanced studies in English from Lahore. Apparently, the Nobel Prize winner knew a thing or two about the value of one's own mother tongue.

Many schools and universities in the US, Canada and UK provide Punjabi language courses. Khalsa schools have Sikhism and Punjabi language in the curriculum. Sikh charter schools have started giving out lessons in the Punjabi language and the Gurmukhi script to the newer generations of Sikhs born abroad. The study of the Punjabi language is available in all Sikh chair programs across American universities. These are opportunities waiting to be seized.

Sikhism and contemporary social issues
Global warming | Environmental degradation | Pollution control

Sikh community is at the forefront of dealing with these issues. The Founding Father of Sikhism Guru Nanak Ji was our earliest and foremost environmentalist. In the *Japji Sahib* (Sikh scripture) he said, *"Pavan Guru, Paani Pita, Mata Dharat Mahut."* It means the wind is our teacher, water our father, and earth our mother.

Late Bhagat Puran Singh of Pingalwara (home for the disabled), Amritsar, promoted the planting of saplings and trees in order to create green lungs. In fact, a study shows fifty-eight historical Sikh Shrines in India and Pakistan are recognized with names of 19 species of trees. They include the likes of Gurdwara Neem Sahib, Reetha Sahib, Tahli Sahib and more (Jaspal 2012). At Harmandir Sahib in Amritsar, a four-hundred-year old tree named *Dukh Bhanjani Beri* is now permanently under the care of botanists and plant taxonomists.

Eco Sikh is in the business of planting trees. Baba Sewa Singh has planted over three hundred and fifty thousand trees. Sant Balbir Singh Seechewal worked for years to clean up the waterways of Punjab. Plastic has given way to stainless steel cups and plates at all Sikh *langars*. Dr Devinder Pal Singh has given us an excellent account of Sikh teachings in the

Guru Granth Sahib Ji about respecting and protecting our environment and our plant biodiversity.

MISCELLANEOUS
Sikh economic model

It may not be out of place to discuss the economic model on religious grounds. The financial rules are set by the state where people live. The institutes set the laws but individual thinking plays a role in how we obey the laws and allocate our resources.

This is where religion has a role in shaping human behavior, on an individual basis.

Let me start with some historical perspectives on economics.

Early humans were dependent on one another for day-to-day necessities of life. The barter system was in vogue before any form of currency made an appearance. As humans started building townships and cities, their needs increased. Officialdom and a system of bureaucracy was introduced to run administrative setups. Village heads, kings and monarchs began to rule. A need arose for a disciplined way of promoting production, consumption and transfer of wealth, a process which we describe as economics, derived from the Greek word meaning household management. All early civilizations needed these kinds of management practices and, with minor differences, laws and regulations came into place.

Manu, the creator of Manusmriti or the Laws of Manu, is considered the first legal advisor in ancient India. These laws were further developed by Chanakya, the ancient Indian polymath, also known as Kautilya. His political treatise—*Arthashastra*—is a magnum opus on political science and economics in India, his work considered an important precursor to classical economics according to publications in the *International Journal of Social Economics* and the *Indian Economic Review*. He was a leading light of political economy and taught at the Indian university of Taxila.

Chanakya was an advisor to the rulers of the Mauryan empire. He advised in many areas of administration, including on the distribution of food to the poor during famines, creating jobs by developing infrastructure—in those days primarily the construction of forts. He was a firm believer in creating strong institutions.

The western father of modern economics, Adam Smith (1776) believed self-interest or "self-love" as the most important incentive in business, commerce and exchange of goods. He was later critiqued by many. Stephan Leacock said of him:

> *Adam, Adam, Adam Smith*
> *Listen to what I charge with!*
> *Didn't you say*
> *In a class one day*
> *That selfishness was bound to pay?*
> *Of all doctrine that was pitch.*
> *Wasn't it, wasn't it, wasn't it, Smith?*

Some of Adam Smith's later comments on sympathy, generosity and public spirit were, however, conveniently ignored.

Today we have economic systems based on capitalism, socialism and the 'third way' as the Chinese system is called. Communism as an economic system has almost failed. Most countries follow a mix of capitalism and socialism.

Sikhism appeared in the 15th century and Guru Nanak Ji, its founder, spelt out his economic philosophy in Mool Mantar where he commented, "*Kirt kar* (hard work), *Dasan Nuvaan Di Kamai* (working with ten fingers of both hands, metaphor for work ethics) and *Wund Shako* (sharing)." In modern times it means working hard and charitable giving. Now you can add paying your share of taxes.

He preached sharing through his famous remarks, "*Ghal Khai Kichh Haathon De Nanak Rah Pacchane Se.*" It means if you earn your living through hard work and share with others, you have found the righteous path. He combined the path of hard work and individual behavioral change in economics by his religious preaching. His economic philosophy can be summed up as Compassionate Capitalism (capitalism in mind, socialism at heart), implying hard work and sharing the rewards. He was against the ill-gotten wealth of rulers. As mentioned before, while on a visit to Eminabad (currently in Pakistan), Guru Nanak Ji refused a dinner invitation from the ruler of the area, Malik Bhago, preferring instead to dine on simple food earned through hard work by Bhai Lalo. Most of the economy at that time was centered around agriculture and related services.

Sikhism has preached steadfastly against greed, ego, pride and advocated honest, truthful living. These are all also good, modern corporate practices. Human beings can debate whether success and failure are predestined but nobody questions *Kirit Kar* (hard work). Subsequent Sikh Gurus continued the same philosophy and the Singh Sabha movement highlighted it. American President Franklin D. Roosevelt followed the same model after the US was swept by the greatest of recessions in the wake of the First World War. He tried to reduce income inequality.

Sikhs are spread all over the world and rules of economics are set by individual states. The behavioral ethics however are set by the individuals, guided perennially by religion and spirituality.

Sikhism and human rights

Right from its inception, Sikhism has stood firmly for human rights, particularly those of the weak, downtrodden and minorities, irrespective of their caste and religion. I will go over some of the human rights issues raised by the

Bhai Kanhaiya

Sikh Gurus much before the United Nations charter of human rights was instituted in 1948. Sikhism has dealt with many social issues as enumerated below:

The invaders, ruler, the ruled and the poor
Nanak dukhiya sab sansar
(The world is in misery).

Guru Nanak Ji was at Eminabad town in 1505 A.D. and an eyewitness to the misery inflicted by the Mughal invader Babar. In his poetry *Babar Vani* in the Guru Granth Sahib Ji he challenged the invader in his own, justice-seeking words. "If the fight is among lions (strong), I will have no regret. But pouncing on a flock of innocent (unarmed civilians) animals is no bravery." Metaphorically he commented, "*Pap di janj leh kabulon thia jooru mange dan wey lalo.*" (Babar has sinned, he has descended from Kabul and demanded the bride by force).

Guru Nanak Ji even asked the Akal Purakh to stand up to the cruelty of the invaders. He was bold enough to chastise the ruling class. In his words, "*Raje sheen mukadam kutte.*" (Kings are behaving like lions, but their subordinates are no better than canines.)

Sikh Gurus supported farmers against high land taxes and the oppressive *Jizya*—imposed on non-Muslims during Mughal rule.

Equality of humankind

The Sikh Gurus preached that all human beings are the same, and are equal. As written in the Guru Granth Sahib, "*Awal Allah noor upaya kudrat kae sab bandey, ek noor tae sab jag upjaya kaun bhaley kaun mandey.*" Sikhism condemned the caste system. The color bias of the west was non-existent in Indian society. Bhai Kanhaiya, a devout Sikh, was assigned to provide water and other help to injured soldiers during skirmishes with Mughal rulers at Anandpur Sahib in 1704. He took care of injured Sikh soldiers as well as enemy soldiers. This humane treatment of enemy soldiers occurred over one hundred and fifty years prior to the first Geneva convention in 1863.

Religious Freedom

Indian society was embroiled in religious discord during the times of the Sikh Gurus. Guru Nanak Ji, the Founding Father, in all his wisdom said, "There is no Hindu, there is no Muslim." He was considered Shah Faqir— *Hindu da Guru, Muslim da Pir* (Guru for Hindus, spiritual figure for Muslims).

The Sikh Gurus believed in freedom of religion and revolted against forced conversion to Islam. The fifth and ninth Sikh Gurus sacrificed their lives in order to uphold the sanctity of religious freedom. The ninth Sikh Guru Teg Bahadur Ji was approached by Kashmiri Pandits to intervene as the Mughals were threatening to convert them forcibly into Islam. When he intervened and negotiated with the Mughal rulers in Delhi, Guru Teg Bahadur Ji had to pay the ultimate price by sacrificing his life. He was decapitated heinously by the devilish zealots since he determinedly refused to convert to Islam.

Tenth Guru Gobind Singh Ji had a loud slogan. It said, *"soora sau pehchaniye jo lade deen ke hait...."* It means brave are those who fight for religious freedom. It was a time in history when religion was all-powerful, and the bigoted ones blinded by it were perpetrating their inhumane acts everywhere. Giordano Bruno, an Italian philosopher, was burnt alive in Rome on February 17, 1600 for refusing to recant a heretical statement. His last words to his tormentors were, "Perhaps you who pronounce my sentence are in greater fear than I who receive it."

Gender equality

Since its inception Sikhism has preached gender equality. About six hundred and twenty-three years ago Guru Nanak Ji had the great foresight to tell this about women, "It is women who keep the race going. We should not consider them cursed and condemned,

when from women are born leaders and kings." Guru Nanak Ji's words spoken in 1499 are more relevant today than ever before. There are many parts of the world where women are fighting for basic human rights, even as I write this book.

The Sikh Gurus were clearly against child marriage and dowry. They were in favor of widows remarrying. The third Sikh Guru had honored women and appointed many women as missionaries. Today many of them function as clergy. This is much before the suffrage movement of women in the western world.

Income equality

Income inequality is as old as the time humans began to settle in towns and cities. There were rulers, administrators, and then the ruled. There were clear income disparities among these segments, with the ruled getting the crumbs and the rulers taking the cakes. For some time, communism tried to counter this, but it died due to its own, ill-conceived ideas. Today's world remains beset with income inequalities.

The occasional voice of sanity can be heard crying out for a more humane society with a minimum universal income, and a less disparate society. Actions, they say, speak louder than words. But in this case, at least, only the deafening silence of inaction can be heard. Guru Nanak Ji was well aware of the poverty that the masses suffered, as well as the ill-gotten wealth of the rulers. On principle he shared a meal with a carpenter named Bhai Lalo but politely turned down an invitation from the ruler of the town. The farmers' agitation in India took place on grounds of inequality in incomes. While some had disproportionately high sources of revenues, others were barely able to eke out a living. The movement was initiated by the Sikh farmers of Punjab and later their counterparts from other states joined in.

Freedom and independence

Freedom is a basic human right. Sikhs lost their lives in very large numbers during the independence movement against the British. The blot of the Jallianwala Bagh massacre is not yet erased from history. When Sikhs aboard the Japanese liner Komagata Maru were turned back from Canada, they were shot in Calcutta and many died. The Ghadar movement led to the hanging of dozens of Sikhs and the incarceration of hundreds. During the Indian emergency Sikhs were sent to jail under the draconian provisions of MISA imposed by Prime Minister Indira Gandhi during the dark days of 1975.

Rights and protection of minorities

In 2021, Kashmiri Muslim students in India were mistreated and beaten after Article 370 of the Indian Constitution was revoked in the state of Jammu and Kashmir. At the time Sikh Gurdwaras provided shelter to these students. Sikhs also provided *Langar* (free food) during the Muslim agitation in New Delhi against Citizenship Amendment Act 2019.

Sikhism and its relationship with other religions

Religion has been an important part of everyday life all over the world in the last many centuries. Religious hatred and wars were common. Sikhism does not believe in forcible conversion and also does not actively promote missionaries. Hence no ill will is created with other religions. This is in contrast to Islam and Christianity.

Sikhism is respectful to all religions The Sikh holy scripture Guru Granth Sahib has representative writings of saints of all religions of India at the time. In addition to the *bani* (religious discourse) of Sikh Gurus, it includes fifteen *bhagats* (holy men), eleven *Bhatts* and four

Gur Sikhs (religious scholars). Since Sikhs have to deal with the religions of the host countries, it is important to know how Sikhs historically dealt with the main prevailing religions.

Sikhism and Islam

The marauding Muslim invaders had started entering the Indian subcontinent much before the birth of Sikhism in the 15th century. The earliest occupation of India was by Sultan Muhammad bin Qasim in the 12th century. There was subsequently a gradual rise of the Mughal empire that lasted a few centuries and it declined when the British entered India, first as traders, and then as colonialists. The last Mughal emperor Bahadur Shah Zafar was deposed in 1857.

Sikh engagement with Islam has been varied. After his defeat to Sher Shah Suri, emperor Humayun came to seek guidance from Guru Angad Dev Ji. His son, emperor Akbar, shared food with Guru Amar Das Ji at a *langar*. Muslim *pirs* (holymen) and the masses had a good relation with the Sikh Gurus. In sharp contrast, the ruling Muslim rulers were much against the rising popularity of Sikhism.

Sikhism's Founding Father Guru Nanak Ji was considered Baba Nanak the faqir, the Hindus' Guru and the *pir* of Muslims. He was equally revered by Hindus and Muslims. Rai Bular, a big land owner and a Muslim chieftain from Talwandi (later named Nankana Sahib), donated eighteen thousand five hundred acres of land to the followers of Guru Nanak Ji. The fifth Guru had high regard for the holy men of Islam and requested the *pir*, Mian Mir, to lay the foundation stone of Harmandir Sahib, the most sacred Sikh shrine on planet earth.

The fifth Guru while compiling the holy Guru Granth Sahib Ji inducted verses of prevailing religious figures of the time including those of Muslim holy men such as Sheikh Farid and Kabir. The sixth Guru Hargobind Rai Ji had a mosque built at the town of Siri Hargobind Pura near the river Beas. Pir Bhudhu Shah, a Muslim holy man, sent his two sons and an army to help the tenth Guru during the battle at Panghani in 1688. Two Muslim brothers, Nabi Khan and Ghani Khan, helped the tenth Guru to escape in disguise as a Muslim *pir* (holy man) at a time when Mughal forces had laid siege to the town of Machhiwara in Punjab. The Nawab of Malerkotla, Sher Mohammed Khan, a Muslim ruler, pleaded with the Governor of Sirhind, Wazir Khan, for sparing the lives of Sahibzada Fateh Singh and Sahibzada Zorawar Singh—the two younger sons of tenth Guru Gobind Singh Ji—in 1704 while he was planning to brick them alive. Khan did not pay any heed.

The ruling Mughals were all for mass conversion to Islam and did not like the rise of Sikhism. The fifth and ninth Gurus were, therefore, tortured to death because they wanted to protect the religious freedom of Sikhs and Hindus. Outraged and infuriated by the repeated barbarism of the Muslim rulers and their generals, the Sikh community retaliated sharply by wreaking havoc inside the Mughal kingdom. They were ably led by the legendary Sikh warrior Banda Bahadur Singh. Later, a secular Sikh kingdom was established under Maharaja Ranjit Singh who had a Muslim wife, Moran Sarkar, and a Muslim foreign minister Fakir Azizuddin. During the Anglo-Sikh wars the relationship between the Sikhs and the Muslims turned for the better. They were further strengthened when they united during the freedom movement against the British.

But the bonhomie and camaraderie between Sikhs and Muslims has been short-lived. Partition of India proved to be once more very divisive and large-scale rioting saw killings on either side of the divide in Punjab. Sikhs and Muslims once again were pitted fiercely against one another during those macabre moments. In general, Punjabis on both sides are in favor of good relations, at least on the surface. As a goodwill gesture, the Kartarpur Sahib corridor was opened up in November 2019, months before the coronavirus pandemic devastated the world. It is at Kartarpur Sahib that Guru Nanak Ji retired before his heavenly journey. Punjabis in general and Sikhs in particular are a peaceful community. They are good citizens who are willing to adapt themselves to new circumstances wherever they migrate.

Punjab Na Hindu Na Muselman, Punjab Tan Vasda Guru Dey Nam
(Professor Puran Singh)

Sikh-Muslim animosity has considerably reduced and no further discord has occurred in the last seventy years, since India's partition. The hatred of generations can be attributed to behavioral epigenetics that are caused by changes occurring on the surface of genes. This can be hereditary and transmitted to subsequent generations. With the lack of an environment filled with hatred, the epigenetic phenomenon will disappear over subsequent generations and Sikhs will reestablish the same relations with Islam as they have with other religious and ethnic groups. Time, as they say, is a great healer.

While things have cooled down between the Sikhs and Muslims after the episodic history of wars and manslaughter, Islam itself is under severe pressure in western countries due to frequent incidents of terrorism. British Parliamentarian David Amess was recently stabbed to death. Twelve people were shot dead by extremists in the office of a French newspaper, while numerous fatwas (religious death warrants) have been issued against Muslim authors deemed to be blasphemous by the orthodox clergy. As I write, three cities in Sweden are burning as locals are battling Muslim populations. Caught in this crossfire of rising global hatred against Muslims are the Sikhs whose turbans have often given them a mistaken identity.

Sikhism, Christianity and the British

It is important to understand the historical relationship between the Sikhs and the British, particularly in the context of Sikh migration to various countries including the erstwhile colonies of the empire. Engagement between Sikhs and the British started during the time of Maharaja Ranjit Singh. The British had subjugated Sikh

> [For the British, the end justified the means. They uninhibitedly used the carrot-and-stick policy, but more to divide the Indians and rule through communal discord and disharmony. The British did win the two wars against the Sikhs but the losses they suffered were devastating]

principalities of Patiala Nabha, Jind, Kalsia and Faridkot. The Maharaja was acutely aware of British intent and design and had, therefore, signed treaties with them. He had, side by side, initiated the process of strengthening his army with the help of western generals. The Sikh kingdom fell in shambles after his death and Punjab was annexed by the British during the two Anglo-Sikh wars fought between 1845 and 1848.

Then began a phase of ups and downs in the relationships. The youth in Punjab and Bengal, particularly the college students, were being stirred up against the Raj. The Sikh community began to get organized to seize control of the shrines from mahants, the caretakers. The Singh Sabha movement was very active in its efforts at rejuvenating the Sikh religious doctrines. It is important to review the events that were to subsequently shape the freedom movement of India.

1. Sikhs lost the second Anglo-Sikh war and were subjugated in 1848.
2. They accepted their subordinate relationship and when encouraged by the British decided to join the Imperial army. In turn, the British declared the Sikhs as a martial race.
3. Sikhs helped the British to quell the sepoy mutiny that took place in 1857-1859.
4. Namdhari Sikhs agitated against the British in 1872.
5. Sikh migration to British colonies and dominions began in 1880 including to Singapore, Malaysia, Hong Kong, East Africa, Fiji, New Zealand and Australia.
6. The development of canal colonies began in 1885, primarily for the benefit of Sikh farmers.
7. The Ghadar movement (1914-1919) in North America and the Komagata Maru incidents in Canada and Bengal (1914) were the beginning of uprisings and rebellions against the Raj.
8. The Sikhs in India supported the British war efforts during the First World War (1914-1918), even while the Ghadarites based in California and in British colonies around the globe wanted to stop them from doing so.
9. The Jallianwala Bagh massacre of April 13, 1919 vigorously stoked the fires of a freedom movement.
10. In 1920, the Sikh Gurdwara movement and the Akali Dal were in place.
11. On March 23, 1931, following the Lahore conspiracy trials, Bhagat Singh and his companions were hanged. That further galvanized the freedom movement.
12. Sikhs and Indians helped the allies during the Second World War fought between 1939 and 1945.
13. Sikhs now live in Great Britain with respect and dignity. A large Sikh population prospers in that nation. Hatred levels have come down. In the last few years several Sikhs have made it to British Parliament. Several leading businessmen have come up from within the Sikh community.

For the British, the end justified the means. They uninhibitedly used the carrot-and-stick policy, but more to divide the Indians and rule through communal discord and disharmony. The British did win the two wars against the Sikhs but the losses they suffered were devastating. At one point they wanted to give up fighting the brave Sikhs. Henry Hardinge, the governor-general of India (between 1844 and 1848) nearly lost his life during the first Anglo-Sikh war in 1845. The win eventually was a matter of chance as revealed by contemporary poet Shah Mohammed in his book Jangnama (1846). *"Singhan ne ghorian de wang numbuan lau nature sute,"* were his words. It means that the Sikh battered the white army and squeezed out their blood, just like you squeeze juice out of a lemon. The intrepid Sikhs were declared a martial race and given preference during recruitment in the British army. The British created canal colonies for the Sikh farmers and took them overseas as security guards and policemen. Their fabled valor came in handy during the two world wars. When it came to the princely states, the British played Jekyll and Hyde with gay abandon. Maharaja Bhupinder Singh of Patiala was conferred the title of Farzand-i-khas (special son) while Maharaja Ripudaman Singh of Nabha was forced to abdicate his throne.

British reprisal for all activities they perceived to be against the empire was swift. The Sikhs were punished for the Namdhari movement, Komagata Maru voyage, the freedom movement for which the Jallianwala Bagh massacre took place. They did not spare the Ghadarites either.

Christian missionaries were very active during the British rule and used the soft power of charity, resulting in conversion to Christianity. This was more effective in the lower socio-economic order of Indian society. Very few Sikh families converted to Christianity. Higher education in England and marriages to Anglo-Saxon women, however, did lure some Sikh men to convert. Some of them added Samuel to existing Sikh names.

The British appeared to be favorably disposed towards the Sikhs. They, however, could not do any favor to the Sikhs during the partition of India. The only choice the Sikhs had was to remain an integral part of India. Their aspirations for a kingdom or a separate state were gone with the British.

Sikhism and Puritanism in Christianity have similarities. Puritanism as advocated by John Calvin was for purification of the Catholic Church and Sikhism was purification of Hinduism and other prevailing religions of India. It is interesting that the early Puritan Protestants set up colonies where the expectation was that the young would work for the welfare of the old. This kind of filial piety is also a part of Sikh philosophy.

Sikhism and Hinduism

M A Mcauliffe   Kahn Singh Nabha

Hinduism is the dominant religion in India accounting for over eighty percent of the population of 1,400 million. The Sikhs, Muslims, Christians, Buddhists, Jains, Zoroastrians, termed minorities, make up the rest twenty percent.

Sikhism is an offshoot of Hinduism. The ninth Sikh Guru saved Hinduism by sacrificing his own life by refusing to convert to Islam. Since the Mughals could not convert him, they were unable to convert other Hindus. Historically, Sikhs and Hindus have lived cordially. But while Sikhism is a monotheist religion, Hinduism remains a polytheist one.

This difference has been the subject of numerous debates and writings. The Singh Sabha movement went at lengths to explain the differences between Sikhism and Hinduism. Bhai Kahn Singh of Nabha wrote a booklet titled *Hum Hindu Nahin,* meaning we are not Hindus.

Max Arthur Macauliffe (1841-1913) also shared the concern that Hinduism will finally absorb Sikhism and likened it to boa constrictor of Indian forest. That concern is no longer valid and Sikhism has established itself as a stand-alone religion on its own merits. In spite of the evident differences, Sikhs opted to stay with Hindu India and not with the Islamic Republic of Pakistan after partition in 1947. Perhaps the brutal history of the Mughal times had a part to play in this decision.

BJP has a Hindutva agenda and it is a matter of concern for all minorities. Sikhs currently are all over the world and fear no threat. They are important for the security of India due to their location on the north west border and significant presence in the defense services.

Sikhs overseas are a powerful force. Their struggle against any form of perceived oppression and disrespect in India will continue. The Khalistani issue—demand for a separate Sikh homeland called Khalistan—is yet to die down, much against the annoyance of India that has been made clear to Canadian and British authorities. In fact, it has from time to time kept the BJP and the Sangh Parivar on the edge.

SIKH HEROES

In the Merriam-Webster dictionary, the word 'hero' means someone who is admired for his great and brave acts, or fine qualities, and willing to accept even bodily harm for a worthy cause. American poet and literary critic Adam Kirsch (2021) redefined the American hero. In his words, "A hero is someone who is willing to give up these things (wealth, fame, power) and more, to do what is right."

"These dead shall not have died in vain"
(Abraham Lincoln Gettysburg 1863)

Below is a brief description of Sikh heroes in the past in India and abroad.

1. Sikhs are acutely aware of the martyrdom of the 5th and 9th Gurus. Bhai Mati Singh, Bhai Mani Singh and approximately thirty or more others were tortured to death for religious and other animosities (Khalsa Sukhminder). Also, two sons of the 10th Guru were killed in a battle and the younger two were bricked alive. There was the capture and torture of Banda Singh Bahudur. Many Sikhs were killed during the Ghallugharas (holocaust). Every Sikh in this period is a hero for saving Sikhism. They rejuvenated Khalsa during those difficult times and created the Sikh Raj.

2. Those who lost their lives during the two Anglo-Sikh wars. Sham Singh Attariwala and many other Khalsa generals and soldiers are among them.

3. After the annexation of Punjab by the British, the real heroes were the Namdhari Sikhs (offshoot of Sikhism). They were blown off by cannons used by the British in January 1872. Their leader Sat Guru Ram Singh Ji was sent to Myanmar to die. He was the first to declare the fight for the independence of India on April 12,1857, a month before the great Indian mutiny of May 1857. He also declared the boycott of British products in favor of *swadeshi* or local products.

4. Sikhs who sacrificed their lives under the leadership of Lachhman Singh Dharowal in order to wrest back control of Sikh Gurdwaras from Mahant Narain Dass in Nankana Sahib, now in Pakistan.

5. The martyrs of the Jallianwala Bagh massacre of April,13 1919, that included Sikhs and other Punjabis.

6. Martyr Bhagat Singh and his associates Rajguru and Sukhdev, the freedom fighters tried and hanged in the Lahore conspiracy case.

7. The Sikhs from North America who were either shot dead or sent to the gallows during the Komagata Maru episode and the Ghadar movements. Many were sentenced to life imprisonment.

8. Shaheed Mewa Singh was served a death sentence in Vancouver, Canada, for the assassination of W.C. Hopkinson in 1914. The latter was an anti-Sikh immigration officer who was trying to save murderer Bela Singh, a traitor on the payrolls of the Canadian immigration department.

9. Udham Singh faced death sentence in 1940 for the London killing of Michael O'Dwyer, a former lieutenant governor of

Punjab and the mastermind behind the Jallianwala Bagh massacre.

10. Shaheed Karnail Singh Benipal who was shot dead in 1955 by the Portuguese army during a peaceful march for freedom of Goa. All those who sacrificed for the freedom of India and who lost their lives during the partition are heroes.

11. Creation of Punjabi Suba required agitations and serving of jail terms by many. Chandigarh, the rightful capital, was not given to Punjab and is shared with the state of Haryana. Besides, a few Punjabi speaking areas were given to neighboring Haryana.

12. Darshan Singh Pheruman (Sikh Wiki) did a fast-unto-death for getting Chandigarh as the sole capital city of Punjab. He also demanded that the neighboring Punjabi-speaking areas that had gone to Haryana after the splitting of greater Punjab be returned to Punjab. He died in October 1969 after having gone without food for seventy-four days. This event which should otherwise have been fresh in the minds of the Sikhs has been forgotten. Regrettably, Darshan Singh Pheruman remains an unsung hero.

13. Demand for Khalistan and the subsequent death of Sant Jarnail Singh Bhindranwale and many Sikh youths. Some consider Bhindranwale a hero, others differ. The same can be said for Satwant Singh and Beant Singh, bodyguards of Mrs Indra Gandhi who killed her.

14. In modern democratic societies helping the poor and needy is a heroic deed (Kirsch 2021). The late Tarlok Singh, ICS, rehabilitation commissioner of Punjab for settling refugees of 1947 after the partition of Punjab, worked long hours with limited resources and facilities to carry out a mammoth task. Late Bhagat Puran Singh ji of Pingalwara (home for disabled and homeless) at Amritsar and Ravi (Ravinder) Singh of Khalsa Aid deserve great honor. Khalsa Aid is an international Sikh NGO that has been providing food, clothing and other provisions to victims of natural disasters, famines and wars.

15. During the farmers' agitation of 2020-2021, over five hundred Sikh farmers died, some claiming their own lives because they were burdened with debts. They are all heroes.

Sikh exceptionalism

Sikhism is exceptional in its philosophy and way of life. I say this, even after knowing fully well that self-praise is no recommendation.

Exceptionalism is defined in the following terms:

1. The condition of being exceptional or unique.
2. The theory or belief that something, especially a nation, does not conform to a pattern or norm. (The American Heritage dictionary of English language, fifth edition.)

The United States adopted exceptionalism as a national virtue, with some opposition from others. American exceptionalism, in its positive connotation, is used to extol the virtues of a society made of immigrants characterized by liberty, egalitarianism, democracy, Republicanism, and individualism. This has been criticized negatively by others, given the way early settlers treated Native Americans, blacks and later Catholics, Jews and Asians, including Sikhs. This term has been used earlier, but merited more attention after Joseph Stalin used it. Stalin had deposed Jay Lovestone from the leadership of the Communist Party of the US, a post the latter had held for two years. During Lovestone's visit to Moscow in 1929 a confrontation with Stalin took place during an interview. According to *The New York Times*, Lovestone, 29, managed to flee with the help of false identity papers as his life was in danger.

Exceptionalism may be a purely American phenomenon. I am using it as a general term that has a complimentary connotation and wonder if this has been applied to any other nation, organization or religion in the above context. For a society, religion, and organization to be exceptional, it has to have all the above virtues and more. Does the Sikh community and religion stand up to be exceptional in that regard? This is an effort to explore that. This however, is not any effort to undermine values of any other religion or ethnic group.

Sikh religious philosophy began with *Nam Jap* (pray), *Kirit Kar* (work hard), and *Wund Shako* (share resources). This was supplanted with secularism, income and gender equality, abolition of caste, and creation of Khalsa to fight injustice and cruelty of a ruling class on Sikhs and the underprivileged in Indian society.

Guru Nanak Ji, the founder of Sikhism, commented against ill-gotten wealth when he was visiting one of his followers, Bhai Lalo. He was, therefore, aware of income inequality. Sikhism fought for human rights and the freedom to practice a religion of one's choice.

Charitable giving or *Daswund* (donating 10 percent of one's income) has been emphasized in the Sikh tenets. Guru Nanak Ji commented *"Ghal Khai Kichh hathon de Nanak rah Pehchane Se."*

It means, working hard and giving donations puts you on the path of righteousness.

Through his highly evolved and divine vision, Guru Nanak Ji also started the institution of *langar* (free kitchen), a uniquely Sikh religious tradition. Today many Sikh organizations are doing charity. At the international level, the Khalsa Aid society is helping victims of disasters as well as victims of war.

Equality of mankind was well emphasized by Guru Nanak Ji, much before anthropologists rejected the concept of race differentiating human kind. Guru Granth Sahib quotes and promotes the idea of Bhagat Kabir: *"Awal Allah Noor Uppaya Kudrat De Sab Bande Ek Noor Te Sab Jagg Upje Kaun Bhale Kaun Mande."* It means all human beings are the same and nobody is better, and nobody worse. Sikh *Ardas* (prayer) emphasizes *Sarbat Da Bhala* (Goodness for all). The Sikh concept of *sangat* (congregation) signals democracy while *pangat* (eating in *langar* with everybody sitting on the floor) promotes equality without considering anyone as higher or lower.

Guru Nanak Ji the founder of Sikhism was probably the first to raise the issue of gender inequality. He preached respect for the female gender and commented, *"So Kyon Manda Aakhiye Jit Jamey Rajan."* It means how can we talk poorly about a woman, the one who delivers kings.

Protection of the environment has been an integral part of Sikh theology. Guru Nanak Ji said, *"Pawan guru, pani pita, mata Dharat mahat."* Air is guide, water is father, earth is mother. Sikhism has owned that environmental theme since its very beginning.

Eco Sikh is a recent movement that in cooperation with other religious organizations and the United Nations has set out to create green spaces by planting trees and reducing environmental degradation.

Sikhs have had a major contribution to the freedom movement of India, whether we look at the Namdhari massacre, Ghadar Party rebellion, Indian Independence League, Akali Party, the martyrdom of Bhagat Singh and his associates. The Sikhs and the rest of the Punjabi community suffered when Punjab was divided. The rest of India was freed. But perhaps the rest of India has been less than gracious to the community that has sacrificed a lot for India's freedom.

All of the points I've made above justify the exceptional status of Sikhs in India. How about the role of Sikhs in bringing the above values abroad, and to the US? While American exceptionalism is tainted with the history of atrocities against Native Americans, followed by discrimination against Jews, Catholics and other immigrants, Sikh exceptionalism indeed does stand tall with its head held high.

Being a Sikh, I run the risk of being accused of wearing rose-tinted glass and writing things that are favorable.

You may judge me once you're done reading this book. ∎

CHAPTER 6

EARLY SIKH MIGRATION TO NORTH AMERICA

(Late 19th century - 1965)

The American continent was inhabited by indigenous tribes called by different names. These tribes themselves came from Africa and walked across the hypothetical bridge at Bering Strait connecting Russia with Alaska and gradually occupied North, Central and South America.

The next wave of migrants were European explorers by sea and Puritans who landed at Jamestown Virginia, Plymouth, Massachusetts and other places in the US. The British and Dutch were followed by others from different parts of Europe. Hispanic Mexico owned a major part of Southwest America, even before the pilgrims came.

The United States is a land of opportunity. People from various countries enter the US as permanent residents by legal or illegal means. Some come in as refugees and others as asylum seekers. The Asian migration started with the Chinese. They were followed by Japanese, East Indians (Sikhs) and Filipinos. Many other countries followed later.

Why did the Sikhs want to migrate?
Young man, go West

Following the Second Anglo-Sikh War, a fierce military conflict between the British East India Company and the Sikh Empire, Punjab was annexed in 1848-49. This left the Sikhs considerably demoralized. Besides, the population of the province had sizably burgeoned and landholdings had become divided. It did not help that famines had become quite frequent in Punjab. Matters were further exacerbated by a series of epidemics of malaria, smallpox, cholera and plague that broke out with alarming regularity between the 1850s and the early decades of the 20th century. Life had become very tough, and the patience of the Punjabi population had reached the end of its tether. Cremations in my ancestral village and in the canal colonies of Punjab had become a daily routine. The population had become morally and physically enervated, and could take no more. I remember my grandfather telling me that he just about managed to save his family by leaving the village for a year.

Sikh migration in chronological order

Hong Kong had few Sikhs in 1840 before Punjab was annexed by the British. Maharaj Singh was the first Sikh brought to Singapore in 1849 by the British as a political prisoner after the second Anglo-Sikh War in 1848. Sikhs were later brought by the British as security guards and policemen to Hong Kong (1881).

Maharaja Duleep Singh was brought to England in 1854. His mother Rani Jind Kaur came in 1860. The general migration of Sikhs to Great Britain started in 1910.

Sikhs first came to Panama to work in transoceanic railroads in 1855 and later in 1904 to dig the Panama Canal.

Two Sikh Gill brothers Phuman Singh and Bir Singh came to New Zealand earlier and others followed from 1880 to 1910. Jiwan Singh was probably the first Sikh to reach Australia around 1880.

Risaldar Major Kesur Singh is reported as the first Sikh to migrate to Canada in 1897.

The British brought Ramgharia Sikhs as craftsmen, and for the construction of the Kenya-Uganda railroad in 1897. Others followed between 1905 and 1920.

Bakshish Singh Dhillon along with three companions came to San Francisco, US, from Hong Kong in 1899, though there is a report in the 18th century of an Indian servant of ship captain Phillips in Salem, Massachusetts.

Sikhs came to Fiji as a group of 70 in 1904. The Fiji currency has a turban-wearing Sikh to honor the Sikh community's contribution to Fiji.

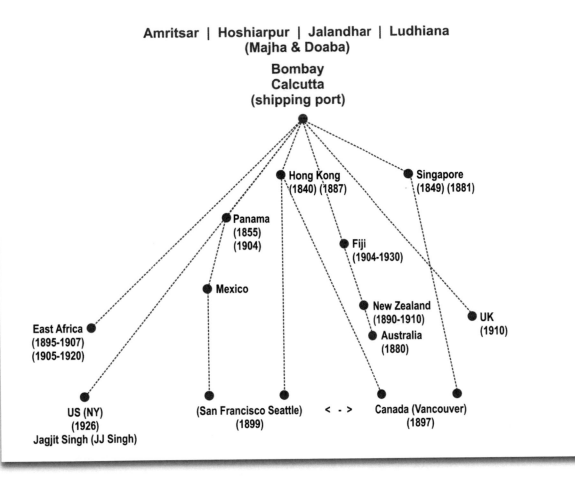

Also, the British had decided to forcibly sell products manufactured in their country to India. They had broken the back of India's cottage and domestic industry and had started imposing higher Muamalat, a land revenue tax, on farmers. Pushed to the wall, Sikh farmers, especially from the severely affected Jalandhar and Hoshiarpur regions within the Doaba, began mortgaging their land to money lenders who became the new owners. A lethal combination of acute financial and health-related woes made the Sikhs look desperately for better opportunities westward.

In order to stop farmers from becoming tenants in their own land, Sir Chhotu Ram of Punjab's legislature pioneered the passing of the Punjab Relief Indebtedness Act, 1934 and the Punjab Debtors Protection Act, 1936.

During times of extreme trials and tribulations people create songs that tell the story of the times. It was not uncommon to hear the Punjabi farmer sing these lines:

Pagri sambhal, jatta lutia gia maal tera (Be careful, your losses are mounting big time!).

In the US things were no better during the early years of the twentieth century. Riots and agitations against the large landholders and plantation owners were commonplace. Here too the farmers found a way to deal with the misery by composing their own song. The lyrics, as available in the International Book of Folk Songs, are as follows:

When the farmer comes to town
With his wagon broken down,
Oh, the farmer is the man who feeds them all.
If you'll only look and see,
I think you will agree
That the farmer is the man who feeds them all.

The farmer is the man,
The farmer is the man,
Lives on credit till the fall;
Then they take him by the hand
And they lead him from the land,
And the middleman's the man who gets it all.

Oh, the lawyer hangs around
While the butcher cuts a pound,
But the farmer is the man who feeds them all;
And the preacher and the cook
Go a-strolling by the brook,
But the farmer is the man who feeds them all.

The farmer is the man,
The farmer is the man,
Lives on credit till the fall;
With the interest rate so high,
It's a wonder he don't die,
For the mortgage man's the man who gets it all.

When the banker says he broke
And the merchant's up in smoke,
They forget that it's the farmer feeds them all.
It would put them to the test
If the farmer took a rest,

Then they'd know that it's the farmer who feeds them all.

The farmer is the man,
The farmer is the man,
Lives on credit till the fall.
His pants are -Wearing thin,
His condition, it's a sin,
He's forgotten that he's the man who feeds them all.

Even though conditions remained quite harsh and severe, climatically and otherwise, by and large the economic situation of Sikhs and Punjabis were better than others in the rest of India. But still, prevailing traditions meant that the youngest in the family had no hope of inheriting land, and the chances of getting married were very slim. So, it was normally the youngest, unmarried male that would venture out to explore new horizons, with a clutch of friends in similar unenviable positions from the same village.

Sikhs ventured out into many parts of the world, but they did not go as indentured workers under the British colonial system that mainly recruited migrants from the eastern parts of United Provinces and Bihar, and from the southern parts of India. The indentured workers were sent to the Caribbean islands like Trinidad and Tobago, Demerara (modern day Guyana), Saint Vincent and the Grenadines, Jamaica, Grenada and onwards to places like British Honduras in Central America. They were sent to Fiji in the Pacific, to Mauritius in the Indian Ocean, to South Africa, Malaysia, and Singapore. The French who had a presence in southern India and in Chandannagar in Bengal recruited indentured workers for the Reunion Islands, Guadeloupe, Martinique and French Guiana. The Dutch took them away to what was Dutch Guiana, modern day Suriname. The Danes also sent some workers from India to St. Croix in the Caribbean. Sikhs also migrated to Australia and New Zealand.

The British moved Ramgharia Sikh craftsmen to East Africa. They also recruited

A Sikh hawker in Goulburn Valley, Victoria

Sikhs in the police and for security duties in Hong Kong, Singapore and Malaysia. Sikhs also migrated to places like Argentina for farming, and to Panama to play a part in the building of the nation's canal. Today, they are in every continent, and stand out for their hard work, their turbans, their social work, apart, of course, for their enormous capacity for enterprise and charity.

This book, however, focuses mainly on Sikh migration to the US and Canada. To begin with, both nations had porous borders, their people spoke English, and had a common connection with Great Britain that colonized Canada, but failed to do so when it came to the US.

One also wonders why Sikhs alone thought about migration which was not through the indentured route? As things stood, in spite of the general economic malaise in British India where the rulers were sucking the lifeblood out of the subjects, Sikhs and Punjabis were economically considered better off than those in the rest of India, as mentioned earlier.

The reasons for their migration must have been varied. One would have been that the large-scale unemployment among Sikh youth could present a tinderbox like situation following the annexation of Punjab and rapidly declining economic conditions. The clever British knew that a way needed to be found to prevent the crisis from precipitating. So, they decided to recruit Sikhs in the Imperial army in a preferential manner. They also opened agricultural development in what came to be known as the 'canal colonies.' They started encouraging the migration of Sikhs to other British colonies. There was also the fact that Sikhs were quite willing to emigrate since historically, due to frequent barbaric invasions from the Northwestern side, they had experienced an unsettled existence that had resulted in many mini-migrations within the Indian subcontinent.

Canadian Pacific Empress Line advertisement in 1930 for the Empress of Asia *(Collection of Dr Wally Chung)*

How did Sikhs know about North America and Canada?

According to a publication of the California State Polytechnic University at Humboldt, Andrew B. Hammond purchased the Samoa sawmill, the largest of its kind in Humboldt County, in 1900. In order to overcome the shortage of mill workers caused by the abolition of slavery, Hammond, based out of Astoria in Oregon, went scouting for labor in India soon after his new acquisition. When this requirement of Hammond went public in Punjab, many Sikhs volunteered to go to the Pacific West. They were also encouraged by news brought in by shipping agents about the great opportunities that lay in store in that part of the western world.

Information on the bright prospects in the Pacific West also came to the Sikh soldiers who were fighting for the British Empire alongside their American and Canadian

Imperial army ship from Hong Kong to Vancouver, British Columbia, Canada on way to London for Diamond Jubilee Celebration of Queen Victoria 1897

counterparts during the Boxer Rebellion in China, a violent uprising by a secret Chinese society known as the Boxers against foreigners between 1899 and 1901. Many nations at the time had sent troops to quell the attacks. A contingent of Sikh soldiers on duty at the Diamond Jubilee of Queen Victoria that celebrated her sixtieth year of ascension to the

LEFT: British India Passport. **RIGHT:** Sikh passengers arrive at Seattle, Washington by ship S.S Minnesota on June 23,1913

Sikhs arrive by ship at Vancouver, Canada

LEFT: Risaldar Major Kesur Singh. **RIGHT:** Gravestone of Buckam Singh at Kitchener, Ontario, Canada

British throne also likewise learnt of opportunities in the Pacific West from their counterparts in the American continent, as they did a few years later from similar interaction when the queen passed away and King Edward VII was crowned in 1902. Among others, Edward VII also assumed the title of Emperor of India. What was encouraging for the Sikh soldiers was the respect they received from the uniformed men from the US and

Canadian armies, something they were not accustomed to from the British who treated them rather shabbily, no better than mere subjects of an enslaved nation.

Who migrated?

The migrants were the Sikhs from different walks of life. The first to migrate to North America were retired soldiers of the Imperial army as well as policemen and security guards from Hong Kong, China and Singapore. The second largest group was made up of young men from the farmlands of Punjab. A significant number of Sikh students came to various universities in the US.

Not everyone, of course, was headed to North America. A small number of Sikh political activists or convicts were sent by the British to various colonies of the empire including Malay, Burma and Andamans. Some landed in Australia and made a living by hawking items to farms, far and away. When the nation opted for the White Australia policy, Sikhs started looking for alternative destinations. Some of the Sikhs who got wind of the new applicable social conditions in racism-inflicted Australia from fellow passengers, changed ships and set out for other destinations. The Sikhs who ventured away to lands far away were undaunted by the changing circumstances. "*Vaikhu Jau*," became a common response. It means, "We'll see what happens." (Kaur, 2020). Some went to Fiji, but almost none to the Caribbean islands where indentured workers were taken by the British. The Sikh community benefited when the Ramgharia craftsmen migrated to East Africa. Some then moved on to work in the construction of the Uganda railroad between 1895 and 1902.

As word spread about the economic opportunities in the US and Canada, farmers mostly from the Doaba region, made their move. The shipping industry agents pitched opportunities abroad with pamphlets in the countryside. Many, who worked in the construction of the Panama Canal, availed the opportunity and walked through Central America and entered the US from Mexico, mostly illegally. They settled mainly in the Imperial Valley of the US.

Even after anti-immigration laws were enacted, students continued to be allowed. They entered in significant numbers, many with the intention of settling down permanently. The number of businessmen migrating, however, remained small.

It is important to remember that even before the American Civil War (April 12, 1861 to April 9, 1865) there were obstacles to the entry of Asians into the US. Tax was imposed on foreign workers in 1852, even though labor was in high demand. Only free white people could be considered for citizenship by a law passed in 1870. During this time Sikhs were by and large unaware of the opportunities in America. It was only around 1899 that they started going to the Pacific West.

Between 1904 and 1907, a significant number of Sikhs had entered Canada and the US. Most of these people were sojourn migrants, and were not looking to stay back permanently since they had left families behind. They wanted to make money, return home, buy more land, and raise a pucca, brick house. But the large majority of those who returned to India found it difficult to adjust to the village life, the colonial oppression of farmers, and the frequent family disputes. They also feared for their personal safety, and chose to return to the Pacific West. That is how sojourn turned into permanent migration. While some early migrants remained *Sabat Surat* Sikhs—they kept their turbans and did not cut their hair, many did not do so, possibly to fit in with western society.

In years to come, several laws were passed that discouraged the entry of Asians into the US. The California Alien Law of 1913 and the Barred Zone Act of 1917 were meant to discourage Chinese and Sikh immigration. No Asian could become a US citizen according to a law enacted in 1924.

The common perception, however, is that Indian and Sikh settlers were working only in farms and the lumber industry. But that does not quite present the correct position. There were highly educated Sikhs and other Indians in the US. Lala Har Dayal Mathur, Bhagat Singh Thind, Dalip Singh Saund, Vaishno Bagai and D R Devi Chand lit up the American skies with their intellect. There were several more who later became an integral part of the revolutionary Ghadar movement.

Lala Har Dayal who was a writer and philosopher gave up a faculty appointment as a lecturer in Indian philosophy and Sanskrit at the Stanford University around 1911-1912 when his activities came to light. He had earlier turned down a career with the Indian Civil Service. He was very close to the Sikhs of the Stockton area and became one of the prime movers of the Ghadar movement that took place to free India from British rule. Bhagat Singh Thind was a PhD in theology and English literature from the University of California at Berkeley. He was a one-time president of the Ghadar party, and served in the First World War for the US as a sergeant. He is the very first turbaned Sikh to serve in the American army. In spite of the time served in the US army, he had to fight a long battle for American citizenship, so discriminatory were the laws at the time. Thind had sought citizenship on the grounds that he was from the white Aryan race. He received a citizenship with sixty-six others which was later rescinded in the case of forty-two, including Thind. He was third time lucky though, and got citizenship on this third attempt.

Dalip Singh Saund, a PhD holder in mathematics from the UC, Berkeley, was the first Sikh and Indian to become a Congressman. According to an article in *The Daily Guardian*, Saund served the 29th District of California between January 3, 1957 and January 3, 1963. He remains, admirably enough, the very first Asian-American, the first Indian-American, the first Sikh-American and the first member of a non-Abrahamic faith to be elected to the US Congress. Kartar Singh Sarabha was also a student at UC, Berkeley. There was a raft of other Indian students whose brilliance shone through in various American universities.

This initial phase of Indian immigration was interrupted by anti-Asiatic laws until emigrants got a new wind following the passage of the Luce-Celler Act of 1946. The third phase took place when President Lyndon Johnson passed a generous immigration law in 1965. This allowed many Sikhs and other Indians to come to the US. The fourth phase was a large chain immigration of family members of US citizens who migrated to make America their permanent home. The 21st century has seen an upsurge of Sikh youth leaving India for higher studies in the US, Canada, Australia and the UK, with the ultimate aim of settling down in these countries.

History of Sikh migration to North America

According to a publication of the University of California at Riverside, Captain Stephen Phillips, one of the earliest ship captains to sail to Indian ports on US flag vessels in the 1780s and 1790s, settled down in Salem, Massachusetts around 1800. During his excursions he traded mainly with the East India Company and managed to hire the services of a Sikh sailor whom he nicknamed George. When in 1800 Phillips retired from his business at the young age of about thirty-six, he somehow persuaded George to be his servant in the US. It has been recounted how George usually wore the long white tunic of the people of New England, along with loose trousers and a red sash. He also tied a blue turban, and must have been a rare sight in the newly independent United States of the time. The German writer Friedrich Gerstäcker has also spoken about the presence of Sikhs in the mines of California during the days of the Gold Rush, around 1854.

According to the publication *The Colonies and India*, Risaldar Major Kesur Singh of the Imperial Indian Army became the first Sikh to enter and subsequently settle down in Canada. He arrived in Vancouver from Hong Kong on board the Empress of India in May 1897. The ship was on way to London for the celebrations of the Diamond Jubilee of Queen Victoria. In 1997, Kesur Singh's arrival a hundred years ago was marked with celebrations across Canada.

In April 1899, Bakshish Singh Dhillon, Boor Singh, Sohan Singh and Waryam Singh—four tall and turbaned Sikhs recruited by the British military and police and stationed in Hong Kong—sailed on a Japanese flag vessel to San Francisco. These handsome young men were from the Punjab countryside, and the local press and public remained in awe of them. In fact, an onlooker at the Pacific Mall Deck exclaimed in astonishment that the local policemen were really no match for the towering Sikh visitors.

As mentioned, between 1904 and 1907 there were a significant number of Sikhs living in Canada and the US. Some participated as soldiers in the Chinese Boxers rebellion of 1899-1901. Some worked in lumber mills and lived in small habitations along the Columbia River between Astoria and Dalles, with a significant number at St. Johns suburb of Portland, Oregon. They had to move when Hume mill, a division of Hammond mills, was burned down in 1922. A few of them worked on the construction of the Central Pacific Railroad and later moved to the Sacramento Valley in places like Yuba City and Marysville. Some Sikhs who worked on the construction of the Panama Canal walked right through Central America and entered the US, perhaps unauthorizedly, to settle down in the Imperial Valley, California.

Around 1919, Vaishno Das Bagai from Amritsar, Punjab, paid a lot of money to secure American citizenship and arrived in the US with his wife Kala and their three children. Bagai wanted to live freely. Bagai, a Punjabi Hindu from Amritsar, was a store owner in San Francisco. When his citizenship was terminated following a Supreme Court ruling and he was not allowed entry into a house he'd purchased by paying a large sum of money in a white neighborhood, a deeply anguished

Bagai, failing to see light at the end of a dark tunnel, took his own life. His wife Kala turned into a human rights activist. In September 2020, a street was named after her—the Kala Bagai Way—in Berkeley. D R Devi Chand, mentioned earlier, immigrated to Vancouver. Once there, he encouraged many more Punjabis to come to Canada in the early 1900s to find labor at the sawmills. The most outstanding among all was Mayo Singh from Paldi in Hoshiarpur district. He went on to become a rich and successful lumberman in British Columbia, Canada. Paldi is the only town in Canada that is named after a Sikh immigrant, in this case Mayo Singh.

Jacoby (1956) has come up with approximate numbers of East Indians in the US in the first half of the 20th century.

1. There were a few legal immigrants before the First World War. After work got over on the Panama Canal in 1914, few came to the US from Central America. There were only six Sikh females, two of them young girls brought to the US by their brother who migrated to the US.

2. Between 1920 and 1924, one thousand students came to the US for studies. No other immigrants were allowed because of the prevailing laws.

3. Between 1920 and 1930 an estimated three thousand East Indians entered the US illegally.

4. Between 1930 and 1945, no legal entries of Asians were allowed. Illegal immigrants continued to work their way into America through Mexico, and some through the northern borders with Canada.

5. In 1946, the Luce-Celler Act allowed hundred immigrants from India to come to the US every year.

6. By 1950, the US Census counted there were 2,650 East Indians residing in the country. That figure, of course, could not take into account a large number of illegal immigrants already present. Small numbers had earlier returned to Punjab between 1914 and 1933.

7. In 1965, President Lyndon Johnson passed

generous immigration laws that opened the floodgates of immigration for Sikhs and other Indians. It resulted in chain migration. Sikhs also emigrated to the US from East Africa, Fiji, Great Britain and other nations.

In stark comparison to the farmers and laborers who had come in large numbers at the turn of the 20th century, the new post-1965 immigrants were highly-educated professionals. Today, most Sikh immigrants are in coastal cities and some reside in the larger cities inland. Sikhs, especially those that are from the younger generation, are an integral part of the social, economic and political fabric of the US. As mentioned earlier, Dalip Singh Saund was the first Sikh elected to the US Congress. After a gap of many years we have two Sikh mayors in medium-sized cities. Gurbir Singh Grewal is director of enforcement at security and exchange commission of the U.S. Nikki Haley was US ambassador to the United Nations and a former governor. Daleep Singh has joined as a deputy national security advisor.

Sikhs are adapting to their host societies gradually and this is a subject matter taken up later in the book.

ASIAN EXPULSION

Early Sikhs to the US and Canada were sojourn migrants. They later changed their mind and went on to stay permanently in North America. Labor unions and Governments of the US and Canada used every means possible to deport them back to their home countries.

Filipinos and some migrants from other countries did go back. In the case of Sikhs, the Canadian government suggested that they be sent to British Honduras, presently known as Belize. The government of British Columbia was concerned that Sikhs would become public expense due to rising unemployment in the province. A delegation that included two members of the Sikh community visited British Honduras following which Sikhs rejected the offer.

No Honduras for Canadian Sikhs
"No Honduras for us"

It was autumn in British Columbia in 1908. A stunning canopy of colorful trees and maple leaves filled the landscape in and around Vancouver. By any stretch of imagination, it was a beautiful sight to behold. It was also a reminder of the cold and snowy winters ahead. Unemployment had begun to rise rapidly within the East Indian community, and it was only a matter of time before it could snowball into a full-blown crisis. Ample evidence of how things could go wrong had been seen and felt during the previous two winter seasons. Vancouver and British Columbia did not wish for a repeat of the "public charge"—a term coined for those who become a burden on citizens and taxpayers—the East Indians had become during the last two winters due to lack of employment opportunities.

J.B. Harkin, the private secretary to the Minister of the Interior, was tasked to come up with a report that could suggest ways and means to deal with the impending crisis. It would be an understatement to say that over the years Vancouver's society had become more than just nettled by the influx of Asians in the Pacific West. In fact, exactly a year ago in September 1907 a riotous mob had run amuck in the US port town of Bellingham, merely 55 miles south east of Vancouver, and driven out East Asians after torching their homes and chasing them down all the way to the railway station. Now in Vancouver unrest was brewing and things were not looking very good as far as the East Indian community was concerned.

There were around 3,000 Indians in the Vancouver district, an overwhelming majority of them Sikhs from Punjab in British India. They were mainly engaged as labor in sawmills, farms, railway construction, and for clearing land on a contractual basis. A handful of them even cultivated fields that they had come to own. Harkin had sought the assistance of William Charles Hopkinson, a police inspector from Calcutta hired by the

Canadian immigration department for his proficiency in Hindi. Hopkinson reported to Harkin in September 1908 that of the 3,000 Indians, nearly 1,000 were already out of work, and by winter the number was expected to swell to 2,000. These were alarming figures as far as the Vancouver authorities were concerned. Questions began to be asked by the people of the area about who would look after the East Indians during the harsh winter months if they remained unemployed. Bearing the expenses of boarding, lodging and meals was going to be a considerable public charge.

Harkin knew that the Indians did not wish in any way to return to India, unless, of course Canada shut all doors on them. This, though, was unlikely and deportation on a large-scale was not something that the Canadian authorities were looking at. At the same time no one wanted the East Indians to become a public charge. Other options needed to be worked out, and one of them was to explore the possibility of sending some of them to work in the British colonies in the West Indies.

The Canadian authorities believed that the West Indies could prove an alternative place to relocate the East Indians for several reasons. Firstly, under the colonial indentured system, Indian labor was being taken to many nations in the Caribbean to work primarily in the sugarcane and other plantations. Secondly, East Indians were likely to feel more at home in the tropical climes of the West Indies rather than the severe, Arctic-like winters in Canada. Apart from the West Indies, alternate destinations such as Fiji, Hawaii, Cuba and Panama were looked at closely. The British colonial office in London was involved at every step, after all it remained the overseer of all the colonies of the empire where the sun famously never set. Finally, a proposal was made for settling some of the unemployed East Indians of Vancouver in British Honduras.

The imperial authorities in Britain suggested that Canada should bear the expenses of a small delegation of East Indians and Canadian officers to British Honduras. In October 1908 Harkin called a meeting in Vancouver that was attended by Rev. John Knox Wright who had spent a number of years in the West Indies among East Indians, Capt. C.J. Brook, a retired officer of the Indian Army settled in Canada, J.H. McGill, an immigration agent, and Hopkinson. An offer was made to the East Indian community for a visit, and two members—Nagar Singh and Sham Singh— were chosen for undertaking the journey to British Honduras.

Harkin and Hopkinson along with the two East Indian men arrived in the British Honduras capital of Belize on October 25, 1908 and met with Acting Governor A. Collet, officiating in the absence of Governor Swayne who was away in England. The British Honduras authorities wasted no time in making an offer to immediately grant ten acres of land to settle 100 East Indians near the new Government railway. The offer was subsequently raised to accommodate 200 East Indians by granting, of course, more land. The period of indent would be anywhere between one and three years, depending on what the labor wanted. They'd be required to mainly work fifty hours a week on railway construction and other public works. Wages would be eight dollars a month along with rations that would include flour, rice and other articles. Alternatively, wages could be twelve dollars a month without rations. Accommodation would be free. An offer was also made to employ twelve Sikhs in the British Honduras police force. The delegates were shown around the principal districts of the country, both in the north and the south. They were taken to towns, plantations and even the jungles in order to get a feel of what conditions were like.

Harkin and Hopkinson left Honduras along with Nagar Singh and Sham Singh and reached New Orleans, Louisiana on November 6, 1908. While Harkin left for Ottawa from there to report to his bosses, the rest left for Vancouver. On November 30, 1908, Harkin was back in Vancouver. They soon called a meeting with the East Indian community heads. It became apparent that moving to Honduras was not an acceptable proposition for the East Indians. Wages in Honduras compared poorly with those in Canada, a nation where employed East Indians made between fifty cents and a dollar a day. Some made even more. "No Honduras for us. It is full of yellow fever and the wages are very low," was the common refrain.

Nagar's diary

In his diary, Nagar Singh had written that during the visit he had an opportunity to talk to many East Indian laborers in British Honduras. Wherever he'd gone he heard one common story—that work was very hard to find, and when it did come, the pay was barely enough for a hand-to-mouth existence. The standard compensation varied between a shilling a day to a shilling and half a day. A shilling at the time was worth twenty-five cents, far less than the money the East Indians made in Canada. He narrated the story of an East Indian man with whom he'd conversed in his native tongue. When Nagar Singh asked him if things were all well in British Honduras, the man said he was starving and it was no different for most other East Indians who'd been living in the colony for thirty to forty years. "Why did he not till land?" Nagar asked him. The man responded by saying that eight years ago he'd bought a piece of land for about ten dollars. After clearing it, he had grown plantains, coconut, oranges and lemons and yet had barely eked out a living. Today when he wanted to sell off his land, he was being offered five dollars. The price had halved in eight years, such were the poor economic conditions. He also noted in his diary that Hopkinson had been trying to prevent him from speaking to the locals, an issue over which he had a serious argument with the Canadian immigration official.

Nagar Singh also learnt that a man who received rations from his employers made between seven to eight dollars a month, and the one who didn't, made anywhere between eleven and twelve dollars. If a man fell sick and needed to be hospitalized, charges were deducted by the employer at the rate of half-a-dollar a day. An average man paid three dollars a month for renting a place to stay, five dollars a month on rations, and four dollars a month on water if rains failed. He also found out first hand that mosquitoes were rampant and people had to use mosquito nets. Fever was rife, especially in the months of June and July, months during which the locals had to purchase water from a company which brought it in a boat.

He had the opportunity to travel through the country a bit. He saw plenty of sweet potatoes, coconuts and, of course, giant mosquitoes that attacked the face and arms of humans with unbridled ferocity. They were a huge nuisance during his travels inside British Honduras. On October 30, 1908, Nagar Singh had a chance to go inside a jungle on horseback. He noticed plantain crops and sugarcane fields. He also saw "coolies," as indentured East Indians were called, laboring on a railroad. He was told by one of them that they were paid forty-five cents a day for their back-breaking job. Nagar Singh in his diary wrote, "The humming of the mosquitoes sounded like the humming of trees during high wind. Me thinks these mosquitoes suck one dollar of life blood from each coolie per day working there for forty-five cents."

On their way back to Vancouver, Hopkinson wanted Nagar Singh and Sham Singh to write down that British Honduras was a good place. Hopkinson wanted to send the signed document to Ottawa to prove that the visit had been successful. Both Nagar and Sham refused on the grounds that they'd no authority to write down such a thing. It could only be done after speaking to the Sikh Temple Committee in Vancouver. Besides, a bribe charge was leveled against Hopkinson for trying to lure the two Indians into giving a good report. Hopkinson, says a report signed by Sava Singh, President of the Managing Committee of the Sikh Temple in Vancouver, even threatened the two travelers that the entire East Indian community would be deported to India if they failed to write down what he asked them to. Also, the country, according to the testimony of Nagar Singh and Sham Singh at the Sikh Temple, was like Andaman Islands, the island where British Indian convicts were sent.

Quite clearly, British Honduras was not the destination that the East Indians in Vancouver would leave for. They would stick together in Canada, and rough it out in the winters.

"The humming of the mosquitoes sounded like the humming of trees during high wind. Me thinks these mosquitoes suck one dollar of life blood from each coolie per day working there for forty-five cents."
—Nagar Singh, Sikh delegate to British Honduras from Vancouver in 1908

Citizenship refused and revoked

In the early part of last century, sixty-seven Indians were granted citizenship. But the majority were flattered only to be deceived, as the Supreme Court revoked forty-two of the citizenships granted to Indians. Bhicaji Balsara was one of the earliest to get citizenship. He was a Parsi (Zoroastrian) and claimed to be from the Aryan race with origins in Iran. Bhagat Singh Thind who had an honorable discharge from the American defense forces during the First World War was at first refused citizenship. On appeal, he claimed to belong to the Aryan race and was granted citizenship. This was later revoked by the Supreme Court. He finally received his citizenship on his third attempt. This is a landmark case.

Some went back

Even though the US and Canada remained attractive destinations for permanently settling down, the plethora of anti-Asian riots, and the general economic slump in North America made some of them return back to Punjab. An estimated six thousand Sikhs left on a permanent basis as they did not wish to tolerate racial hatred, discrimination on the work front, and premeditated hostile attacks. Some of them were also well-off economically at home, and so the process of reverse migration gained momentum. Others left for India from the Pacific West during the Ghadar uprising—an estimated 527 of the 616 East Indians who returned to India were Sikhs—and during the movement to improve Gurdwaras.

We need you. We will have you

After the Second World War there was a dire need for workers as the economic boom had begun. The Luce-Celler Act of 1946 allowed immigration from India and other countries in limited numbers. Once the 1965 Immigration Act came into place, things improved and hundreds of East Indians and Asians migrated to the US.

The present generation of Sikhs has made a mark in all walks of life. They are members of various organizations. They are also well placed in public life, as mentioned earlier.

Beg-me immigration

There has been a gradual fall in birth rates in many countries including the US and Canada. In every likelihood there will be a continuous flow of migrants to these countries with work permits and immigration. How much of it will take place, only time will tell.

When did American and Canadians come to know about Sikhs?

Salem, Massachusetts had become an important US port in the 18th century. As mentioned earlier, Captain Phillips, one of the first ship captains to sail to Indian ports on US flag vessels, had hired the services of a Sikh sailor. That was reported by William Bentley in his dairies. The German writer Frederick Gerstacker has also spoken about the presence of Sikhs in the mines of California during the days of the Gold Rush, around 1854. Turban-wearing Sikh soldiers were noted in Canada at the time of the diamond jubilee celebration of Queen Victoria in 1897, and again during the coronation of King Edward VII in 1902.

The first Sikh to enter Canada is Risaldar Major Kesur Singh who was part of the Indian army attending the 1897 diamond jubilee celebrations. Buckam Singh was the first Sikh to join the Canadian expeditionary force of the 20th Infantry Battalion in 1915 and was injured in the battle at Flanders. According to *Sikhmuseum.com*, Buckam, who enlisted himself as a Christian in the army since there were no positions available for Sikhs, is buried at Kitchener, Ontario, his grave the only known one in America of a Sikh soldier from the two World Wars.

The first documented recognition of a Sikh arriving in the US is that of Bakshish Singh Dhillon, Boor Singh, Sohan Singh and Waryam Singh. All of them arrived on April 16, 1899 in San Francisco on a Japanese flag vessel. The local public and press looked at them in awe, they were tall, well-built and turban-clad. All of them were retired soldiers and policemen from Hong Kong. One of those who stood mesmerized watching the four tall Sikhs walking about at the Pacific Mall Deck commented that the local American policemen were hardly any match for these towering Sikhs.

Awareness about Sikhs also grew when they settled in Astoria, Oregon to work in the saw mills. It was a time when the local press reported the first ever cremation, that of Rauma Singh. Bhagat Singh Thind then went on to make a splash by becoming the first turbaned Sikh to join the US defense forces.

The 1907 riots against Sikhs and Chinese in Vancouver, Canada, and a few miles south in Bellingham, US, further made people aware of the Sikh presence in North America, though not in a very flattering way. Inflammatory articles headlined *Turban Tide* and *Hindu Invasion* in American newspapers did not do the cause of the Sikhs any good either. The Sikhs were also to be seen at lumber mills around the Columbia river and around Yuba City and Marysville in California. Their numbers were growing, so were their detractors.

Mental health issues of Sikh immigrants

No mental health studies on Sikh migrants in the US were done since the need did not arise. There was no evidence of homesickness, or any kind of agitation caused by apartness from their families back home in Punjab. The initial lot of Sikh migrants were mostly single young men, fully prepared for a life of adventure. Many of them migrated in groups and, therefore, belonged to the same village in Punjab. They were socially able to back each other up in a crisis. There were no cases of isolation, or deprivation.

I'm pretty much sure, though, that in spite of their tough and rugged countenance, they must have missed their culture, families, food and festivals back in Punjab. After all, the fact that they belonged to Punjab was the foremost factor that made them bond together. The building of Sikh Gurdwaras, with time, improved the social environment for them, and made it more meaningful and convivial to mix with one another. The Gurdwaras even offered initial shelter to those who arrived newly to the US.

The early Sikhs were the victims of at least three large-scale attacks, all of them racially motivated. They faced them with fortitude and raw courage in an alien land. They displayed no form of post-traumatic disorder syndromes, nor were there any perceptible psychiatric issues that were reported among them. The frustration and pain caused by the racial attacks and snubs made around one hundred and fifty Sikhs take a decision to sail back to Calcutta in August 1910. They wished to return home and were not prepared for the racial slurs and profiling of the white community. Besides, their economic conditions were quite good in Punjab and they didn't have to toil for a living in a hostile environment.

We have earlier discussed the case of Vaishno Das Bagai who claimed his own life after paying a large sum of money for his family to immigrate to the US and subsequently being denied citizenship.

On the whole, mental health was not an

issue that was a cause for a great deal of worry for the Sikh migrants. They had far more formidable matters and daunting challenges to deal with during their life in North America.

Sikh identity

Nanak Panthi Sikh identity is no different than any other Indian or South East Asian identity. At the time of the tenth Guru, Sikh identity became synonymous with the Khalsa with the 5Ks. The turban and unshorn hair became the two most visible symbols of identity for Sikhs. When Risaldar Major Kesur Singh entered Canada in May 1897 as part of the imperial army contingent, the turban was in full view. As we understand from historical records, he was the first Sikh to make Canada his new home, in what was then called the New World. Around the same time, Bakshish Singh Dhillon and three other Sikhs spoken about earlier, all turban-clad, made their way to the lumber yards of Oregon in April 1899, after initially arriving by ship in San Francisco. That was the beginning of Sikh migration to Canada and the US.

The early Sikhs were sojourn migrants who had plans to make some money in the west and return to buy a plot of land and raise a pucca house back in Punjab. At the time they all preferred to wear the turban, even in a hostile, western environment. Passengers aboard the Komagata Maru ship and visitors to the Sikh Gurdwara at Stockton, California, were turban-clad. Those who joined the Ghadar movement in the Pacific West wore turbans.

Things changed when Sikhs decided to settle down in Canada and the US permanently. Many of them, as a result of the rising tide of violence and assaults, chose not to stand out in the crowd by wearing the turban. Derogatory terms such as ragheads were levelled against them. Many who entered illegally through Central America since the US had stopped Asian immigration, removed their turbans and shaved-off their beards to hide their identity, lest they be deported. One such migrant Sikh was interviewed by professor Bruce LaBrack in 2005. He said, "I was quite willing to die for my religion, but was afraid of being deported." There were stories of major emotional suffering that these migrants endured during this process of giving up their turbans. Many would break down, cry and howl, as they felt they were letting themselves down. A part of them died when they gave up the turban. There was a report of about twenty Sikhs who broke down severely after they shaved their beard to enter the US illegally from Mexico.

Religion and Sikh migrants

Most of the early Sikh migrants were highly religious. The Singh Sabha movement of the latter part of the 19th century had an important part to play in religiosity. They strictly adhered to the tenets of Sikhism, believing in one God, Waheguru or Akal Purakh. That was a time in history when men were believers in God and atheism and agnosticism were alien concepts, even among the westerners.

After the Sikh Gurdwara was established in Stockton in 1912, many non-Sikhs also started visiting the place on religious occasions. Sikh Gyanis (preachers) visited communities far and away to meet with the Sikh folks in the remote countryside. The early migrants wore turbans and were *Keshdhari* Sikhs. They carried a lot of respect for Akal Takht, SGPC and the Akali political party.

In the US and Canada in the early part of the 20th century, the term 'Hindoo' was used for all Indians, irrespective of their religion, and this remained the case until the partition of India in 1947. The Sikh-Muslim relations that had begun to heal after the atrocities of the Mughals in the 17th century once again became very embittered after partition. The new nation of the Islamic Republic of Pakistan was created on religious lines and the majority Sikh population decided to move over to India, a majority Hindu nation.

Bhagat Singh Thind was an outstanding Sikh spiritual scholar of the time. He completed his PhD in theology and English literature from the University of California at

Berkeley. He was deeply impressed by the great thinkers of the time, especially men like Ralph Waldo Emerson, Walt Whitman and Henry David Thoreau. He wrote extensively on spirituality and theology. He also lectured widely in the US, and cultivated a large number of followers. His spiritual teachings were inspired by the wisdom he gathered from the words of Guru Nanak and Kabir Das.

Sikhs and Punjabis who married Hispanic and Anglo-American women, became Church-goers. Their families would make the occasional trip to Stockton Gurdwara, though. Under the influence of their Sikh fathers, hybrid children would visit the Gurdwara but generally followed their mothers to the Church. The mothers, unlike the fathers, had their extended family in the US and were Church-going, and, therefore, this had a greater influence on the children. Many of the hybrid children and adults did not receive due respect at the Sikh Gurdwara, particularly after the large-scale migration of Sikhs post-1965.

Sikh challenges in a new land

Humans emigrate in order to get a better life. But the associated movement comes accompanied by challenges. Like any other group of immigrants, the Sikhs too faced numerous challenges in the new land. The host society found them culturally very different, in particular the Sikh turban stood out everywhere. In turn, the Sikhs found the religion, skin tone, language, traditions and identity of the host society strikingly different from their own. The difficulties that arose as a result are enumerated below:

1. Distant, new land that presented an uncertain future.
2. In the absence of regular immigrant or citizen status, many Sikhs lived in fear of being deported at any given moment.
3. Even though most early Sikhs in North America came from farming backgrounds, they were neither able to lease, nor buy any land.
4. Lack of communication was a vastly limiting factor—the Sikhs, largely uneducated, knew no English, the language of the host societies.
5. Communication with the homeland was non-existent. Even in the late 1960s, by which time I was in the US, it took an entire day to book a call to India. Postal mail services were available, but it took several weeks before a letter or parcel could reach Punjab in India.
6. Sikhs belong to a monotheist religion and theology. They did not have a Sikh Gurdwara in Canada or the US, until, of course, the early part of the 20th century.
7. Color bias was deeply ingrained in an American society that had been accustomed to slavery for nearly four hundred years. From the very beginning, Sikhs fell in the in-between zone when it came to skin tone. They were neither black, nor white, and were labelled as brown Caucasians by the local population. Color bias existed at the time, and continues till today, both in Canada and the US.
8. Gender deficit was the order of the day since most of the Sikhs who migrated were young, single males who had no female companionship.
9. Due to visa restrictions, returning to Punjab to marry was difficult. Some ended up marrying Hispanic women, and converted to Christianity. An entire generation was, therefore, lost to the Sikh community due to interfaith marriages.
10. Immigration and citizenship laws remained unfavorable till the middle of the 20th century.
11. Discrimination on the basis of race and color was a daily occurrence. What made matters worse was the fear caused by a sense of inferiority since Sikhs believed they came from a slave nation. Then there was the danger of race-based violence that lurked around the corner, and the anxiety of being raided by immigration agents.
12. Life in labor camps and shack houses with community restrooms and kitchens were insulting for the proud Sikh farmers.

Sikhs and host society

Due to porous borders allowing for unhindered movement, Sikhs in Canada and the US remained one community. There were job opportunities on either side, at the same time each country had its own set of laws. Both countries were influenced by Britain. Canada was a British dominion. There were, of course, two different perceptions of Sikhs.

One was the perception of the employer in the private sector. The other was the perception of those who sat in administrative buildings and whose pay cheque came from the taxpayers' money—that is the Government officials. While the private employer wanted the Sikhs because he was paying them far less than what he would have to pay their white counterparts, the Sikhs were not very liked and were unwanted by those whose jobs they were unwittingly taking away. The labor unions forced the Government to enact laws that would keep the Asian hordes away. There were other difficulties too, that the Sikhs faced. Let's list them:

1. **Living standards**: Most Sikhs, unable to afford good housing because they came from a poor country, lived together in shacks meant for single men. It wasn't something that they liked, but nonetheless like birds of the same feather, they flocked together. Living in groups was therapeutic mentally. With time and resources, living standards improved.

2. **Civil society**: The locals perceived them as uncivil and lacking in basic manners. They were given to spitting while walking on side roads and walkways. Many of them did not feel that it was outrageous to be answering nature's call against the sidewalls, roadsides, or bushes. Not using public restrooms was seen as offensive by the white folk. The turbans were mocked at—ragheads and toggery were words thrown at them all the time. Not trained at not staring, the Sikh men were often guilty of ogling at the white women, especially their legs. It wasn't difficult to guess what was going on in their minds. To their utter humiliation, this is what was reported in a local Canadian newspaper: "An unwholesome group of starved, decrepit humanity, which was making attempts to foist upon the (white) community aged, infirm and impecunious persons." (Verma).

3. **Employers**: The employers were happy with the hardworking Sikhs who were being paid far less than their white colleagues. They were used as strikebreakers or scabs.

4. **Local labor**: They were unhappy with the Hindoo (a term that was used recklessly irrespective of religion), Chinese and Japanese labor undercutting their wages. This widespread discontent resulted in two of the worst riots that took place in the Pacific West in 1907—at Vancouver, Canada, and Bellingham, US. Anti-Sikh riots also took place in Marysville, California and at St. John, Oregon. The Sikhs were driven out of their homes, and their properties were extensively damaged. Fortunately, no death was reported.

5. **Government authorities**: Laws were passed against further influx of labor from Asia. While the Japanese Government was able to work out some favorable deals, the Sikhs, being slaves, received no help from the British masters. In fact, the Englishmen knew of the anti-British feeling among Sikhs and were wary of their growing population in the US and Canada. British cunning may well have been at work when anti-immigration laws were framed to keep the Sikhs away from North America.

6. **Police, local administration, neighbors**: With time, Sikhs befriended their neighbors, who like them were also immigrants to a new land. Some of the standout Sikhs of the time have to be Kehar Singh and his brother who farmed in Clovis, California. They had also learnt the fine art of wine-making from an Italian neighbor and enjoyed home wine-evenings even during the prohibition in the US that lasted between 1920 and 1933.

At the time, according to *Britannica*, there was a nationwide ban on the production, importation, transportation and sale of alcoholic beverages. The brothers were peaceful and honorable citizens. It is said that police sergeants joined them for a glass of wine or two during the prohibition. Kehar Singh and his brother were good Samaritans, they looked after the farm of a Japanese friend who was interned during the Second World War.

Rala Singh and his RalaMelon firm selling melons and onions became a household name first in Phoenix, Arizona, and later all over the US. Over the years, Sikhs developed great love and respect for America that had given them a new home, new opportunities and a chance to grow impressively in their chosen walk. They are a hardworking and peaceful lot, and have managed to win the hearts of the American people.

7. **British influence**: Even though there were instructions from the British to treat the Sikhs poorly in Canada and the US, the Sikhs soldiered on in their adopted land undeterred by the odds. The kinship brought about through the Sikh faith and Punjabiat provided them with emotional well-being. They were buoyed when the first two Sikh Gurdwaras in Canada (Vancouver, 1904) and US (Stockton, 1912) came up. The Gurdwaras were a place to congregate, and for newcomers a place where they could have a short stay after their arrival in a new land. Even Hindus and Muslims were welcome, and an atmosphere of congeniality and camaraderie prevailed.

SIKHS AND THE LOCAL PRESS

Before the arrival of Sikhs from Punjab, the Chinese and Japanese had already made their presence felt in North and South America. In Canada and the US, in particular, the local politicians, racist organizations and the news media who had already bellowed and belched about the "yellow peril" caused by the Chinese and Japanese immigrants, started indoctrinating the public about the dangers of the 'Hindoo invasion' and how it would jeopardize the future and opportunities of the white race in America. Other contemptuous terms such as 'yellow terror, yellow specter, turban tide' became common. One can only imagine that it wasn't the friendliest of environments that the Sikhs encountered at the turn of the 20th century in North America.

Yellow peril

In the late 19th century, Jacques Novikow, a Russian sociologist, came up with the term 'The Yellow Peril' in an essay. This was to project a misconceived threat to the western world from China and Japan, the two nations with the yellow races. The term was alarming enough for the last German emperor Kaiser Wilhelm II to encourage European empires to colonize China through invasion and conquest, especially since Japan had defeated Russia in the Russo-Japanese war fought between 1904 and 1905. Historically, the term 'yellow peril' can be linked to the time Genghis Khan and his descendants conquered Central Asia and Eastern Europe, subjugating the white race in the process. In the late 19th and early 20th century, however, the term 'yellow peril' was raked up irresponsibly to create a threat perception from the Japanese and Chinese immigrants to the US and Canada that did not exist. This perception was later misused to pass stringent laws to prevent Asian migration to North America.

Hindu invasion
The Pacific Monthly, 1907

The term Hindu was devoid of any religious connotation, instead it was applied randomly to all immigrants from India, irrespective of their faith. Fred Hockley first used the term while writing in *The Pacific Monthly* in 1907. He was referring to the East Indians in British Columbia, Canada. He interviewed many Sikhs with turbans who were engaged by the lumber companies that were doing roaring business in the Pacific West. He discussed with them the poverty, hunger, epidemics and the caste system in India. He did not fail to write in an eulogizing manner about the tall Sikhs and their strong bodies and Caucasian features. He witnessed a cremation of a Sikh man who had died. Henry Gladstone, a retired Britisher who had settled in British Columbia, is known to have said that he was rather surprised to see Sikhs doing manual labor in Canada, while in India they enjoyed the status of high-caste soldiers and policemen. He predicted that they would find it hard to assimilate in Canada and would return to India. His prediction, of course, was way off the mark!

Overland Monthly, April 1908

It was Agnes Foster Buchanan who in the *Overland Monthly* wrote an article titled, "The West and the Hindu invasion." She had reviewed the earlier migration of the Chinese and the Japanese that were followed by that of the East Indians. She interviewed a fine-looking Sikh named Binga Singh who worked in a boiler room in an iron factory and spoke English with a great deal of fluency. She wrote about the turban, and the Indian food habits. When she asked Binga Singh about his immigration status, he replied that all was well. Before a judge, however, he refused to remove his turban and repeat the same thing on oath.

The journalists regularly misspelt the names of the Sikhs as they went by the phonetics, rather than the actual way they were written. The misspelt names are to be found in some county records as well.

The tide of turbans
Forum Publishing Company 1910

Herman George Scheffauer, German writer and poet, wrote a three-page article about turban-wearing Asians for the *Forum Publishing Company* in 1910. He saw Sikhs, but did not interact with them. He mentioned how their physical appearance was different from that of the Chinese and the Japanese.

Hindus too brunette to vote
The Literary Digest, March 10, 1923

In various writings that appeared in the first decade of the 20th century it became evident that the Canadians and the Americans found the Sikh race to be Caucasian. According to *The Literary Digest* of March 10, 1923, when it came to suffrage, an article titled "Hindus too brunette to vote here"

appeared. It followed the Supreme Court decision to deny citizenship to Asians.

It pleased the local citizens no end when it was announced that the two thousand acres of land that the Sikhs owned through their hard-earned labor would be confiscated by the state. Another eighty-six thousand three hundred and forty acres of land that had been leased out to them would also be freed up. It was cause for inappropriate celebrations!

Hindus driven out
New York Times, January 27, 1908

At Live Oak, Marysville in California, seventy Hindus residing at two homes were attacked in January 1908. They had just recently been discharged after duties with the Pacific Railroad Company. A local mob chased them out of their homes and compelled them to leave town. The East Indians complained that one thousand nine hundred and thirty dollars that they had on them were taken away forcibly by the members of the mob. This was the kind of societal harmony that prevailed at the time!

Anti-immigration laws
United States

1. As per the Naturalization Act of 1790, only free white people of good character were eligible to become naturalized citizens of the US. This law ruled out citizenship for native Americans, indentured servants, slaves, free blacks and Asians.

2. The foreign miners license tax was imposed in 1852, specifically on foreign workers.

3. In 1874, a law was enacted to prevent the Chinese immigrants from becoming citizens in America.

4. The California Alien Land Law of 1913 made it impossible for Asians to own land, and have it leased out to them for the longer term.

5. The Immigration Act of 1917, also known as the Literacy Act or the Asiatic Barred Zone Act, required an applicant for immigration above the age of sixteen to demonstrate clear reading and writing

LEFT: A rare photo of Bhagat Singh Thind as sergeant with other soldiers.
RIGHT: Bhagat Singh Thind US defense services

Bhagat Singh Thind with wife Vivian

skills. Along with them, ineligible for entry were, "idiots, criminals, alcoholics, convicts, epileptics, anarchists" and others viewed as "undesirable." This law could easily be misused and there was scope of misinterpretation.

6. Strained application or the immigration law of 1924 restricted the immigration quota to two percent of immigrants already in the US, or the native born of any nationality whose names appeared in the US Census of 1890. It instantly put the brakes on immigration from India and Southern Europe.

7. The anti-miscegenation laws in the US were in place as far back as 1691, enacted first by the colony of Virginia and subsequently by other states. They prohibited inter-racial marriages. This was meant to segregate races, and banned any kind of sexual intimacy and was applicable for the black slaves, native Americans and people of brown color. In 1967, the US Supreme Court declared this repressive law as unconstitutional. When the Sikhs first arrived in the US, they had limited choice to marry due to the old laws.

Balwant Singh Brar set a fine example of Sikh kinship. He was an electrical engineer who had been in the Second World War and was disabled. He was granted American citizenship and so was eligible to own land. He bought land on behalf of some friends in Yuba City who could not do so legally. When the laws were changed, he returned the land he had held on their behalf to them.

Canada

Some outrageous examples of Canadian hatred of Asians can be found in the words of Prime Minister Wilfred Laurier who said, "The situation with regard to the Hindoos is serious." His labor minister Mackenzie King who would later become a Prime Minister mentioned, rather unsubtly, "The Hindu is not suited for the

LEFT: Vaishno Das Bagai with wife Kala Bagai and kids.
RIGHT: Vaishno Das Bagai's suicide note in a local newspaper

climate of this country." The leader of the cooperative common federation J.S. Wordsworth had this to say, "They are decidedly grotesque and sadly out of place in Canada." All of them were referring to Sikhs, partly because of the alien habits they had brought with them.

This hatred resulted in anti-Asian laws. Let's take a look at them below:

1. Japanese Immigration Protection Law, 1896.
2. Chinese Immigration Act, 1903.
3. Increase in head tax from $100 to $500.
4. General Immigration Act, 1906.
5. Continuous Journey Act, 1908.
6. Requirement for Indians entering Canada

to possess $200. The Japanese at the time were expected to carry only $40. This was meant to discourage Sikh immigrants.

Favorable immigration laws
United States
The Luce-Celler Act of 1946 [HR 3517, Public Law 483]

This was proposed by Republican Clare Booth Luce and Democrat Emanuel Celler in 1943. On July 2, 1946, President Harry Truman signed this into law. It allowed one hundred Filipinos and one hundred Indians to emigrate to the US each year.

In this context mention needs to be made

In 1946, President Harry S Truman signs into law the Luce-Celler Act. J.J. Singh, standing third from right, was an Indian businessman who had lobbied for the law successfully

J J Singh (*Courtesy Family Collection*)

An advertisement for Singh-Singh Cottons in the Pittsburgh Post-Gazette in May 1939

about Jag Jit Singh, a.k.a. J.J. Singh. He was born in undivided India's Rawalpindi (presently in Pakistan) in October 1897. By age twenty-two he had decided to throw himself into India's freedom struggle following the Jallianwala Bagh massacre of April 13, 1919. He fought in the First World War and landed in New York in 1926. The same year he participated at an exhibition in Philadelphia where he displayed silk fabrics, embroidered works and handlooms, all imported from India. He'd earlier successfully done business in the UK. He opened a store

President Lyndon B. Johnson signs the Immigration Act of 1965 on Liberty Island in New York Harbor with a view of the New York City skyline in the background

in Philadelphia's Walnut Street and became a successful businessman. Soon he had another one on New York's Fifth Avenue. The fashionable and well-heeled in New York sought out his exclusive dresses and gowns, and J.J. Singh became a name to reckon with in the charmed and elite circles of the city.

In December 1941, he became president of the India League for America. He, according to sources, was close to Clare Boothe Luce, and helped draft the historic Luce-Celler bill that was signed into law by President Truman in 1946. The law granted citizenship to over four thousand East Indians residing in the US, and also established an annual quota for one hundred Indians and an equal number of Filipinos to immigrate to the US. His granddaughter Sabrina Singh who was the regional communications director for Hillary Clinton's 2016 presidential campaign also advised Senator Kamala Harris during her political battle in 2020.

The Immigration and Nationality Act of 1965 also known as the Hart-Celler Act [Pub L 89-236]

This was a federal law by the 89th US Congress and signed into an act by President Lyndon B Johnson. For moving into the US, the law abolished nationality origins—the prejudiced foundation of America's one-sided and unfair immigration policy since 1920.

There are many special visa programs such as H-1B for specialty and trained workers, EB-5 for business investment, ones for refugee status, and others.

Canada

The visa types in Canada include those for permanent residency, family class, economic, humanitarian and compassionate grounds, and regular immigrant visa which is through a point system applied to levels of education, language, employment, including an arranged one, age, and adaptability. To qualify, one needs sixty-seven out of a maximum possible one hundred points.

A Sikh man (right) surveys the damage done to Asian shops in the aftermath of an anti-Asian riot in Powell Street, Vancouver, 1907

HISTORICAL EVENTS
Anti-Asian and anti-Sikh riots
The Bellingham Scar

Bellingham, the northernmost city in the contiguous United States (i.e. excluding the state of Alaska), was to provide a watershed moment in Sikh history in North America. In 1904, just around the time Asians were migrating in droves to the Pacific West and Northwest, Bellingham had been coalesced into a single entity from four settlements—Whatcom, Sehome, Fairhaven and Bellingham. Hundreds of Sikhs had left British military jobs in India and had landed up in North America on the Pacific shore. Along with them were young farmers, looking to change the destiny of their lives. Their first port of call was inevitably Angel Island in the San Francisco Bay where once stood an active immigration station—today it is a national landmark. Angel Island was the equivalent of the more known Ellis Island on the East Coast. After quarantining at Angel Island, the

Asian immigrants would move into California, or set out northwards, to places such as Bellingham in Washington state and beyond.

The town of Bellingham offered an abundance of opportunities in mining, railroad construction, cannery and lumbering. The Seattle Civil Rights and Labor History Project at the University of Washington points out that the Bellingham Bay Lumber Company (later merged with the parent company Bellingham Bay Improvement Company) was the largest employer of Sikhs and others from Punjab. The other major employers were the Larson Lumber Company Mill on Lake Whatcom and the Whatcom Falls Mill Company. Most of the Punjabi labor in Bellingham had given up their light guns with long barrels for the axes and saws that would serve them well in the Pacific Northwest and Canada.

Until September 4, 1907, Bellingham had some 250 East Indian workers, mostly Sikhs. But on that particular date their lives would change dramatically, it has already gone down

Anti-Hindu (Sikhs) newspaper cartoons

Arch of Healing and Reconciliation
(In remembrance of the 1907 Bellingham riots)

as a black day in modern American history. In the evening a mob of white working men chased, heckled and then mercilessly thrashed two East Indian workers in one of the town streets. It didn't take long after that for the tinder box of hatred and racial aggression to explode. Around 500 marauding white men headed menacingly towards a boarding house that was occupied by several Asian mill workers. Without warning, they began smashing down windows, driving the place's terrified occupants out of bed and on to the streets and down to the tide flats. The mob went searching for every dark-skinned East Indian that was there, from house to house, mill to mill. When they found them, they drove them away to the train station. They

minced no words and the message was delivered sharp and clear—the community was both undesirable, and unwanted.

The Cascadia Weekly has recounted some of the horrors in one of its editions in the year 2007, a hundred years after the Bellingham riot took place. At the time it appears that the Seattle Republic had publicly lowered its head in shame and written, "It is always a safe bet that the white man is ever ready to do violence to some class of human beings if they happen to have a darker skin than their own." The New York Times was less opinionated and more factual. It said, "Six badly beaten Hindus are in the hospital, 400 frightened and half-naked Sikhs are in jail and in the corridors of City Hall, guarded by policemen, and somewhere between Bellingham and the British Columbia line are 750 other natives of India, beaten, hungry and half-clothed, making their way along the Great Northern Railway to Canadian Territory and the protection of the British flag...the city is quiet today, but there is a strong undercurrent of opinion which apparently approves the action of the members, and it may be found impossible to prosecute the leaders."

The Bellingham Reveille was less than penitent, in fact it quickly assumed a hostile posture. A day after the incident it argued that the purpose of the riots was to "move on, to get them out of town, and scare them so badly that they will not crowd white labor out of the mills." The Bellingham Herald managed to stoke the fires of discord even further. "The Hindu," it said, "is not a good citizen. It would require centuries to assimilate him, and this country need not take the trouble. Our racial burdens are already heavy enough to bear. … Our cloak of brotherly love is not large enough to include him as a member of the body politic. His ways are not our ways; he is not adaptable, and will not in many generations make a good American citizen."

The irony in those words in the Herald does hit out at the soul of a more inclusive and democratic America today. The Hindus and Sikhs as a group have the highest household income in the USA, more than that of white Americans. Their successful entrepreneurial careers, celebrated academic excellence and scientific temperament have been hailed within the USA time and time again. Just about a century down the line the words of the Bellingham Herald truly ring hollow.

The Asiatic Exclusion League was formed in 1907 and it took Bellingham no time to turn into one of the hotbeds of the AEL's activities. There were over 800 AEL members in the town at the time of the September 4 riot. Bellingham's labor unions that were loyal to the AEL, not unexpectedly, remained highly obdurate and unrepentant after savagely driving out the East Indian community. The words of its leaders were not carefully chosen, their remarks remain uncharitable until this day. They said that the AEL "would guard the gateway of Occidental civilization against Oriental invasion."

Bellingham, like many other towns and cities along the Pacific coast, was seen as a gateway to America since it served as a maritime harbor. To drive home the message that they meant business, the AEL members even wrote to President Theodore Roosevelt, threatening that if Asian immigration to the Pacific Northwest was not curtailed, bloodbaths could ensue. Little wonder then that along with the Sikhs and Hindus, other Asian groups like the Filipinos, Chinese and Japanese fled Bellingham the day after the riots, never to return again.

Anti-Sikh riots occurred later at Oakville in Marysville California in 1908 and at St. John Oregon in 1910. But Bellingham's record of racial bonhomie in the early 20th century was nothing to trumpet about.

The Komagata Maru incident—racism's pinnacle

We have power to exclude and to deport certain immigrants…who do not come up to a certain standard either physically, intellectually or morally and whom we deem to be unworthy of Canadian citizenship. We have power to deport Hindus or anyone else if we are of the opinion that they come within any of the classes I've referred to…

Wilfred Laurier, Prime Minister of Canada, April 1908—*The Canadian Encyclopedia*

The legendary Komagata Maru episode, eponymously linked to the ship carrying East Indian emigrants, could well have been known by a different name.

Originally when it was launched as a British-built cargo steamship in 1890 and purchased by the German owner Hansa Line, it was named the Stubbenhuk. In 1894, the ship went to another German owner, the Hamburg America Line, and its new name became Sicilia. In 1913, the ship's ownership changed again—the new owner was Shinyei Kisen Goshi Kaisha who renamed the ship as the Komagata Maru, a name that was retained until 1924, two years before it was ship-wrecked in Hokkaido under another name, Heian Maru. Traveling at an average speed of about 20 km per hour across the vast expanse of the Pacific Ocean, the Komagata Maru with 340 Sikhs, 24 Muslims, and 12 Hindus aboard, arrived at the Burrard Inlet of the Coal Harbour in Vancouver. The passengers included two women and four children. All of them had origins in the undivided Punjab Province in British India. Baba Gurdit Singh, a Singaporean businessman, was the vessel's charterer.

The prime characters

Fred Wellington Taylor, better known as Cyclone Taylor in his earlier days as a

On board the Komagata Maru—Inspector Reid, H. H. Stevens and Walter Hose

celebrated ice hockey player, was at the time serving in Canada's immigration department. He would eventually go on to retire as the Commissioner of British Columbia and Yukon. Taylor was the first immigration official to meet the ship, constructed some six years after he was born. He was under instructions to wait, and not allow the ship to dock as the then Canadian Prime Minister Robert Borden was personally seized of the matter.

By the time the Komagata Maru arrived, the Asiatic Exclusion League (AEL), a radical anti-Asian organization set up in 1907, had already turned very active in Canada and the US. They were not averse to rioting and arson, and were never in need of a great deal of provocation to foment trouble. The AEL's ever-expanding members aggressively pursued the agenda of stopping all Asian emigrants from entering the shores of Canada. One of its ardent supporters, Henry Herbert Stevens, a Conservative MP, had been robustly campaigning for the exclusion of Asians. Sometime in 1914 he's believed to have even mentioned that Canada would not be able to

preserve "the national type" if Asians were allowed to enter the nation. That the Komagata Maru arrived full of Asians was understandably not to his liking.

Stevens was chiefly responsible for getting Malcolm R.J. Reid a job as a Vancouver immigration agent. Reid had no prior experience in the field, nor was he in the civil service. His was essentially a patronage appointment. Naturally Reid waited for a chance to return Stevens the favor. The Komagata Maru arrived at an opportune moment and Reid wanted to show Stevens that he was ready to bend over backwards to comply with the MP's uncompromising racist ideology. He did go on to play an active role in disrupting the journey of those in the Komagata Maru. Reid was also made the chairman of a board of enquiry to look into the legality of allowing passengers in the Komagata Maru to disembark, and get into Canada. It turned out that every decision he took was premeditated.

Much after the ship had sailed away, however, Reid found himself in troubled waters. He was unceremoniously removed from his position in Vancouver on the direct intervention of Prime Minister Borden, so large and embarrassing had become the file of growing charges against him in Ottawa. Cyclone Taylor, Reid's junior, did not quite get along well with his boss either, more so since the agent had the unsavory habit of sharing official and confidential correspondence with Henry Herbert Stevens which the immigration department did not approve of. After all, Stevens was a politician and was not a part of the immigration system which placed a high priority on confidentiality.

At the time the Komagata Maru sailed in, British Columbia had a premier by the name of Richard McBride. According to information available in the publication *New Westminster Record*, the parent advisory council of a school named after McBride has, at the time of writing this book, unearthed some very discomforting facts about his past, and those have been shared with the local district. The council has also asked that the school be renamed. The reasons for the parent advisory council's hard stance are not hard to fathom, and its findings are quite unpalatable for those who are in favor of upholding human dignity. It turns out that during the twelve years that he remained premier, McBride, who was also a four-time MLA, remained unwaveringly in favor of a White British Columbia. Deplorably enough he wanted to shut out the "Asiatic hordes" including cheap Japanese and Chinese labor in order to prevent competition in "everything the white man has been used to calling his own."

He also spearheaded several legislatures for not just steeply taxing companies that hired Chinese labor, but also denying voting rights to Asians and the First Nation people. Besides, his somewhat misogynistic side came out in the open when he shrilly campaigned for denying women their voting rights. Given this not-so-flattering background, it didn't come as a great deal of surprise that when the Komagata Maru sought permission to dock, McBride was heard telling those around him that, "to admit Orientals in large numbers would mean the end, the extinction, of the white people." It was an official line he'd been pursuing since 1911 when the Conservatives had formed the federal Government. McBride had that particular year made a plea to Prime Minister Borden to legislate against Asian immigration and thereby honor an election promise.

As McBride raised the pitch of his anti-Asian campaign targeting those on board the Komagata Maru, Stevens and Reid found a way to enter the ship that was awaiting docking rights. Both the protégé and the mentor were accused of ill-treating the passengers. They were joined on board, among others, by Walter Hose, a man who would one day retire as the Chief of Naval Staff in the Canadian Navy.

On behalf of the immigration department, William Hopkinson was entrusted with the task of interpreting what the Punjabis on board the Komagata Maru said after being questioned. In essence he was a police inspector from Calcutta who had come to Canada around 1908 while on leave. Having been born in Delhi and raised in northern India where his father was posted, he could speak Hindi with a certain degree of fluency. He may have also understood a spattering of Punjabi, without speaking the language itself. According to documents published by the *International Council for Canadian Studies* and the *Pacific Historical Review*, Hopkinson soon became a multi-tasking agent, much in demand. While continuing to work for the Indian Imperial Police's CID, he was also drafted into the immigration branch of the Canadian Government as an inspector and interpreter.

He reported to his seniors, stationed both in Ottawa and London. Even the US immigration saw much merit in enlisting him for his services. His main task was to provide information on the Ghadarites (see separate section in this chapter) who had grouped largely along the Pacific West Coast to start a movement to dethrone the British from their empire in India. Hopkinson depended on Indian informers most of the time. Two of them, Punjabi residents of Canada, were

Komagata Maru Shaheed Ganj, Budge Budge

murdered in August 1914. In October 1914, five months after the Komagata Maru came to the Pacific shores of Canada only to be turned back, Hopkinson, the interpreter who liked to spy, was shot dead by Mewa Singh Lopoke in a court in Vancouver where he'd gone to testify during trials. He was thirty-four, and had clearly lived a dangerous life.

The voyage and after

According to a publication of the *University of British Columbia Press*, the Komagatu Maru set sail from what was the British Hong Kong on April 4, 1914 with 165 passengers on board. Four days later it docked at Shanghai, picking up more passengers. Six days after sailing from Shanghai it reached Yokohama. It left the Japanese port on May 3, 1914 and reached Coal Harbour in Vancouver on May 23 with 376 on board. On reaching that point the ship was denied docking facilities. It remained in Canadian waters for two months, during which period only 24 persons were allowed to enter Canada. These are likely Punjabis who'd been living in Canada for a while and were returning to the country after an overseas trip.

There were multiple reasons for the refusal of entry. Firstly, Canada officially practiced a white policy and Asians were being targeted on a regular basis for reportedly taking away jobs and opportunities of the Caucasian men. Besides, they were seen as an inferior race and were much maligned in local media and public platforms for not just the color of their skin, but their habits, mannerisms, and propensity to form clusters and live in crowded conditions.

In 1907, the year the Asiatic Exclusion League was formed, anti-Oriental riots had taken place, bitterly straining race relations. In January 1908, by what came to be known as an Order in Council, the Canadian establishment moved resolutely to restrict Asians from entering their country. The order prohibited immigration of people who, in the opinion of the Interior Minister, had not come from the country of their birth, or citizenship, by a continuous journey. Also, they were barred from entering Canada if they had not purchased tickets prior to leaving their country of birth, or nationality. The Canadian authorities knew

A few passengers from the Komagata Maru that were allowed to disembark

well that it was impossible for any ship to make a continuous voyage between India and Canada. Given the great distance, stopovers were necessary in Hong Kong, Japan, or Hawaii.

Besides, through another regulation, immigration officials in Canada were empowered to turn back any Asian who arrived with less than $200, a princely sum of money in 1914. This rule did not, however, apply to the Chinese and Japanese who were alienated and kept out through other stringent measures.

Overruling of anti-Asian laws

Things were different just months before the Komagata Maru arrived on the shores of Canada. In November 1913 a Canadian judge overruled an order that had been issued for the deportation of 38 Sikhs. The immigration department had drawn their powers based on the Order in Council, thereby directly impacting the Sikhs and Punjabis who'd arrived in Canada via Japan on a Japanese passenger liner named Panama Maru. Ships that frequented the route between India and Canada needed stopovers due to the great

distance. By invoking the Order in Council, the immigration officials maintained that the Sikhs had failed to carry out a continuous journey from India. Also, they said the immigrants did not have the necessary $200 that each of them required to possess to enter Canada. The Canadian judge found the immigration department's order unfair, and inconsistent with the wordings of the Immigration Act itself. He, therefore, annulled it.

This victory in a Canadian court, no doubt, raised the hopes of Indian immigrants. They began to believe that the system was not totally against them, and justice was possible. The court's annulment of the immigration department's order also implied that future immigrants from India who came to Canada via Japan, Hawaii, or Hong Kong—in other words without a continuous journey from India—would be allowed to enter the North American nation. The Panama Maru case would also have, no doubt, lifted the spirits of all those who chartered and sailed in the Komagata Maru. In any case they were also convinced that Canada would not deny entry to passengers from a

British colony. In the worst-case scenario, the Canadians would know that Sikh troops in British India could rise in rebellion and threaten the very stability of the British Empire.

Baba Gurdit Singh

Gurdit Singh Sandhu, better known as Baba Gurdit Singh from Singapore, had chartered the Komagata Maru from Hong Kong, a British colony he had visited in January 1914. According to *The Canadian Encyclopedia* and other journals of repute, he was appalled by the exclusion laws in Canada and wanted Punjabis to emigrate to what the Canadians claimed was solely "a white man's country."

Sardar Rattan Singh, Gurdit Singh's grandfather, had once refused the offer of a jagir—a feudal land grant—by the British shortly after the annexation of the Punjab. Rattan Singh was a high-ranking military officer in the Sikh Khalsa Army and had battled bravely against the British during the First and Second Anglo-Sikh Wars fought between 1845-46 and 1848-49 respectively. Rattan Singh's son Sardar Hukam Singh, Gurdit's father, had left India and settled in British Malaya as a contractor. Gurdit Singh was born in Sarhali in Amritsar district in the undivided province of Punjab in 1860. It seems his family could not join his father in Malaya until many years later. Gurdit Singh kept up correspondence with his father, the little elementary education he'd privately acquired helped him in doing so. He eventually visited Malaya in 1885 and like his father became a contractor, carrying out business activities in that country as well as neighboring Singapore. When he returned to Punjab in 1909, he was taken aback by the punishing conditions under which people were being forced to labor in British India. Many of his near and dear ones worked extraordinarily hard simply to get a few meals, and they

Gurdit Singh with a pair of binoculars aboard Komagata Maru

Passengers aboard the Komagata Maru. Baba Gurdit Singh is in a light-colored suit, next to a young boy

received no remuneration for their work. Deeply rankled by this type of harsh exploitation at the hands of the British rulers, he wanted people in Punjab to rise and revolt, or in the least seek out new pastures to settle down in. He himself started helping out people from the Punjab province to move to Canada in the early years of the 20th century. And then he chartered the Komagata Maru in 1914, little knowing that its tumultuous journey would prove to be a turning point in Sikh history.

In the early years of the 20th century, a few thousand Punjabis, mostly men, had migrated to British Columbia. At the time they'd discovered that wages in Canada were far higher than they could've ever wished for in India. Looking at the huge opportunities in Canada they started writing letters to friends and relatives to join them there. Those returning to India from Canada also gave vivid details of how life could change, from abject penury to joyful abundance. But little did the early settlers from India in Canada realize that resentment was brewing strongly against them, mainly because of their economic success. The Bellingham riots (see earlier section) ripped apart the social fabric in a small town in the Pacific Northwest, exposing the deep racial divide. Prejudice, both cultural and racial, prevailed in large measure. It was fast becoming evident in the first decade of the 20th century itself that life for Indians in the Pacific coast was not going to be a bed of roses, and there would be many thorns on their road to prosperity.

Gurdit Singh's initial philosophy of helping people leave India was that the "visions of men are widened by travel, and contacts with citizens of a free country would infuse a spirit of independence and foster yearnings for freedom in the minds of the emasculated subjects of alien rule." In early 1914, while in Hong Kong and just before chartering the Komagata Maru, he had publicly supported the cause of

Onlookers at the Vancouver wharf in July 1914

Ghadarites and that of the Ghadar Party. Initially named the Hindi Association of the Pacific Coast, it was an organization founded in June 1913 by Indians in the US and Canada with the explicit aim of liberating India from British rule. It is possible that the Komagata Maru had nationalistic Indian men who wanted to be a part of not just the prosperity of the West Coast, but also the Ghadar Party. That suspicion also may have played a part in the Canadian decision to turn the ship away, based likely on British intelligence.

When the passengers were being ill-treated aboard the Komagata Maru waiting to dock at Coal Harbour, it required the intervention of Martin Burrell, the then Minister for Agriculture, to ensure that things did not escalate out of control. He was the one who liaised with the shore committee and ensured that the ship was sent back without any violence.

The principled Joseph Edward Bird

One of the most intrepid and respectable characters in the Komagata Maru episode was forty-six-year-old Joseph Edward Bird, the principal lawyer for the passengers of the ship. Bird was a senior partner in MacNeill, Bird, Macdonald and Darling, a Vancouver law firm. He had been hired by the Khalsa Diwan Society, the oldest Sikh society in Greater Vancouver, for his previous successful defense of passengers who'd arrived in the Panama Maru. According to documents available with the *Simon Fraser University*, Bird's association with the Khalsa Diwan Society had been facilitated by Husain Rahim, a Gujarati businessman who'd arrived in Vancouver in 1910 and managed the Canada-India Supply and Trust Company for Sikh investors. Rahim, along with others, was also on the shore committee that collected thousands of dollars to aid the men, women and children aboard the Komagata Maru.

When Bird took up the case, he was just not espousing the cause of the Indians on board the Komagata Maru, he was also at the same time fighting his own community that had turned against him sharply. Bird knew that the dice was heavily loaded against him. Almost the entire Vancouver, and beyond, wanted the ship to return. The acrid headlines of the *Vancouver Sun* made the sentiments of the local white community clear. They screamed that "Hindu invaders are now in the city harbor on Komagata Maru." And yet Bird soldiered on, making every attempt to convince Reid—head of the board of inquiry—and the other Canadian officials that legally the passengers could not be kept out. He argued that since the Indians on board were British subjects, they should be allowed to land in Canada, which also had been a colony run by the British. The authorities who heard him were not convinced. Apart from Richard McBride, the premier of British Columbia, the other man who was opposed to allowing Indians into Canada was Truman Smith Baxter, the mayor of Vancouver. So, Bird stood little chance against such a formidable opposition. Reid and his board insisted that the right of admission to immigrants belonged to the country alone, and none else. Deliberately, the board moved very slowly, frustrating Bird by the hour. At the same time the authorities decided that they would starve the passengers on board without adequate food and water. It was a tactic that would eventually wear down their bodies, and importantly their collective will, and make them agree to turn back. Bird lost the case, not on the grounds that his clients represented by one of the Komagata Maru's passengers, Munshi Singh, were dark in skin tone, but because there were irreconcilable cultural differences between Canadians and Indians that could not be bridged at the time.

The return and the gruesome after

After losing the case in spite of his best arguments and largely due to the utter intransigence of the Canadian authorities, Joseph Edward Bird became a marked man. He received threats in Vancouver and had to leave town with his family for a while, before returning to take up more cases for the Khalsa

Truman Smith Baxter, Vancouver Mayor who also opposed the entry of the passengers inside Canada

Diwan Society when things cooled down.

Meanwhile, the HMCS Rainbow, initially built for the Royal Navy of Britain and subsequently transferred to the Royal Canadian Navy, that had been called in to keep close watch on the Komagata Maru was ordered to escort the ship out of Canadian waters. Before that supplies were provided on board so that the starving men, women and children would survive their journey back to India. The return journey began on July 23, 1914, exactly two months after the Komagata Maru had sailed into the Burrard Inlet of the Coal Harbour in Vancouver. Exactly five days after the ship sailed into the Pacific, the First World War broke out on July 28, 1914. Ironically enough, as a part of the British India Army, an estimated one million Sikhs were to put their lives on the line defending the very British Empire that was ill-treating Indians at home and overseas. An estimated seventy-five thousand were killed on duty, but their heroic sacrifices never got the attention that other martyred soldiers from the "fairer" regiments may have received.

One can only imagine the condition of the passengers inside the Komagata Maru, including Baba Gurdit Singh, its charterer, as the Japanese vessel made its way across the oceanic waters towards India. No doubt, their resolve to somehow free themselves of white supremacists must have raged in their minds and hotly debated on board. Little did the passengers know that there was more trouble waiting for them. The dark clouds that would have gathered from time to time over the Pacific may have given them ominous signs of things to follow.

On September 27, 1914, as the Komagata Maru entered the Calcutta harbor, it was intercepted by a British gunboat. In the eyes of the British, the passengers of the ship were not just lawbreakers who'd tried to escape India without authority, but were also political agitators who were out to stir up a rebellion in the Pacific West. Baba Gurdit Singh was the first to be arrested when the ship docked at Budge Budge on the eastern banks of the Hooghly river. One of his fellow passengers resisted this move and a policeman was attacked. In no time a riot broke out and the police fired indiscriminately. Nineteen passengers lay dead. Gurdit Singh managed to escape, but most of the others were arrested and imprisoned, or sent to their villages to be kept under arrest for the duration of the First World War.

Remembering Komagata Maru

In 1952, a memorial dedicated to the Komagata Maru was set up by the Indian Government for the martyrs in Budge Budge with Prime Minister Jawaharlal Nehru himself inaugurating it. In September 2014, a hundred years after the history-making journey of the Komagata Maru, special five rupee and hundred-rupee denominations were released.

On the Canadian side, a plaque commemorating the incident was placed at a Sikh Gurdwara in Vancouver in July 1989. It coincided with the 75th anniversary of the Komagata Maru's departure from Coal Harbor, Vancouver.

May 23, 2008, has become another historic day. The Legislative Assembly of British Columbia passed a resolution, unanimously, that announced: "This Legislature apologizes for the events of May 23, 1914, when 376 passengers of the Komagata Maru, stationed off Vancouver harbour, were denied entry by Canada. The House deeply regrets that the passengers, who sought refuge in our country and our province, were turned away without benefit of the fair and impartial treatment befitting a society where people of all cultures are welcomed and accepted."

Few months later in August 2008, Prime Minister Stephen Harper appeared at the 13th Ghadri Babiyan Da Mela in Surrey, British Columbia, and declared, "On behalf of the Government of Canada, I am officially conveying as prime minister that apology." He was, of course, referring to the Komagata Maru incident. On its 100th anniversary, a stamp was released by Canada Post on May 1, 2014. Besides, many towns and cities in British Columbia have declared May 23 as the Komagata Maru Remembrance Day.

And on May 18, 2016, Prime Minister Justin Trudeau, provided a formal and full apology for the incident in the House of Commons. It was to prove beyond a shadow of doubt that the Canadian Government of a hundred years ago, including the likes of Richard McBride, Henry Herbert Stevens, Malcolm R.J. Reid, Truman Smith Baxter, men who held positions of great responsibility, were prejudiced, unjust, and woefully wrong

Komagata Maru Memorial at Coal Harbor, Vancouver, Canada

when it came to upholding the dignity and honor of fellow human beings.

Sikhs and California's Ghadar Movement (1913-1918)

Inside the mind of the Ghadarite

What would it be like to walk a few yards in the shoes of a revolutionary? What kind of song would he hum? What pace would his pulse race, his heart beat? What would it take to sacrifice one's youth for the nation's sake? What would it be to bristle with patriotism at the utterance of *aazaadi*, the Indian revolutionary's clarion call for liberty? What can it be that makes the mind of revolutionary tick?

What would it be like to leave home, and near and dear ones, and go and live in hiding, waiting for a day when there arrives enough strength in the will and enough force in the flesh to rise and take on the oppressor, and break the shackles of debilitating serfdom?

The answers aren't easy. But some things are certain. If his cause is big enough, the revolutionary is willing to pay the ultimate price with his life. He will give up material life to seek freedom for his people. Freedom from oppression and tyranny. Freedom from injustice. Freedom from penury. No matter how great the peril, or how difficult the goal, he'll strive tirelessly.

The true revolutionary will usually stake his all to break the shackles of tyranny and oppression, injustice and penury, and breathe that air of freedom. In the words of Jamaican legend Bob Marley, "better to die fighting for freedom then be a prisoner all the days of your life."

Oh, if only there were such patriotic heroes today!

Injustice and oppression, the motivators

That is why revolutionaries make compelling stories. Just to know why they did what they did. Not all revolutionaries are successful in what they attempt. Not all escape alive. Not all live to see their dreams come true. In South Africa, Steve Biko did not. In Latin America, Che Guevara did not. In India, Subhas Chandra Bose did not. In order to smell the air of freedom, the revolutionaries do stake their very last breath. Such sterling stuff, that which filmmakers rush to immortalize in motion pictures.

The more one gets into it, the more it becomes clear that the mind of the revolutionary is sparked, shaped and set into action by injustice and oppression. History doesn't lie. When the route of peace is cut off, the road to revolution has usually been the answer. Sometimes it has been the only answer. Revolutionaries like to walk the path of armed resistance, talk the language of warfare, revenge and force to take on their opponents. Usually, the greatest foe is the state, the symbol of tyranny that must be brought down and shattered. Revolutionaries create a cause that they can sell and that which people can easily buy.

Discrimination and patriotism

The minds of the revolutionaries that floated the Hindustan Association of the Pacific Coast and later the Ghadar newspaper in November 1913 were similarly sparked. Their cause was big enough, and they were willing to lay down their lives. They were stoked by the undying flames of patriotism. They were fueled by a deep desire to set their motherland free from bondage. The Ghadarites, as we call the Ghadar revolutionaries, lived overseas and were tormented by bitter racial discrimination. Being Indian was enough to be vilified and abused publicly, and not just for the color of their skin. In the land of plenty, they were just filthy coolies spoiling the American environment. Because of their slave-like status in India, they were easily disparaged and ridiculed in America. They always worked hard and there was plenty of monetary gain to be made in return. But the pain of suffering ridicule, being reviled publicly and oftentimes being assaulted, completely offset all that gain. As they kept doing financially better, draconian laws came into place to keep them away from entering the USA and Canada. For the Ghadarites, it was a

PROCLAMATION

WHEREAS: Astoria, Oregon is the oldest American settlement west of the Rocky Mountains, founded in 1811; and

WHEREAS: By 1911 Astoria had a working waterfront that included fishing, canneries, and lumber mills that contributed to the economic vibrancy of the city; and

WHEREAS: Workers in these industries included in large part immigrant laborers from China, India, and Finland; and

WHEREAS: The Hammond lumber mill in Alderbrook listed about 100 Punjabi Sikh Indians working alongside Finnish immigrants from 1910-1922; and

WHEREAS: The Punjabi Sikhs were inspired by the success of the American Revolution against Great Britain, and by Finland's struggle for independence from Russian occupation; and

WHEREAS: The Punjabi Sikhs met at the Finnish Socialist Hall in 1913 and formed the Ghadar (mutiny) Party; and

WHEREAS: Supporters of Ghadar, thousands of whom living in the United States and Canada, returned to India, and inspired their countrymen to fight for their independence from Great Britain, which was achieved in 1947; and

WHEREAS: The Ghadarites fought and died not only for the freedom of their home country, but also for the innate rights of the immigrant worker to lead a dignified and discrimination-free life; and

WHEREAS: 2013 is the 100-year anniversary of this historic meeting that recognizes the universal right of sovereign nations to independence and self-rule.

NOW, THEREFORE, I, Willis L. Van Dusen, Mayor of Astoria, do hereby proclaim 2013 as a celebration of the

CENTENARY OF THE FOUNDING OF THE
GHADAR PARTY IN ASTORIA, OREGON

IN WITNESS WHEREOF, I have herewith set my hand and caused the Seal of the City of Astoria to be affixed this *18TH* day of March, 2013.

_____
Mayor

discriminatory world, both at home in India, and away in America.

Hindustani Association of Pacific Coast

In July 1912, Indians working in different mills in the Portland (Oregon) area formed Hindustan Association with Sohan Singh Bhakna, a lumber mill worker, as president, G.D. Kumar as secretary and Kanshi Ram as treasurer. They invited Har Dayal who visited them a few months later. Sohan Singh Bhakna and Udham Singh Kasel went to Astoria and established a branch of Hindustan Association with Bhai Kesar Singh Thatgarh as president. At the end of May, 1913, Har Dayal along with Bhai Parmanand visited St. John, Oregon, and addressed meetings of Indian groups in the neighboring cities of Bridal Veil, Linton and Wina and on June 2, went to Astoria along with Sohan Singh Bhakna and others. At a meeting of some patriotic and enlightened Indians, Har Dayal passionately spoke about throwing the British out of India and securing liberation by all means at their disposal. It was at this June 2 meeting that the Hindustani Association of the Pacific Coast was formed with a major objective of liberating India from British colonialism with the force of arms, just as Americans had done more than a century ago, and help establish a free and independent India with equal rights for all. Sohan Singh Bhakna, was elected President of the association, Kesar Singh Thathgarh was Vice President, Har Dayal, was General Secretary and Kanshi Ram was treasurer. Har Dayal provided leadership for the newly formed association and was the central figure and the force behind the new organization. It was also decided to start a newspaper to be named 'Ghadar' after the 1857 Ghadar in India. In December 1913, during a conference in Sacramento, attended by representatives from Oregon, Washington, California and Canada, the executive committee was expanded. Jawala Singh was elected as vice president and several others from California were included in the committee.

Punjabis had come to the United States with the highest of expectations. But they were

The Independent Hindustan (newspaper)

disillusioned when they faced hostility, humiliation and racial prejudice from the American people and were disheartened by the failure of the British Indian Government to provide help when they became victims of violent acts from American hoodlums. They felt that they could fight for their rights and live in dignity in America if their own homeland was not under foreign rule. When the Hindustani Association of the Pacific Coast was formed, Punjabis whole-heartedly supported its objectives of liberating India from colonial rule, enthusiastically became its members, liberally helped with finances and willingly agreed to fight a revolutionary war for India's freedom.

The headquarters of the Hindustani Association of the Pacific Coast was established at 436 Hill Street in San Francisco and was named Yugantar Ashram. It served as a base for coordination of all the activities of the association. Later, a building at 5 Wood Street was purchased and the headquarters was shifted there. The association launched a magazine appropriately titled *Ghadar* for free distribution to promote the aims, objectives and activities of the organization. In the first issue of the *Ghadar*

Founding leaders of the Ghadar party

Kartar Singh Sarabha, one of the earliest student leaders

Gulab Kaur from Manila, Philippines, a woman leader

journal, the editorial declared:

"Today there begins in foreign lands, but in our own country's language, a war against the British Raj.
What is our name? Ghadar.
What is our work? Ghadar.
Where will Ghadar break out? In India.
The time will soon come when the rifles and blood will take the place of pen and ink."

Leaders and followers

The Punjabi farmers and the lumbermill and construction workers formed the backbone of the Ghadar movement. They were led by many intellectuals like Lala Har Dayal, Ram Nath Puri, Tarak Nath Das, P.S. Khankhoje, Dalip Singh Saund, Bhagat Singh Thind, Maulavi Barkatullah, Sant Baba

Wasakha Singh Dadehar, Baba Jawala Singh, Santokh Singh, Sohan Singh Bhakna.

Character and spunk

The Ghadarites were young men with dreams, and plenty of courage. The bulk was made up of Punjabi farmers that had arrived in the west coasts of USA and Canada in the first decade of the 20th century. The intellectual capital came from young Indian students and teachers in prestigious institutions such as Berkeley and Stanford. They came mainly from Punjab, and a few from Maharashtra, from Bengal, and other parts. Together they rose, and gave the call for Ghadar—meaning mutiny—to free India. Force was their way, and storming the empire's citadel, the final goal.

In 1913, at Yugantar Ashram, the Ghadarites gave the call for *aazaadi*. In many ways, it was the precursor to the other known pre-Independence revolutionary movement by the Azad Hind Fauj under Bose. An estimated eight thousand overseas Indians, mainly Sikhs, played a direct part in the Ghadar movement.

Remember, it was also a time in Indian history when Mahatma Gandhi was away, yet to return from his life-changing experience in South Africa. The method of Satyagraha that he practiced there was as yet an alien concept to Indian minds. The armed revolt of 1857 in India and the American Revolution of 1776 in the USA were the ideological templates available to the Ghadar revolutionaries. In both instances, the adversary was the same—Britain's repugnant colonial machinery. The Ghadarites knew that allowing the British to trample the subjugated citizens all over India, allowing them to milk India systematically, and drive Indians deeper into penury and debt, would plunge their motherland indefinitely into serfdom. And that is why their daring is so compelling. "The sin of silence when they should protest makes cowards of men," said Abraham Lincoln. The Ghadarites threw silence to the winds and roared in unison.

The Ghadar newspaper

Ghadar literally means revolt or mutiny and

A group photo of the early members of the Ghadar party

was published in Urdu, Hindi, Punjabi, among other languages. The first issue of the journal Ghadar was in Urdu and was published on November 1, 1913. An edition of the journal was brought out in Punjabi in Gurmukhi script in December 1913 and in May 1914 a Gujarati edition of the journal was also published. It carried articles on the conditions of the people of India under British rule and also on problems of racial prejudice and discrimination against Indians in the United States. The magazine contents expressed the community's pent-up anger and suppressed feelings and exhorted like-minded people to join the association. Through the magazine, the Indian people were called upon to unite and rise up against British rule and throw them out of India. The activities of the association were intense and incessant. The *Ghadar* magazine became very popular among Indians, its circulation and influence increased rapidly. Over a period of time, the Hindustani Association of the Pacific Coast itself became known as the Ghadar Party.

Within a short period of time, the weekly magazine became a sought-after periodical for revolutionary and patriotic ideas. Besides *Ghadar*, other publications were brought out to raise the consciousness of the Indian people for revolt against the British. One of them was a collection of poems and songs titled *Ghadar-di-Goonj* which became very popular among the Punjabis. The poems were composed by amateur poets and reflected the discontent and the surging anger against injustice and oppression by the British. Ten thousand copies of this pamphlet were published and distributed. The poems were memorized and recited at gatherings. They exhorted people for an armed rebellion to gain freedom of their country. Publications from the Yugantar Ashram became very popular and were eagerly awaited. They were sent to Indian revolutionaries in India, Europe, Canada, Philippines, Hong Kong, China, Malaysia, Singapore, Burma, Egypt, Turkey, and Afghanistan. The weekly *Ghadar* magazine, being the principal patriotic literature, reached many people; even if one copy reached India or to a fellow revolutionary elsewhere, multiple copies were made for circulation.

In the past, several attempts were made in the UK and Canada to mobilize the Indian

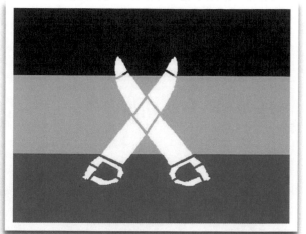

Insignias of the Ghadar party and printing press

community for India's independence. But it could not become a mass movement as both countries were under the British. After the Ghadar Party was formed in America, many volunteers started devoting full time to publish *Ghadar* magazine which was sent free every week to over five thousand people in the USA, Canada and other countries. The contents of the journal awakened the consciousness of the readers and poems published in *Ghadar* newspaper excited them to liberate their motherland. The visible effects of the *Ghadar* publications started to manifest in India and abroad. Many committed volunteers opened branches of the Ghadar party in various countries and worked tirelessly to promote the objectives of the party. They had imbibed the fire of revolutionaries and were motivated to fight for freedom for their motherland. The movement became the symbol of political consciousness of the overseas Indians. The influence of the Ghadar movement was so powerful that when called upon, many overseas Indians returned to India to fight for India's freedom.

The Ghadarites expressed their frustration of being a part of a slave nation in no uncertain terms in one of their publications. Their words portray their immeasurable pain, hurt and humiliation.

Some push us around, some curse us.
Where is your splendor and prestige today?
The whole world calls us black thieves,
The whole world calls us "coolie."
Why doesn't our flag fly anywhere?
Why do we feel humiliated?
Why is there no respect for us in the whole world?

Our patriots, their terrorists

History through the eyes of the British administrators typecasts these revolutionaries as criminals, terrorists and seditionists, simply because they had the audacity to challenge the empire. The fact is that like anywhere else in the

Photos of some of the 400 Ghadar Martyrs.
Kartar Singh Sarabha was the youngest to be hanged

world, they were freedom loving people, nothing more, nothing less. Quite a few of them had withstood hostility to become rich by working very hard. They owned large tracts of farmland in the USA and Canada. Some diversified into other businesses, including trading. The majority that went to North America was able to bring about a sharp and positive turnaround in its own economic fortunes, compared to what things were at home in India. Yet, for the sake of freedom, for the sake of their motherland, they gave up their business interests, their enterprise, their land, their wealth and their youth. What great heroes they were. What they could never give up, though, was the springing, eternal hope to accomplish the larger dream—to see India free one day.

Short-lived story

Not all stories have happy endings. The romantic story of the Ghadar patriots was destined to be ephemeral, and not unexpectedly. The Ghadarites had daring, but the British had tact, guile, ammunition,

Ghadarites in chains at the Amritsar railway station 1938. Baba Sohan Singh Bhakna is seen second from the right

specially set up fast-track courts, and horrific jails. It was almost a mismatch. Each time they tried to make a dent, the Ghadarites were vanquished even before they could reach the gates of the citadels. Each time they tried to bombard their bastions their efforts blew up in smoke. The enemy's wherewithal was too much for the young, brave men. They were arrested and thrown inside jails unfit for humans. Significantly, the British espionage system delivered when it mattered, time and time again. Most of the men feeding this well-oiled spy system were, tragically enough, Indians themselves. They were the gaddaars—traitors—to the core who let down the patriots and their own country over and over. Political leaders, elite and rich landowners, had no desire to be part of this freedom movement. Some Sikh gurdwaras were even praying for the success of the rulers in the war.

Stamp of Ghadar

Indian Prime Minister Dr Manmohan Singh released a stamp commemorating the centenary of the Ghadar movement at the 10th Pravasi Bharatiya Divas at Kochi, Kerala on January 8, 2013. It was followed by a Ghadar Oration by Professor Harish Puri, author and professor. In 2013, at the Indian Republic Day function at the Consulate General of India in San Francisco, a Ghadar stamp was released by the late community leader from California, Mr Inder Singh, and the then Consul General of India.

As of now, let's all live with the simplicity of it all. The patriotic members of the Ghadar party had powerful dreams. Some died without seeing their beloved India free from foreign rule. Some lived to see the beauty of their dreams come alive through India's Independence in 1947 nearly 28 years after the movement had been completely crushed by the British. It was a moment in time when all they'd lived for, all they'd given up their youth for, had come true.

Ghadar indeed, it was.

Mela Gadri Babian Da

The British wanted to crush any movement for the freedom of India. This massacre was revenge against any such movement.

The Ghadar uprising that involved the Sikh population of the Pacific West and those in the British Indian Army had rattled the British Empire. The heroic Ghadarites who had the courage but not the means to take on the force of the empire were crushed. Their brave attempt to free India from colonial rule had started in 1913 but was crushed by 1919 (see earlier section). After swift trials in special courts, forty-eight Ghadarites were sentenced to death and were hanged. Many hundreds were imprisoned for life, the majority in the cellular jail of Andaman and Nicobar Islands. By 1919, two draconian laws were also in place—the Defence of India Act, 1915 and the Rowlatt Act, 1919, both meant to completely curb the fundamental rights of Indians to such an extent that India came to

Reginald Dyer,
the Butcher of Amritsar

Udham Singh who assassinated
Michael O'Dwyer

Bullet marks on the walls at
Jallianwala Bagh, preserved carefully

be equated with a slave nation.

Punjab was the epicenter of the Ghadar movement. It included a revolt within the British Indian army whose men from regiments stationed at Rawalpindi, Jhelum and Peshawar bombed cantonments in Mianmir and Ferozepur. The Ghadar movement gained impetus when students, lumberyard and mill workers, and farmers in the Pacific West, mainly Punjabi Sikhs, joined in large numbers. They gave up their vocations and decided to overthrow the British. Indians within the British army who were spread across various colonies of the empire were motivated to revolt, and fight for the cause of a free India. The Ghadarites weren't equipped with the firepower to take on the British, but they clearly had the will to do or die. They were exceptionally brave and daring men.

In November 2019, at the 28th Mela Gadri Babian Da held at the Desh Bhagat Yadgar Hall in Jalandhar, the centennial year of the Jallianwala Bagh massacre was commemorated by intellectuals and the intelligentsia, and local people. They were paying homage to the revolutionaries who laid down their lives in the Ghadar movement.

Early immigrants and marriage Anti-miscegenation laws in the US

As mentioned earlier, the US had a law in place in 1691 that prohibited inter-racial marriages. It was first enacted in the colony of Virginia and then applied to other states.

The 1917 wedding photo of
Valentina Alvarez and Rollie Singh

Group photo of Punjabi-Mexican couples

This was meant to segregate races, and banned any kind of sexual intimacy and was applicable for the black slaves, native Americans and people of brown color. In 1967, the US Supreme Court declared this repressive law as unconstitutional.

Due to unfavorable immigration laws, the Sikhs who entered the Pacific West did not wish to return to India to find a spouse. That would have jeopardized their chances of a possible re-entry. Many had entered illegitimately through Mexico. Their choices for marrying were, therefore, quite limited. Sikh marriages that took place at the time were as a result of individual selection and not community choices. That would depend on the level of education, economic status, religiosity and visa status. The highly educated Dalip Singh Saund and Bhagat Singh Thind married local white women, for instance. On the other hand, Bakshish Singh Dhillon who had immigrant status returned to Punjab to find a bride. His spouse Rattan Kaur arrived in the US in 1910, arguably becoming the first Sikh married woman to enter the shores of America. In 1924, Puna Singh and his wife Nand Kaur came from Utah to settle down in Yuba City and started a dairy farm. This is the first married sikh family to move to Yuba City. Like Bakshish Singh Dhillon, the turbaned Kehar Singh, a well-settled farmer, went to Punjab to get married late in life. That was a time when the Luce-Celler Act permitted

The gravestone of Mota Singh and his wife Consuelo Singh

A Punjabi Mexican family

limited immigration for East Indians to the US.

For Sikhs, approving a picture-bride was ruled out as the girl would be required to undertake a long train journey from Punjab to Calcutta, then take a ship to Hong Kong where the layover could take months, and then take another one to the US west coast. The stringent laws also meant that the Sikhs could not take a chance to return home to get married, their re-entry into the US or Canada was not guaranteed at all. Many of them, as discussed before, who came from Panama settled for Hispanic women as brides. Over five hundred such marriages have been recorded, most of them in the Imperial Valley of California (Leonard 1992).

Why Mexican women opted for Sikh men is a question that has not been answered with any degree of satisfaction. While it is true that Mexicans and Sikhs were colleagues in the agriculture fields and labored together, it is not clear whether there was a shortage of Mexican men at the time. By marrying Sikhs from time to time, Mexican women made their preference for the brown man over the black African-American man abundantly clear. Were the Mexican women unreasonably enamored by the hardworking, handsome and thrifty Sikhs? Was alcoholism

a serious issue among Hispanic men? In any case, it is hard to believe that the Punjabi Sikhs were all sober men. Some of them indeed had a reputation of drinking quite heavily too. Besides, in the prohibition-era, drinking was forbidden and surely the men who labored in the fields, irrespective of nationality, must have been law-abiding citizens too and could not have been drinking themselves to death. Like the Sikhs, the Mexicans too were disliked by the white men. Like Sikhs, they too had a close-knit patriarchal society. Like the Sikhs, they also fell in the category of brown people.

Interviews in later years with the offspring and descendants of the Sikh-Mexican marriages were to provide some clue about why the Hispanic women liked the Sikh men. For instance, one male descendant revealed that the Sikh fathers were thrifty, a very admirable quality indeed. His mother would, in fact, go to the extent of searching his father's purse when he was asleep (Bruce LaBrack, 2005). His cousins and nieces opted to marry friends and co-workers of Sikh relatives. The Hispanic wives were devout Christians, at the same time they frequented the Sikh Gurdwara at Stockton. Hybrid marriage homes had pictures of both Guru Nanak and Jesus Christ. The marriages, even if they had a poor approval rating from society, worked quite well.

Hybrid marriages have been in vogue throughout history, especially during times when the men did not find companions from within their communities. British employees of the East India Company, for example, who worked in tea estates married local Indian women. Their off-springs came to be known as Anglo-Indians. This was because in the 19th century a ship journey back to England to find a wife was a time-consuming affair. The situation changed in the 20th century when shiploads of girls from England arrived in India to find well-settled ICS, civilian and army officers in India (Gilmour, 2018).

Hybrid and cross marriages

The benefits of hybridization are well-known in plants and in some animal species such as mules, a cross between a horse and a donkey. Studies by Montagu (1947) among racial groups that had hybrid marriages revealed that the offspring more often than not displayed "hybrid vigor." Since the Sikh-Hispanic marriages were small in numbers, no proper assessment of the offspring could be made.

If one goes back in history, it will be clear that Punjab's population is largely a byproduct of cross marriages and hybridization, chiefly because of the state's northwesterly location. Mingling and mixing with the early Aryans, Greeks and Mughals and later the British resulted in a unique race, sturdier and stronger than most other people of India. This intermixing did generate enough hybrid vigor. The Punjabis are natural adventurers, brave, and blessed with the spirit of enterprise. It fires the imagination no end to think how the Punjabis who lived so far away from the seas of western and eastern India had the daring to make long oceanic voyages and go away to far-off lands in quest of a better future. It could not have been easy.

Half and Halves

According to *The History of California's Punjabi-Mexican Communities* by Jordan Villegas published in *Latina.com*, the first recorded marriages between Punjabi men and Mexican women took place in 1916. It was legal for a Punjabi man to marry a Hispanic woman at the time. But not always did it go off well. There is reportedly an instance of a group of Mexican men abducting two Mexican sisters who'd married Punjabi men in the Imperial Valley. The women were taken to Mexico, locked and beaten up by their captors who hadn't taken kindly to their fondness for East Indian men. Karen Leonard, a professor of anthropology at the University of California at Irvine, in her book *Making Ethnic Choices: California's Punjabi Mexican Americans* says, "Many Punjabis married the Mexican women that worked on their land because of their cultural similarities and proximity. And when they'd show up at the county record office, they could both check 'brown.' No one knew the difference."

Marriage ceremony

The first Sikh Gurdwara in the US was established in Stockton, California in 1912. Marriages would get formalized in this place, but not for those who lived far away. There is no official record of any Sikh marriage ceremony from that time, and certainly no photograph of a Sikh groom arriving on a horse to tie the knot. Some Gyanis or Sikh clergy who went out to remote Sikh communities may have performed a few marriage ceremonies. But it is a fair guess that Sikh *maryada* and customs could not be practiced on those occasions. While the farmers in the Imperial Valley were enticed by the Mexican women, primarily because they knew the chances of finding a Sikh bride was remote, those in Yuba City and Marysville preferred Sikh brides since these places had grown into mini-Sikh enclaves. Following the Luce-Celler Act of 1946, Sikhs started going to Punjab to bring back a desi bride.

Children of hybrid marriages

Inter-racial marriages are on the rise in the US. And so are the children from such weddings. In the past the off-springs have been termed mulattoes, mestizos (Spanish and indigenous descent), half-breed, half-and-half, mixed blood, and new people. The off-springs of Sikh-Mexican marriages were by and large known as half-and-half by the Mexicans (see earlier section).

Since the mothers in the Sikh-Mexican marriages were Christians, the children followed them to the Church, and the families adopted Christianity. The fathers or married men who went to the Gurdwara were ignored and overlooked by the newer Sikh immigrants. The off-springs who went to Church also did not receive due respect from the Hispanic congregation. As a result, these children felt isolated by both the Indian and Mexican communities. They went on to create their own group called the Hindustani Club.

In 1984, the *New York Times* did a conference on children of mixed families. In that meeting, Dr. Alvin Poussaint, an associate professor of psychiatry at the Harvard Medical School, pointed out such children were more successful than had been the common impression. Many Sikh-Mexican hybrids celebrated important national occasions such as Indian Independence Day. The annual old-timers dance was held in Yuba City by hybrid families in November each year. The attendance, though, is noticeably on the wane. The hybrid became an inherent part of the melting pot, as described by Dadabhay in 1954. These mixed off-springs could have been Sikhs, but I believe we failed them. Just like the many others we failed, those that are on the fringes of Sikhism—the Sikligar, Ravidassia, Balmiki and the so-called 'other' Sikhs.

Psychological aspects of hybridization

It is a common perception that children of mixed marriages have negative psychological traits. Several studies have been undertaken to get into the nitty-gritty of this perception. Studies by a slew of academics and professors including Dr Alvin Poussaint (1984), Pearce-Morris and King (2012), Astrea Greig (2013) found limited evidence to show genetic negativity among children of mixed marriages. What proved to be of far greater importance for the wellbeing of such children was the ethnicity of their parents, their socio-economic status, the child-rearing practices adopted by the parents, and so on. On the positive side, hybrid children are seen to play a significant role in improving inter-racial connections and relationships. They also enhance tolerance for one another among their community members.

There have been hundreds of outstanding and brilliant individuals who are a byproduct of inter-racial marriages. The list is way too long to mention in this particular book. Two names, though, quickly come to mind—former US president Barack Obama and golfing great Tiger Woods. According to articles in *The Guardian* and *The Telegraph*, Tiger Woods' parents were of mixed heritage. His father was born to African-American parents and had European, Native American and Chinese ancestry. His mother was from Thailand and is of mixed Thai, Chinese and Dutch ancestry. Obama's father was an African from Kenya while his mother, according to Megan Smolenyak, had mainly English ancestry and some lineage from Scottish, Welsh, Irish, German and Swiss forebears.

Divorces

Divorces began to rise when immigration laws became favorable. Many Sikhs divorced their Hispanic wives, and brought back Sikh brides from Punjab. The Mexican spouses were considered inferior to Punjabi spouses. Many men carried their guilt with them when they abandoned their wives and children and ventured off overseas.

Family structure

Until their enclaves were established, the Sikhs lived in scattered parts of the Pacific West, mostly in shared accommodations. With time, hybrid families came up, as has been discussed before. The family structure remained less-than-satisfactory. It all depended on education and marital circumstances. Things began to improve on the family front with the enactment of favorable immigration laws for Asians and Southern Europeans.

SIKH ENCLAVES

According to Ogden (2012), small Sikh

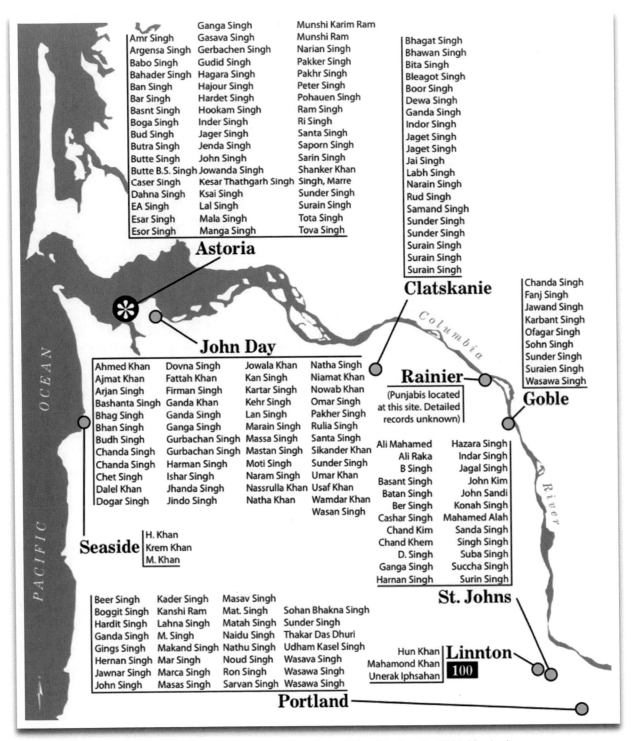

Sikh community that resided around the Columbia river in 1910 (Ogden)

communities were existing along the Columbia river at Astoria, John Day, Clatskanie, Rainier, Goble, St. John, Linton, Bridal Veil, Hood Rivers, Dalles, Winans and Portland. Ogden searched county records and names of those migrants (Ogdens chart). These Sikhs moved to other locations as jobs dried up. Most moved to the more stable agricultural jobs. Tuly Singh and his associates worked in the construction of railroad and were among the first to move to Yuba city where others followed.

Yuba City—The mini Punjab in the US

About forty-three miles north of the Californian capital city of Sacramento is Yuba City. It includes both the Yuba and Sutter Counties in the Central Valley of Northern California, within the Greater Sacramento

Women at Yuba City
(Courtesy: Punjabi American Heritage Society)

area. Yuba City is also the county seat—administrative center—of Sutter County. Its importance is immense when it comes to Punjabi-Sikh migration to the US in the early years of the 20th century. When they arrived here from India, the Punjabi men immediately ran into a system of racial segregation and apartheid. They were hard working and their farming skills helped them find employment quickly. They'd mostly been small peasants in India and were clearly looking for greener pastures in the Pacific West, with Yuba City being one of the places where they started settling in significant numbers. Most of the Punjabi farmers leased or even purchased their own farms. A few of them went on to become highly successful and prosperous farmers.

Between 1917 and 1946, legal immigration from India to the US was barred due to various exclusionist measures and laws. The Immigration Act of 1917, for instance, aimed to severely restrict immigration by language and literacy tests, creating fresh categories of inadmissible persons and barring immigration from the Asia-Pacific region. This act, also called the Literacy Act, and at times the Asiatic Barred Zone Act was amended by the Immigration Act of 1924, also known as the

Johnson-Reed Act. It also put hurdles on immigration from the eastern hemisphere.

Understandably, the growth of the Punjabi-Sikh population in the Yuba-Sutter area was brought down to a trickle. In 1946, the Luce-Celler Act was signed into law by President Harry Truman, allowing 100 Filipinos and 100 East Indians to immigrate to the US each year, and also permitted them to naturalize as United States citizens. A slow but steady migration from Punjab started once more. In 1965, the Immigration and Nationality Act of 1965 was signed into law by President Lyndon B. Johnson. Also known as the Hart-Celler Act, it came as a boon for Asians, including the Punjabi migrants. It removed discrimination against Asians, Southern and Eastern Europeans and other non-Northwestern European ethnic groups that had been a part of American immigration policy. The Punjabi population in the Yuba-Sutter area started growing at a faster clip.

Today, Yuba has the largest concentration of Punjabi-Sikh people in the US. According to the well-known diaspora expert and author, Inder Singh, Punjabis comprise over 10 percent of the total population of about 80,000 in the Yuba-Sutter area. Several are engaged in the field of agriculture and horticulture. They grow about 95 percent of the peach crop in Yuba-Sutter County, and also account for 60 percent of prunes and 20 percent of almonds and walnuts cultivated there.

With the sizable increase in their population, the community has diversified from the core business of farming into various other vocations, including businesses and professions. Many Punjabis have become successful entrepreneurs, venturing into trucking, commercial property, and various other businesses and contribute significantly to their local economy. Several with university degrees have gone into professions such as medicine, teaching, banking and engineering. A number of prosperous Punjabis in the city own palatial houses and drive expensive cars. They endured tremendous hardships and worked very hard to realize their American Dream.

Sikhs have invariably added to the ethnic and cultural diversity of America and have become part of the unique and distinctive multicultural character of the new society. They have contributed to the development of the region's economy at all levels and reshaped the landscape of the cities and towns where they have their homes.

Yuba City is literally a mini Punjab in the USA with three Gurdwaras and a temple. Sat Sri Akal is the preferred form of greeting. Speaking in Punjabi is not considered foreign and the language is officially taught in public schools. A radio program in Punjabi is regularly on the air. The Punjabi American Festival (Baisakhi) is organized every year in May by the Punjabi American Heritage Society which was founded by Dr Jasbir Singh Kang in 1993 to help the younger generation get connected to their roots. The annual event features some internationally acclaimed artistes and hundreds of local ones, including students from California schools, colleges and universities, who perform traditional Punjabi dances such as *Bhangra*, *Giddha* and *Jhumar*. The ticketed event attracts over twelve thousand people and is aimed at promoting a better understanding of the Punjabi community, its culture, and the many

contributions they make to the region. Many business owners rent display booths to put themselves in front of prospective customers.

Yuba City is well-known for its annual Sikh parade which draws a large number of Sikhs from various parts of the United States, Canada, India, United Kingdom and throughout the world. In 1969, the first Gurudwara in Yuba City was started on the 500th birth anniversary of Guru Nanak Dev, the founder of Sikh religion. Since then, on the first Sunday of November, Guru Gaddi Divas (Coronation Day) of Guru Granth Sahib Ji (Sacred Sikh Scriptures) is celebrated by organizing a huge parade featuring many floats. The 34th annual parade in November 2013 attracted an estimated 80,000 to 100,000 people. Two days preceding the event, the 48-hour non-stop recital of Sikh scriptures (Akhand Path) commenced on a Friday. After the concluding ceremony (Bhog) on Sunday, the sacred Guru Granth Sahib Ji was ceremoniously carried onto a lavishly decorated float. As the main float left the Sikh Temple to lead the procession, a rain of flower petals came pouring down from a helicopter circling above the parade. The main float was preceded by five people dressed in orange robes, known as *Panj Piare* or the five Beloved of the Guru. A band of devotees continuously swept the street in front of its path. Many Sikh groups from different parts of the United States put up their own floats which followed the lead float. Several floats had *Ragi Jathas* (bands of religious singers) singing hymns. All along the parade route, enthusiastic devotees put up stalls to serve free refreshments to the bystanders and passersby. Thousands of participants joined the processions and many followed the floats. Several thousand stood along the route and watched.

Langar (free food) is prepared for the participants gathered for this momentous occasion. Feeding a huge number of people is a major undertaking and it is done with the help of volunteers who have the spirit of *Sewa* uppermost in their minds. As many as 200,000 meals are served during the *Guru Gaddi Diwas* weekend. There is no parallel to the event in the United States.

Yuba City looks like a typical city in Punjab on this festive occasion. All kinds of goods imported from India are sold in the Punjab Bazaar, a temporary mini-shopping mall. Thus, the annual parade provides major economic benefits to the community. The city gets its share of revenue in the form of sales and other taxes. The annual event is also a homecoming weekend for many younger Sikhs who have left Yuba City for other parts of the US.

Didar Singh Bains started the parade tradition in Yuba City. He came to the US in 1958 from Nangal in Hoshiarpur and worked as a farm laborer. He and his father bought their first farm in 1962. At one time, he was one of the biggest peach growers in California and was called "Peach King of California." He is arguably the wealthiest farmer among Indians in the United States.

Yuba City has the distinction of having a permanent multi-media exhibition that is housed in the Community Memorial Museum of Sutter County. The exhibition was developed by the Punjabi American Heritage Society and captures the story of over 100 years of the Punjabi community in the United States. The exhibit is appropriately titled, "Becoming American: The story of Pioneer Punjabis and South Asians."

There are also large Punjabi farming communities in other cities in California such as Fresno, Bakersfield, El Centro and the areas surrounding these cities. Some of the farmers have earned name, fame and fortune. A Sikh farmer from Fresno has earned the title of "Raisin King of California." The *New York Times* calls Harbhajan Singh Samra "the okra king of the USA". Samra specializes in growing Indian vegetables such as okra, mooli, tinda, bitter melon, Indian eggplant, methi, among others, near Palm Springs, Southern California.

In 2016, the Sikh community in Yuba City raised $135,000 in order to educate Americans about themselves as well as Sikhism. The money was raised as part of a national campaign. Between 2009 and 2010, and then again between 2013 and 2014, Kashmir (Kash) Gill was elected mayor of Yuba City, the first Sikh to hold this public position in the United States. He also served on the City Council of Yuba City. Between 2014 and 2018, Preet Didbal succeeded Gill and was elected mayor of Yuba City, becoming in the process the first Sikh female mayor in the U.S.

Sikhs have invariably added to the ethnic and cultural diversity of America and have become part of the unique and distinctive multicultural character of the new society. They have contributed to the development of the region's economy at all levels and reshaped the landscape of the cities and towns where they have their homes. At the same time, they have established themselves as a vibrant part of the society that has come to depend on their contributions in the local and national economies.

Stockton

About forty-eight miles south of Sacramento, California's capital city, and ninety miles south of Yuba City, lies Stockton. It is of great historical significance for the Sikhs in America, and the US in particular. The first Sikh Gurdwara Sahib Ji in North America came up in Stockton in 1912. It was founded by the Pacific Coast Khalsa Diwan Society.

The two men who largely funded it were Baba Jawala Singh, a highly successful farmer in the San Joaquin Valley known as the 'potato king' who had leased a five hundred-acre ranch in Holtville, adjoining Stockton, with his business partner Baba Wasakha Singh. In fact, Jawala Singh served as the first granthi of Stockton Gurdwara. According to several historical records such as the *Pioneering Punjabis Digital Archive*, the *Oxford Handbook of Sikh Studies* and others, immigrating Punjabi farmers would perform prayers in a room at their ranch. It had the sacred scripture, the Guru Granth Sahib, also known as the eleventh Guru, after the ten Gurus who lived between 1469 and 1708. It was tenth Guru Gobind Singh Ji who declared the Guru Granth Sahib Ji as the eternal Guru, a spiritual teacher and guide for the Sikhs and Sikhi.

The two farming pioneers from Holtville

Baba Wasakha Singh   Baba Jawala Singh

were to eventually found the Stockton Sikh Temple at South Grant Street. But that in no way diminished the importance of their ranch which was a hotbed of activity when it came to meetings on religious and political matters concerning the Gurdwara. It was the Stockton Gurdwara that played a crucial role in inspiring the Ghadar movement. Before the Second World War, the Gurdwara served not just Sikhs but Hindus, Muslims, Catholic wives and American-born children of the Punjabi pioneers.

Jawala Singh not only formed the Ghadar Party that motivated East Indians in the US, Canada and serving army and construction personnel in British colonies to overthrow the ruling British from India, he also helped sponsor the first Punjabi language newspaper in the US called *Ghadar*. The Stockton Gurdwara sponsored many students who were studying in the Pacific West. One of the most notable beneficiaries was none other than Dalip Singh Saund, the first Sikh American, the first Asian American, the first Indian American and the first member of a non-Abrahamic faith to be elected to Congress.

El Centro

El Centro is in Southern California about 20 miles from the Mexican border. It is the seat of Imperial County and one of the earliest Sikh enclaves in the US. When the early Sikh settlers entered the US from Mexico, quite a few were attracted to the area as it had a newly developed irrigation system that was ushering in a new agricultural economy. There was a time when the Sikh landowners were the richest in El Centro as compared to other ethnicities.

Agriculture remains the major driver of the economy. But while the Sikh enclave at Yuba City flourished, El Centro was a bit of a laggard in terms of its economic growth. The other marked difference between the two cities has been that while exogamy—marriage with Hispanics—has characterized Sikh life in El Centro, endogamy has been the custom in Yuba City.

There is a significant Sikh population around El Centro that has three Sikh Gurdwaras. Toga Singh Sandhu was the founder of the El Centro Sikh Temple, the second one to be opened in California after the one at Stockton. He remained an active member of this Gurdwara for over half a century, holding various positions in its committee. Born in 1902 in Manuke, Punjab, Toga Singh left home at age fourteen with his elder brother for Hong Kong. From there he moved to Shanghai and worked as a security guard at an apartment. In 1923, he came to Mexico after learning of the rich agricultural prospects there. Nine months later he entered the US and became an early pioneer of the Sikh community in this country. He was made an American citizen in 1953, nearly twenty-nine years after he made his way to the US. Before moving to the Imperial Valley, Toga Singh had spent nine years in Los Angeles and had run the La India Café in that city. He sold the café and with the money commenced farming operations in El Centro. Shortly after he started out in farming, Toga Singh returned to India and married Bachan Kaur. The Sandhu family expanded in the US and the couple had four children—Charnjeet Kaur, Charn Singh, Kuldeep Singh and Surinder Kaur. Over the years he sponsored many family members so that they could immigrate to the US. His support was not limited to just his own family, but to others as well. He founded a school, a technical institute and a hospital at Manuke and during a visit to India in 1979 was generously thanked by the local village committee.

Canada

Canada has an ethnic enclave of Sikhs at the Punjabi markets in Vancouver and Surrey, both in the province of British Columbia.

Customs, traditions and festivals

The early Sikh immigrants followed all the customs, traditions and festivals of Sikhs that were prevalent in their homeland of Punjab.

Sikh musicians

Baisakhi, Diwali, Lori are important events in Sikh history, as are the birth anniversaries and martyrdom days of Sikh Gurus. The Gurdwara became the common venue for congregation, *sangat*, *pangat* and *langar*. During leisure time, playing cards perhaps became a pastime, just like in Punjab.

There is no mention of Kabaddi, a Punjabi sport, but Sikhs did take part in local wrestling competitions, with Basanta Singh and Dodam Singh standing out in particular. In the 1970s, at campuses across the US, Bhangra became a rage and spread like wildfire. Today, with the added influence of Bollywood, Bhangra and its fusions are hugely popular not just among Sikhs and East Indians, but also among young Americans as well.

Cremation

Cremation was largely an unknown phenomenon in the US until Rauma Singh (Ram Singh) was cremated at Astoria, Oregon, in November 1906. In subsequent years, a Sikh Gyani ji would perform the last rites during cremation in the presence of Sikhs, or Sikh-Mexicans, as the case may have been. For Sikhs from mixed families, cremation was not easy since the hybrid children were largely unaware of cremation rituals. Someone like Dalip Saund who'd married a local white American girl, was buried by his mixed family at a grave in Hollywood, California.

In the US today, more cremations are being done than ever before. It is the considered view of Abrahamic religions that departed souls will not return and, therefore, their practitioners increasingly find interring the human body a less acceptable option, especially in comparison to cremation. The decomposition after burial can be nauseating. On the other hand, cremation saves money, real estate and the environment too. Bio-cremation uses water-heat pressure and potassium hydroxide, resulting in a greener funeral as compared to cremations where fossil fuels are in vogue.

SIKH YOUTH—PROFESSION AND EDUCATION

First-generation Sikh children had to adapt to the rough and tumble of life. Theirs wasn't a well-heeled upbringing, and most of them followed their parents into agriculture and labor. The children from Anglo-Indian marriages (mainly American mothers and Indian fathers who were well educated) did well in American society, in spite of the deep-rooted color bias that prevailed. These children became educated professionals. This was true of the children of Saund, Thind and few others.

In 1932, Balwant Singh Brar graduated from the University of Michigan with a degree in electrical engineering. In 1923 he had enrolled himself in the Ford Motor Trade School at Michigan and left two years later to study at the University of California, Berkeley. In 1941, he became the first East Indian draftee in the US army. Seven years later he married Parmjit Kaur Gill Brar, the first East Indian who came to California directly from India after the end of the Second World War. On the other hand, Tuly Singh Johal wasn't educated, but his son Gulzar Singh Johal became a physician after graduating from the University of California at Irvine in 1957.

The color bias often meant that Sikh

children were relegated to schools for Hispanics. In any case, due to the Jim Crow laws in place, children had to study in segregated schools. This was until the landmark Brown v. The Board of Education of Topeka ruling of May 17, 1954 by the US Supreme Court held such schools as unconstitutional. In reality, though, segregation was the norm, rather than the exception. It continued to be practiced, and even today there are schools in the former Confederate states that have separate prom nights for black and white students. Could it be that the Saund family moved to Los Angeles from Westmorland, California so that their children could study in non-segregated schools? The official reason the family provided for the move was that they were allergic to the weather in Westmorland.

The children of hybrid families of Sikhs did not fare too well since the parents themselves were less educated. Besides, the children of agricultural and labor families were pulled out of school. Education was certainly not a priority in such families. The parents feared that if provided with higher education their children would give up the Sikh faith, as they would be interacting with a larger, cosmopolitan society on campus. This position was true in both the US and Canada. Many children, therefore, dropped out of high school to work in family farms. If they were unable to marry locally, they were sent to India to find a spouse. Also, when it came to Sikh enclaves, undeniably they did have some advantages, but at the same time they largely deprived the children of the benefits of higher education, and upward mobility that came with it.

SIKHS IN POLITICS
Dalip Singh Saund

The Sikh story in the US can never be complete without mentioning how Dalip Singh Saund fought an uphill battle for the recognition of his community in the US. Saund arrived in Ellis Island in the US shortly after obtaining a bachelor in mathematics from the

Congressman Dalip Singh Saund with John F Kennedy and Lyndon Johnson

Judge Saund at the family home in Hollywood, California, 1960. Clockwise from upper left: Dalip Saund Jr. (son, (holding his son Neil)), Ellie Saund (daughter), Dr. Fred Fisher (son-in-law, holding his son Bruce), Julie Fisher (daughter), Marian Kosa Saund (wife), the Congressman (holding his grandson, Eric), Dorothy Ann Saund (daughter-in-law)

Dalip Singh Saund with chief minister of Punjab Partap Singh Kairon during a visit to Punjab, India

LEFT: Bhagat Singh Thind with India's then Prime Minister Jawahar Lal Nehru.
RIGHT: Mayo Singh with PM Nehru

University of Punjab in 1919. He was born in a small village called Chhajjalwaddi near Amritsar, Punjab. In the US he initially studied agriculture at the University of California at Berkeley before switching over and obtaining a master's degree in mathematics in 1922. He then did a PhD in the same subject in 1924. His studies were sponsored by the Stockton Gurdwara, not far from Berkeley. But after all his degrees and all the mathematical knowledge that he acquired, he ended up becoming a farmer at WestMoreland in the Imperial Valley. He became a success at farming, though.

In 1928, he married Marian Kosa, an immigrant born to Czech parents. The couple had three children. After applying for naturalization, Saund received his US citizenship in 1949, three years after the historic Luce-Celler Act had been passed. The following year he started out as a Justice of the Peace for Westmoreland Township and went on to become a Congressman from the 29th district of California. As mentioned before, he remains the very first Asian-American, the first Indian-American, the first Sikh-American and the first member of a non-Abrahamic faith to be elected to the US Congress. He remained a Congressman between 1957 and 1963.

Even though Saund never openly complained about it, he could not get a job even after a Berkeley education primarily because he was not seen as white. He was in

Rabindranath Tagore seen with local Sikhs in Vancouver, Canada on April 15, 1929

Sikh railroad workers in Washington state in 1900

the US initially at a time when race-based eugenics had tickled the fancy of the average white family in the US. In his early days as a student at Berkeley, and then after that while working on a farm, he, however, continued to wear a turban in spite of the social backlash it caused. By the time he decided to get married to Marian Kosa, a white woman, he had discarded the turban and was a public figure. It was also a time when he wished to settle down permanently in the US. With the turban gone, he became more active in mainstream politics.

But even without a turban, Saund, not a dark man, was denied entry at a hotel because he was not white. The family had earlier registered in the hotel in the name of his wife, a white woman. Unable to enter, the entire family had no other choice but to spend the night in their car. Saund's children were considered brown and, therefore, only allowed to attend a segregated school for Mexican children in WestMoreland, California. All this was proving too much and this is when the family decided to move to Los Angeles. Saund explained that they were leaving WestMoreland because the family had become susceptible to local allergies. His friends, however, believed that the real reason for the relocation was the disdainful color bias that his children had to face in WestMoreland.

Marian Kosa lost her American citizenship under the terms of the Cable Act of 1922 for marrying a brown man. Saund introduced her socially as Marian Rekha Kaur Saund but was unable to popularize the name. He was a liberal Democrat and advocated citizenship for Sikhs and East Indians. When years later he made a visit to his homeland in Punjab, it became a moment of utter joy and pride for the Sikh community. He was a legend in Punjab and for the entire Sikh community in North America. The Sikh population that lives in the enclaves of Yuba City and Marysville, however, has not been able to capitalize on the legacy of Saund and make it really count in the political arena in the US.

SIKHS IN BUSINESS

Earlier sikh migrants were mostly workers in Sawmills and construction of railroad. They later moved to agriculture and other industries.

As a community, some Sikhs made it very big in the US and Canada as farmers. This was not entirely unexpected, given their farming background in Punjab, their ability to work very hard, and the tendency of the average Sikh family to keep the children away from higher education and push them into the farmland.

Kartar Singh is among the first Sikhs who bought farmland in 1913. Jawala Singh and Wasakha Singh were successful potato farmers in Holtville, California. The initial Sikh prayers (*paaths*)

LEFT: Sikh railroad workers in California in 1909.
RIGHT: Group photos of Sikh workers in 1910

Sikh sawmill workers near Vancouver in the early 1900s *(Courtesy Vancouver Public Library)*

Rala Singh of Rala Mellons

Spoony Singh of Hollywood California Wax Museum

Nand Singh seen with his brother. He was the first to buy land in Yuba City, California

were held in a small room in their farm. They were largely responsible for the construction of the Stockton Gurdwara in California in 1912. They also whole-heartedly financed the revolutionary Ghadar Party.

Rala Singh settled in Phoenix, Arizona and grew his watermelon and onion business to an extent that RalaMelons became a household name in the US. At one point, he owned and leased in excess of two thousand acres. Even the great Dalip Singh Saund, about whom we spoke in the earlier section, was able to make a decent living only after he got a franchise to sell agricultural chemicals. He couldn't land a job in spite of his doctorate in mathematics.

In 1959, researcher Scott Littleton found to his surprise that in the Imperial Valley, Sikhs were the richest farmers around. Of the eighty Indian farmers he counted, a staggering sixty-five (eighty one percent) were Sikhs. But the contribution of Sikhs in fields such as finance, law and real estate, or other businesses was nothing to shout about.

Mayo Singh

Outside farming, some of those who made it big include the likes of Mayo Singh and Spoony Singh. The former from Vancouver was nicknamed the 'Lumber King' and was the most successful Sikh industrialist of the time. Spoony Singh (born Supuran Singh Sundher) arrived in America from Jalandhar, Punjab, with his family at the age of two. A *Sabat Surat* Sikh (one with a turban and uncut hair) he went on to create the wax museum at Hollywood. At the time it opened in 1965, a mile-long queue of curious citizens was waiting impatiently to get inside the museum's precincts. Sikhs with the help of Sant Teja Singh created the Bombay Trading Co., Nanak Banking Trust Co., while Husain Rahim, a Gujarati pioneer was in-charge of the Canada-India Supply and Trust Company for Sikh investors.

Sikh organization

Due to the small population of Sikhs in North America, the Sikh Gurdwara has remained the most significant organization for the community. Many non-Sikhs too attend the Gurdwara regularly.

The Ghadar Party founded in the Pacific West became another organization that was mainly run by the Sikhs and funded by them to a very large extent. It was a secular, anti-British organization, and most of its members were Sikh farmers of California and British Columbia.

SIKH PIONEERS AND TRAILBLAZERS

In my community of Sikhs too there have been quite a few pioneers, some of whom I had a chance to meet personally, and others about whom I learnt from their relatives and friends. While those who set out on the Komagata Maru made history after being denied entry into British Columbia where the Canadians officially followed a White Policy, there were hundreds of others too who took pioneering steps for the community. They worked in farms, railroad construction, lumber yards, and in many other places. They sailed away from their motherland to set up their new lives in a faraway nation, and undoubtedly paved the way for future generations to thrive in North America. Below, I recount with much pride, some of their stories.

Bakshish Singh Dhillon

Many years ago, I had the occasion to meet with Kartar Dhillon, daughter of Bakshish Singh Dhillon. The meeting happened during a screening of a movie titled *Turban* by Kartar's granddaughter Erika Surat Anderson at the Sony Metreon in San Francisco. According to the *South Asian American Digital Archive (SAADA)*, Dhillon, along with three other Sikh men,

Bakhshish Singh Dhillon with wife Rattan Kaur and their children

Budh Dhillon, son of Bakshish Singh Dhillon, was in the US defense services

immigrated to the US in 1899. He landed in San Francisco wearing a turban. He later went back to India, married, and his wife, Rattan Kaur, arrived in the Pacific West in 1910. The couple went on to settle in the port city of Astoria, the oldest of its kind in the state of Oregon, and a place relatively free of the racial riots that had become common along the Pacific West. It was from Astoria that Andrew Hammond had gone scouting for cheap labor in India after he had purchased the Samoa sawmill in Humboldt County in 1900. It was also in Astoria that the first meeting of the Ghadar Party was held in May 1913, at the five-storey building—Finnish Socialist Hall—that was completed in 1905.

The Dhillon family recounted stories and interactions between the Finns, who comprised roughly twenty percent of Astoria's population in 1908, and several World War I representatives, in Bakshish Singh Dhillon's house. A catalogue produced by UC Berkeley about Punjabis in California has a prominent photo of the Dhillon family while they were in Astoria. It was a distinguished family that built its home in Astoria after renting land from the mill. Bakshish Singh lived with his wife Rattan Kaur and four of the couple's eight children—Kartar, Budh, Kapur and Karm—attended the local Alderbrook public school.

At the Metreon in San Francisco, Erika gave her audience a firsthand account of the Dhillon family's enormous economic and social struggles against sundry discriminations they had to face on a regular basis. The family eventually moved to San Francisco and became actively engaged in the Ghadar movement. Kartar's brother Budh joined the Ghadar heroes at the tender age of twelve and travelled to several countries to secure help from the enemies of Great Britain during World War I. He studied for some time at the KUTV university in Moscow and during his travels on behalf of the Ghadar party he met Raja Mohendra Partap Singh, another freedom fighter. He eventually retired from the US defense services. His sister Kartar Dhillon became a civil right activist and wrote a book named *Parrot's Beak*. Kartar passed away in 2008. The Dhillon family can rightly be called the first family of migrant Sikhs to North America.

Mayo Singh

Mayo Singh Manhas's story is also quite riveting. He led the life of a true Sikh pioneer in the Pacific West. Born into an agricultural family in the village of Paldi in Punjab's Hoshiarpur district in 1888, Mayo left for Canada at age seventeen to join his elder brother Ganea Singh (real name is more likely to be Ghanaiya Singh) who had arrived in British Columbia earlier. Mayo, though, did not reach Canada directly. Instead, he worked in the US and one day sneaked through the forested borders under the cover of darkness to enter Canada. At the time he wore a turban and was a *keshdhari* Sikh, one with long hair.

It is in Canada that he decided to change his name to Mayo Singh from the earlier Mahaan Singh or Maiya Singh. At the time it was not uncommon for Sikhs to take on western first names. For example, in the Imperial Valley in California, one Inder Singh changed his name to Andreas Singh, and another Magyar Singh to Miguel Singh. At some point down the line Mayo shaved his hair and stopped wearing the turban.

To Mayo's immense credit, he founded the logging town of Paldi in Vancouver Island along with his brother Ganea and cousin brother Doman Singh. He was arguably the most outstanding lumberman in entire British

Mayo Singh with turban

In 1936 it was renamed Paldi after Mayo's ancestral village back in East Punjab.

There are stories about how Paldi came up. When Mayo Singh's potato farm did not yield good results, his curiosity drew him to the lumbering business. He knew no English when he arrived in Canada, so to make up for it, he'd buy English newspapers and find a local schoolboy or two to read the news to him. That way he started picking up the English language, and got better at it over time.

His entrepreneurial and communication skills were such that he could become the lead negotiator while acquiring lumbering rights from the Canadian Pacific Railroad. As his lumbering business prospered and his wealth grew, Mayo Singh began to recruit local Canadians, Punjabis, Chinese and Japanese workers. He established a Sikh Gurudwara, a school and the local post office. You can say that back in the day Mayo Singh was the first Sikh industrialist in Canada.

In September 1935, the *Vancouver Province* carried Mayo's story under the headline Cowichan Lumber King. Mayo was fondly called Santa for his philanthropic efforts in hospitals and local institutions. The University of Victoria, British Columbia, runs a scholarship program in his name. There's a covered walkway named after Mayo Singh at the St. Joseph's hospital in Victoria. He also

Columbia. Besides, Paldi is the only town in Canada that is named after a Sikh immigrant, the rest of the towns have names that have been borrowed from British and European places from where the majority of the immigrants had arrived in earlier days. According to information accessed from the *Working People: A History of Labour in British Columbia* and *The Punjabis in British Columbia*, the town was initially named Mayo after Mayo Singh in 1916. But subsequently it had to be renamed in order to avoid confusion with another town by the name of Mayo in Yukon.

Mayo Lumber Company Ltd

donated generously to institutions in Punjab. When Prime Minister of India Jawaharlal Nehru visited Canada, he did not fail to dine with Mayo Singh, such had become the lumber king's gigantic reputation.

Mayo Singh was related to Jeana Brar, wife of my medical college alumnus and friend Manjit Singh Brar. Jeana is the granddaughter of Mayo's brother. She provided me with a copy of the book that had been written by Joan Mayo, Mayo Singh's daughter-in-law. It was titled, *Paldi Remembered: 50 Years in the Life of a Vancouver Island Logging Town.* Mayo Singh passed away peacefully at his home in February 1955. By then he had made the Sikh community proud due to the immense goodwill he'd generated through his business success, philanthropy and leadership. Today, every Sikh is proud of Mayo Singh's abiding legacy.

Rala Singh (1907-2003)

Rala Melons and onions became a huge brand thanks to Rala Singh who had migrated to the US in 1930 from the village of Pamal in Punjab's Ludhiana district. Sometime in the early 1990s, I noticed the name Rala Singh Farms printed on a large bag of onions at a grocery store in Weirton, West Virginia. It sparked my curiosity instantly. I called up my neurologist friend Dr Jaswant Singh Sachdev who'd settled in Phoenix, Arizona, and expressed my desire to meet Rala Singh.

We eventually did catch up with Rala Singh who was already in his mid-eighties and somewhat of a legend in the region. I did not go into details of his migration to the US during the brief coffee table conversation, but got more information from Daljit Singh Gill who was the son-in-law of his younger brother and had migrated to the US in 1972. Rala Singh was born in village Pamal now part of greater Ludhiana, an industrial city in Punjab, India. Rala Singh had acquired a high school education and done some college courses.

He left for England from Bombay in 1929 with a British passport. He carried one thousand nine hundred silver coins in British Indian currency amounting to one hundred

and twenty-six US dollars at the time. He spent some time in England and came to New York in 1930. He later reached Detroit, Michigan and worked in the Ford Motor Company. He reached Marysville in California in 1931. Then he left for Arizona with his friend Issar Singh in 1935. He worked as farm labor and with the help of his employer leased land. At one point he employed 800 workers on 2,000-acre leased land. He married Elizabeth, a white Anglo-American and had three children. Elizabeth divorced him in 1979 on the grounds that he was sponsoring too many family members from India. He attended Episcopal Church and later in life also went to the Sikh Gurdwara, but went back to his church. He attended the YMCA regularly. He visited India in 1953, 1960 and for the last time in 1974. He died peacefully in 2003 as an unsung Sikh hero, even though his immense contribution as a pioneering Sikh remains etched in the community's history.

Singh Farms

By the mid-1980s I was well settled in my neurology practice in a small town in West Virginia. But being from a Jat Singh farming family in Punjab the burning desire to own a land parcel for cultivation had never really left me. This desire took me and two of my friends in quest of farmland in the west. We flew to Phoenix in Arizona and drove towards the Imperial Valley of California, finding cotton farms en route. At one point we saw a signboard that announced Singh Farms. Naturally curious, we could not resist the urge to call on the owner. Walking uninvited into the compound, we gingerly rang the bell of the house.

The doorbell was answered by a middle-aged gentleman, short and fair. He was both happy and surprised at the same time to see three Sikhs, one of them with a turban. He invited us to his decent living room. He promptly announced that his wife and daughter had gone to Cleveland, Ohio, but he'd gladly cook a Punjabi meal for us. He quickly opened his bar for us for a drink and then he busied himself cooking cauliflower. Even as he cooked, and we quietly exchanged a few conversations among us, our very hospitable host, surprisingly, never queried as to why we'd come down to his farm. He did appear to be a very successful farmer and we did not fail to notice a slew of antique cars parked in his garage. The upkeep of his residence was also top class.

He may have been under the impression that we'd come to collect donations for building a Sikh Gurdwara. Right from the earliest days of immigration this kind of project had been foremost on the minds of most newcomers. But before our host could ask us, I broke the ice gently, and said we're looking to buy a farm. He readily volunteered to talk about the land and commercial crops grown in the area, but at the same time he asked us about our professions. I mentioned to him that I'd come from West Virginia, not very far from Cleveland where his wife's family lived, and that I was a neurologist.

He did not take more than a few seconds to come back with a reply which has stayed with me ever since. He said that had he been a qualified doctor like me, he would not have ventured into farming. *"Jis ka kaam, usey ko saje, aur kare to danka baje,"* were his exact words. It meant that it was always advisable to do the job you are trained to carry out, else you'll have to regret. To be honest, for me medical practice turned out to be the only investment where I did not end up losing any money. We've not kept in touch, but had I met our genial host from Singh Farms again, I'd have told him that much against his counsel I did try to venture out into other businesses, and paid for them very dearly.

In a place far away from Punjab, and even quite a distance away from West Virginia where I practiced, I met this hospitable man who reaffirmed my firm belief that blood is indeed thicker than water. His love for another Jat from Punjab was more than evident. He said his parents had brought him from Banga in Punjab when he was just two years old. Later in life, as a successful entrepreneur, he had the occasion to lead a delegation of American farmers to Punjab at the invitation of the state Government at a time when Partap Singh Kairon was the chief minister.

I dare say, that brief encounter at Phoenix has left an indelible memory in my mind.

Pakher Singh Gill

The life of Pakher Singh Gill is well outlined in a book written by Dr Nirmal Singh Mann, MD. Dr Mann who retired as professor of gastroenterology and liver diseases at the University of California in Davis was known to me personally. Gill, writes Dr Mann, was born in Choorchuk village in Punjab's Moga district. He completed middle school, studying till eighth grade at a Government institution. But he dearly wished to see the world, and travel overseas. To fulfill that desire he undertook a three-day train journey to Calcutta in 1908. He spent two years in what was then the capital city of British India, picked up the Bengali language, and then sailed to Hong Kong in 1910. He then sailed to the port city of Shanghai and spent a few years there before arriving in Seattle in the Pacific West in 1913. Here he became clean shaven, choosing to remove the hair from his head and face. In 1917 he discovered greener pastures in Calipatria in Imperial County. He was about twenty-eight years old at the time and was described by those who knew him as a tall and handsome young man with a gift of the gab, and the ability to speak multiple languages including Bengali and Mandarin. In joining the Ghadar movement, though, he may have found his true calling.

A proud Sikh, he could not suffer insults easily. When derogatory remarks were passed against him by a couple of men who owed him the princely sum of twenty-five thousand dollars for growing lettuce on a large tract of land that he'd leased out to them, he shot them dead. He then voluntarily surrendered at the sheriff's office where he was captured. He remained in prison between 1925 and 1940. Yet, for all the suffering, he was all praise for the American system of administration of justice.

The prime of Pakher's youth had been lost to incarceration. At age 62 he married Juliana, widow of his friend Mota Singh Sandhu. The marriage, however, was not to last very long.

Kehar Singh on arrival in the US

Kehar Singh with his elder brother

Subsequently, Gill went on to tie the knot with a far younger woman named Alicia and the couple became parents to four sons.

Pakher Singh Gill who came to America with a glitter in his eyes and a song on his lips passed away at age 84, in 1973.

Kehar Singh

Much of what I learnt about Kehar Singh comes from a documentary titled *Becoming American: The Journey of Early Sikh Pioneer Kehar Singh*. It was produced by Valarie Kaur, Kehar Singh's granddaughter, a movie maker and social activist.

After migrating from Nomachar in Punjab, Kehar and his brother worked as watchmen for an oil company in Shanghai. They both sailed to Angel Island in California in 1913 but were turned back because neither had the sum of five dollars to pay towards port fees. The brothers turned out to be really resolute, though. Remember those were the days when they were sailing by slower moving ships, and not flying by air. They sailed back to Shanghai, worked to save the money, and returned to Angel Island once more. This time each one had the amount necessary to enter the U.S. They took up work as farm labor and stayed mostly at barns. Shortly after prevailing laws were modified allowing East Indians to own their own agricultural parcels of land, the hardworking brothers were able to acquire their own farmland in Clovis, California. They never gave up their turbans, and made

Dalip Kaur Singh Brar, wife of Kehar Singh

Liquor being dumped into a sewer line during Prohibition

friends easily with their farming neighbors, mostly Italians and Japanese. Kehar, in fact, learnt the fine art of wine production from an Italian farmer and managed to serve wine to police sergeants. During the internment of Japanese families during World War II, the two brothers kept watch over farmland owned by a Japanese family.

Following the relaxation in immigration rules after the Luce-Celler Act became a law in 1946, Kehar went back to his native Punjab, married a young woman in 1950, and returned to California where he raised a family. His wife Dalip Kaur Singh Brar who survived him passed away in February 2013.

Santa Singh Pannu

Santa Singh Pannu was a distant relative of Dr Jagtar Singh Sandhu, a friend of mine who frequently visited him. Santa Singh was born in Lopoke village in Punjab's Amritsar district. At birth his given name was Ranga Singh. He changed it to Santa Singh in order to honor the wishes of an uncle who'd given him two hundred and fifty rupees for buying a steamship ticket to go abroad.

He left India in 1912 after falling out with a neighboring family in his village over a land and irrigation water dispute. He had lost his father early in life, and his mother wanted him to leave the village for the sake of his own safety. She did not wish that Santa Singh embroil himself any further in the dispute.

Santa Singh went to Shanghai and served in the police there for some time before sailing across to Mexico. Dr Piara Singh Pannu, a friend of mine who is related to Santa Singh Pannu and was also sponsored by him for higher studies in the US. He even stayed with Santa Singh Pannu for a considerable length of time. Dr Piara Singh told me that Santa Singh came to Southern California after a brief halt in Mexico. He married a Mexican-origin girl named Lola, and they settled in Carothers, California, where the couple owned fifty acres of land. Santa Singh and Lola had two sons, Frank and Alex, and two daughters, Linda and Christina. Frank, who liked flying, died in a plane crash. His children used the phonetic surname Panno, as the Pannus were referred to.

Santa Singh's lack of education did not come in the way of his becoming President of the Sikh Gurudwara in Stockton, California. Lola passed away in 1968. After her death, Santa Singh had written to his friend Jaswant Singh Kairon, brother of Partap Singh Kairon, the chief minister of Punjab, to arrange for another wife for him from his native state in India, one who could give him companionship for the rest of his days. The Kairon brothers had been students at the University of California at Berkeley and were Santa Singh's friends. But before he could consummate his marriage, Santa Singh passed away in 1971.

Tuly Singh Johal

Tuly Singh from Jandiala near Jalandhar in Punjab lived for ninety years and ten months. He was born Thakar Singh, but in America his name changed to Tuly Singh. Youngest among his brothers, he decided to leave Punjab as was the customary practice at the time those days. The youngest brother had no chance whatsoever of inheriting any land or property, and the prospects of getting married were not very high either. With friends from his village who went by the names of Nand Singh, Basant Singh, Puran Singh and Munshi Singh, he landed in Vancouver in 1906 at the age of 28. Four of them later moved to the US to work on the construction of the Southern Pacific Railroad. They had come to Yuba City for sightseeing and found work with a rancher named Bill Eager. Keen and hardworking, Tuly became a foreman

Tully Singh Johal with his wife

Gulzar Singh Johal, MD, son of Tuly Singh
who was a weightlifter turned ophthalmologist

and was in a powerful position where he could recruit more Sikhs. In 1914 he left for Punjab but remained under constant surveillance by the British intelligence for his loyalty to the Ghadar Party that was trying to overthrow the colonial regime. He left India and returned to the US via Mexico ten years later. After the passing of the Luce-Celler Act he was able to get his family to join him from India. He helped his son Gulzar Singh Johal to pay his way to medical school and become a physician. Along with his Jandiala buddies, he was one of the pioneers who established the Punjabi community in Yuba City and adjoining Marysville in California.

SIKH HEROES IN NORTH AMERICA

We have spoken about the meaning of 'hero' in chapter five. Adam Kirsch writing for *The Wall Street Journal* in 2021, says, "A hero is someone who is willing to give up wealth, fame and power to do what is right." Challenges create heroes. Events like the Komagata Maru and Ghadar—the forerunners that brought about the fall of the British crown in India—discussed in great detail earlier in this chapter, created many unsung heroes. There was no one to write their obituary, there was no one to deliver memorial lectures in their name. No one remembers them on August 15, Indian Independence Day, either. And yet, they were all heroes, fitting in with Kirsch's definition of "doing what is right" perfectly. For want of space, we'll take up the case of only one such

undisputed hero, Mewa Singh Lopoke. He was the one who shot British immigrant agent William Hopkinson for spying on the Sikhs.

Hopkinson, as mentioned in the section on Komagata Maru, had been drafted into the Canadian immigration department for his knowledge of Hindi, and Punjabi to a lesser extent. He'd been an inspector in Calcutta and had spent his early years in Hindi-speaking Delhi. Hopkinson was a mole in the system, and much in demand. Mewa Singh, of course, brought his life to an early end, shooting him dead inside a Vancouver court on October 30, 1914. By then the Ghadar movement had also begun to gather steam.

Since Hopkinson had infiltrated the Sikh and Indian camps in Vancouver through his network of informers, he usually came to know in advance about the plans of the Ghadarites. Even the US agencies sought out this British mole's help. Mewa Singh came to know that one of Hopkinson's sources was Bela Singh who was responsible for the gunning down of Ghadarites—Bhai Bagh Singh, Bhikhiwind and Bhai Badan Singh at a Sikh Gurdwara in Vancouver. Lopoke, unhesitatingly, admitted killing Hopkinson. Here are portions from his long statement, translated from the Punjabi language:

Statement of Mewa Singh Lopoke in a Vancouver court

"I have always been insisting that I need no attorney to defend me. I hope for no justice. I know that I have shot at Hopkinson and I have to die for that. I'm giving this statement for the purpose that the public may know what suffering our community has been through. We have never got any justice from judges, police or from other sources. I am giving my life for this purpose, so that people may know all this."

While walking towards the gallows before being hanged, Mewa Singh Lopoke recited verses from the Sikh scripture. "*Har Jas re mana gaae lae jo sangi hai tero.*" The ninth Sikh Guru Teg Bahadur has called this singing in companionship with God.

While other early Sikh settlers may not

Mewa Singh Lopoke

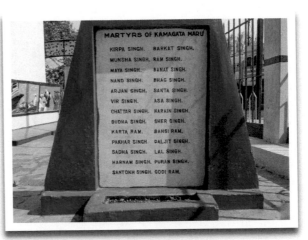

Martyrs of Komagata Maru

have faced bodily harm or death, they do qualify as heroes due to the extreme sacrifice and sufferings they endured. We need to salute the spirit of Risaldar Major Kesur Singh who paved the way for other Sikhs to enter Canada. Risaldars in the British army were economically well-off. Like others of his rank, Kesur Singh would've been rewarded with large land parcels in the newly-developed canal colonies in Punjab.

A ship in a harbor, they say, is safe. But that is not where a ship is meant to be. Instead of falling for those worldly temptations and staying back in Punjab, Kesur Singh opted to explore a territory unknown to Indians. He ventured into a new land with his turban, and discovered that there were striking differences between his language, culture and skin tone when compared to those in the host nation. In many ways, Kesur chose to let go of the shore, in order to find the beauty of the ocean, and a world outside the one he'd known in Punjab. And how different it turned out to be!

In the years to follow after Kesur's 'discovery' of Canada in May 1897, vilified Sikhs, their dignity crushed under the highly subjugating British rule, would go on to remove their turbans, battle stringent immigration laws, cope with absurd, antediluvian stereotypes of race and culture, and migrate. In fact, they also stopped returning to the homeland of Punjab in order to find a suitable life companion. In America, time and again, they rose above their testing, demanding circumstances, went through numerous trials and tribulations, and

admirably enough managed to carve a niche for themselves. They became the stuff that American Heroes are made of.

Leaders like Gandhi, Nehru, Patel and Jinnah are revered in the sub-continent. But when the Ghadarite sons of Punjab returned to India during the First World War to free the nation from British rule, these very leaders were the ones to abandon them. When the Ghadarites needed the support of the top leadership, they let go of their hand, leaving them to become easy fodder for the British rulers.

Their sacrifice went in vain. The Ghadarites abandoned their dreams of a good life in North America, they gave up their possessions, assets, and their growing affluence, so that they could be in India and fight to see the motherland free. And yet the tallest of Indian leaders at the time looked the other way when they arrived. The same leaders readily agreed to partition Punjab in the west, and Bengal in the east. Punjabis and Bengalis paid heavily for the divisions, millions were displaced on either side, nearly a million were killed in Punjab in 1947 during the riots, another million were killed when the West Pakistan army committed a genocide in East Pakistan in 1971. Both Punjab and Bengal have broken free politically and in their own ways are trying to breathe the air of secularism. In these two states, despite its best efforts, the ruling BJP and its allies have been able to make no impact.

Vande Mataram—Love for Motherland. *Bole so Nihal* (Sikh clarion call). These will ultimately prevail.

What Sikhs did for Punjab?

"Love the old country like a mother
and the new one like a bride"

(Arthur Herman in book *Viking Heart*)

In the early part of the 20th century shipping was an established mode of transportation across the vast oceans. Communication was through postal services only. In spite of both these handicaps, the early migrants stayed in touch with their families back home, a tribute to their desire to give back to their motherland.

Those with immigrant visas visited Punjab on family occasions. Many of those settled in Canada were able to make more trips due to less re-entry issues. Their hearts, though, were permanently in Punjab, the homeland, the cherished motherland. Elsa M. Chaney, writing for the *International Migration Review* in 1979, described migrants from most nations as "people with their feet in two societies." They are also termed transnational immigrants.

Below is a brief description of the relationship that the Sikh migrants have had with Punjab:

1. Individual and family aggrandizement: They sent money so that two or three-level brick homes could be built in Punjab. They bought more land in Punjab and leased them out, so as to create a continuous stream of income. They spent plenty of money on marriages. They did *Akhand Paath* (three days of continuous reading of the Guru Granth Sahib Ji), followed by *langar* (community free-kitchen).
Whenever possible they'd buy a horse and a double-barrel gun, all for the prestige of the family in India. Women visitors from Canada would not hesitate to show off their expensive clothing and jewelry. Mayo Singh's father established a money-lending company—Sardar Bholla Singh and Sons Money Lenders—at village Paldi, post office Mahilpur, district Hoshiarpur, in Punjab.

2. Sikhs helped family members and those from the same villages to migrate to Canada and the US, mostly legally. Rala Singh from Phoenix, Arizona sponsored nineteen family members and friends, and helped them settle in the US.

3. Sikhs donated money for public causes, schools and Gurdwaras.

4. They did not hesitate to discuss the virtues of free societies such as Canada and the US. The Sikhs and other Indian migrants went a step further to organize an anti-British political entity called the Ghadar Party. Even though the Ghadar movement was crushed by the force of the British empire, and also in large measure due to the step-motherly treatment its sons received at the hands of India's top political leadership, it at least helped to open the eyes of our subjugated citizens to look forward to a new India.

5. After favorable immigration laws like the Luce-Celler Act were passed in 1946, interaction with families back home improved considerably. Air travel was available, and landline telephones helped in the communication process. Transnational weddings became common. Money transfer facilities became available. When India became free in 1947, it turned out to be a sweet and ecstatic culmination of the dreams of millions. Independence was celebrated with much gusto and zeal, and above all hope. The first generation that had gone through half a century of struggle, now felt far more settled with their dreams of a free nation having come true.

6. Newer generations of recent immigrants are likely to have a far more positive effect. Love for Punjab continues to flow in their veins, as evidenced in the support to the recent farmers' agitation. More than repatriation of money, there was a shift in the thought process, an enlightenment influenced by family members abroad.

Sikh assimilation

The general subject of Acculturation and Assimilation has been described earlier in chapter four. Most of the early Sikhs in North America were sojourn migrants. They came to make money and return home to build a pucca home, or buy a plot of land. They, therefore, were in isolated existence until such time that they collectively decided to stay back in North America on a permanent basis.

For religious, cultural and political needs, they created Sikh enclaves. These enclaves made assimilation slow and smooth with less cultural shock.

This change was not easy. Generally, the turban had to make its way out of the Sikh attire to make assimilation easier, although the pain of its removal remained an intrinsic part of every Sikh who gave it up. Several Sikhs shaved off their beards and cut their hair. When they did so, many would cry out in anguish. They were paying a price for fitting into an alien society. Many with hybrid marriages had little choice but to convert to Christianity. They took the hard decision of marrying local non-Sikh women as the ones from their community were not available. Favorable immigration laws beginning first in 1946 and followed up nineteen years later by a more liberal one in 1965 were God's gifts. Sikh reinforcements made their way from India, including educated ones. More Sikh women migrated, helping the gender ratio to become more balanced. For Sikh men, marrying within the community became far easier than it was for the early settlers. The Sikh community owes a lot to Canada for its policy of multiculturalism in immigration. For Sikhs, Canada is home away from home. This will happen in the case of the US too in the near future.

Sikh achievements in the past

The 1968 book *The New Frontiersmen* by G.S. Aurora is an apt title for the Sikh community as such. In the author's case, he was writing on Sikhs who had emigrated to the UK. They richly deserved the term, and lived up to the title of the book in no uncertain ways in North America as well. They overcame numerous social and legal hurdles including racial discrimination, riots, unfavorable immigration and citizenship laws in the US and Canada.

We've spoken of Dalip Singh Saund who became the very first Sikh in the US Congress.

Bhagat Singh Thind became a scholar of divinity and went on to pen eight books. Wasakha Singh and Jawala Singh ran potato empires near Stockton. Rala Singh's melons and onions in Phoenix and around made him a legend. Spoony Singh set up the famous wax museum in Hollywood, California.

Even though Sikhs made America their home, they stayed very loyal to the mother country, and continued to agitate against the British. It was the pioneering spirit of the Sikhs that made them set out for Canada on the Komagata Maru. When the trip failed, they returned and many were shot dead in Budge Budge, Calcutta.

It was the daring and the will to free India that made Sikhs and other Indians form the Ghadar Party, and stir up patriotic emotions among Sikh army men serving in British colonies around the world. Their movement also failed, and those held guilty of sedition and anti-national and anti-imperialistic activities were hanged, sentenced to life, or simply shot dead. In the face of a daunting British empire, the heroic attempt of a small group of Punjabi Sikhs and other east Indians deserve far more credit than they have ever received in the past. There were heroes in every sense of the term.

Summary

This then is a brief summary of the events and themes covered earlier in the chapter. They include the hardships, challenges and sacrifices of the early Sikh migrants to North America. It was a bitter-sweet mix of adventure and torment.

The challenges faced by Punjabis and Sikhs go back hundreds of years in history. They were the guardians of the northwestern gateway to India and dealt gallantly with the invading hordes from Central Asia and West Asia.

Migration for Sikhs was an economic issue. They were stifled by the lack of opportunities in Punjab, the restrictions put on land holdings, the atmosphere of servitude before the British. The west provided far better opportunities, at least economically. The daily wages in Canada and the US were three to four times higher than in Punjab. They had the freedom to practice their religion in these countries. But, the "life, liberty and happiness" as professed in the American constitution was not theirs to be. In the first half of the 20th century, they did not have property, land or citizenship rights and were looked down upon as lesser people. Much was written in the local media about how they were unsuited for western culture. Until, of course, more favorable laws came along, and they were able to cement their place in North America.

In the US and Canada, Sikhs and Punjabis were initially welcomed as labor in lumber mills and in the construction of railroads. With time, as their numbers swelled, a sense of insecurity started brewing among the local white population. This resulted in racial riots in Vancouver, Canada, and in Bellingham, Washington, St. John, Oregon, Live Oak and Marysville in California. Laws were passed to discourage Asian immigration, and also for making it very difficult for Sikhs to move into Canada and the US in the future.

Even highly educated Sikh folks like Dalip Singh Saund and Bhagat Singh Thind, both educated at the prestigious University of California at Berkeley, could not land proper jobs. While Saund went on to become the first Sikh and Indian Congressman in the US, Thind authored eight books on divinity. He had also been the first turban-wearing Sikh in the US defense. Yet he'd to fight tooth and nail for his citizenship by virtue of having served the US military. On his third attempt, he received citizenship.

This kind of utter discrimination and ill-treatment was largely a result of the East Indians' slave-like status in India. The Komagata Maru incident and the Ghadar movement left indelible marks in Sikh and Indian history. Undoubtedly, they were to set the tone for the British to consider leaving India.

The colonial office in Britain worked with the Canadian dominion administration to dislodge the Sikhs in the Vancouver area to British Honduras in Central America. A two-member delegation travelled to that country along with the Hindi-speaking Canadian immigration agent William Hopkinson and J.B. Harkin, the private secretary to the Minister of the Interior in Canada, flatly refused to live in British Honduras, modern-day Belize. When favorable immigration laws were passed, life began to change for the Sikhs and East Indians.

Due to strict immigration laws, the early Sikh settlers were unable to return home to find a bride. Hence many marriages with Mexican women took place. The mixed-families became Church-goers and were permanently lost to the Sikh community. The children of these hybrid families found themselves between a rock and a hard place, neither the Sikh community gave them the respect that they deserved, nor were the Mexicans overtly charitable to them.

When the early Sikh settlers wore their turbans proudly, the local press criticized them strongly, stooping low enough to term them as 'ragheads.' Incendiary headlines such as Turban Tide did not do their cause any good. They suffered riots at numerous places along the Pacific West. In spite of the difficulties they faced, they remained tough, brave and undeterred. The initial settlers were devout Sikhs, but with time things began to get diluted as greater assimilation began. The turbans were given up to gain more acceptability. Many converted after they married Mexicans. The culture and religion were sacrificed in the melting pot of the Great American Dream.

But not all was lost. Sikhism continued to spread wings in the Sikh enclaves. Friendlier immigration laws helped Sikh cause. There was no dearth of grit, determination and hard work when it came to work. They succeeded in spite of the greatest of odds. Where lesser people would've given up and thrown in the towel and returned, the Sikhs hung on with fortitude, and allowed the hope in their hearts to spring eternal.

It has taken close to sixty years for Indian Sikhs to become American Sikhs. It is time to celebrate this assimilation. The past must not be forgotten, but its lessons must be used well to ensure a glorious future.   ■

Why did the Sikhs want to migrate?
Following the Second Anglo-Sikh War, a fierce military conflict between the British East India Company and the Sikh Empire, Punjab was annexed in 1848-49. This left the Sikhs considerably demoralized. Besides, the population of the province had sizably burgeoned and landholdings had become divided. It did not help that famines had become quite frequent in Punjab. Matters were further exacerbated by a series of epidemics of malaria, smallpox, cholera and plague that broke out with alarming regularity between the 1850s and the early decades of the 20th century

How did Sikhs know about North America and Canada?
According to a publication of the California State Polytechnic University at Humboldt, Andrew B. Hammond purchased the Samoa sawmill, the largest of its kind in Humboldt County, in 1900. In order to overcome the shortage of mill workers caused by the abolition of slavery, Hammond, based out of Astoria in Oregon, went scouting for labor in India soon after his new acquisition. When this requirement of Hammond went public in Punjab, many Sikhs volunteered to go to the Pacific West. They were also encouraged by news brought in by shipping agents about the great opportunities that lay in store in that part of the western world

CHAPTER 7

1965 TO THE PRESENT
SIKHS IN THE UNITED STATES

The Sikhs started entering the US and Canada at the very end of the 19th century and the early years of the 20th century. Their numbers, expectedly, have increased over the years. The major migration, of course, took place after the passing of the Immigration Act of 1965 by President Lyndon Johnson. The Sikh identity is characterized by medium height, brown to dark-colored skin, Caucasian features, and in some cases turban-clad males. At this point in time, turban-wearing people in the US and Canada are Sikhs.

Geographical locations

The Sikh population has variable distribution across the US. For the purposes of looking at this distribution, we can consider three primary geographical locations.

A. **Sikh Enclaves**: Sikhs are relatively densely spread in different parts of California where the original settlers from the community had migrated to, and others had followed. These enclaves are similar to other religious and ethnic communities such as Chinatowns, Orthodox Jewish colonies in and around New York City, Muslim populations around Detroit, Cubans around Miami, Koreans around Los Angeles, among others. These enclaves have been a part of American immigration history. These enclaves are not to be mixed up with the First Nation territories, officially earmarked for indigenous people, the very first and original settlers in the Americas thousands of years ago.

Sikh enclaves, reasonably populated, are to be found in Yuba City/Marysville areas of the Sacramento Valley in California, and the town of El Centro in the Imperial Valley, both in the US state of California. The last name has seen a dwindling of the Sikh population in recent years, primarily a result of lack of opportunities and the inability to pull in the newer immigrants. Small clusters of Sikh professionals are to be found in the Silicon Valley in Northern California.

B. **Medium to large cities**: There is a significant Sikh population around the greater New York, Chicago, San Francisco, Los Angeles, Houston and Atlanta areas. All large cities have a number of Sikh Gurdwaras.

C. **Mountain states and the southern USA**: Fewer Sikhs live in these places even though, overall, the population of the US in these parts is on the rise, given that larger cities and coastal towns, besides the Midwest, are becoming unaffordable for small business owners such as those who run gas stations, fast-food outlets, and convenient stores.

Sikh community today

There has been a gradual shift in family structure as Sikhs permanently chose to settle in the US. The families will eventually adapt to the family structure of the host country which too is undergoing changes of its own. The broader details of the Sikh family are to be found in chapter five. The extended family, overall, is being replaced by the nuclear family.

Sikhs are now in their fourth generation in North America, spanning about one hundred and twenty-five years since Risaldar Major Kesur Singh first arrived in Canada in 1897, and the first Sikhs arrived in the US in 1899. The first generation (original Sikh settlers) is a part of the melting pot. The second generation (1965 onward) is in the 'sandwich' and 'salad' phase (see chapter four). The third and fourth generations are going through the process of adaptation and assimilation. This is hastened by amalgamation and delayed by transnationalism, globalization, communication and the phenomenon of Sikh enclaves.

The early Sikh migrants were less educated and worked primarily as labor. They gradually moved to agriculture. The current generation of Sikhs is highly educated and are to be seen and heard in all walks of life. The third and fourth generations are less interested in religion, and, therefore, make less visits to the Gurdwara. Their food habits, taste in music, interest in sports, and hobbies are different from their parents, what we'd typically say is a result of a generational gap. They cannot speak, read or write the Punjabi language. The families are less patriarchal and the concept of marriage is changing. These families are in the process of selling their assets in Punjab and India, since the new generation is not equipped to deal with relatives and the endless red-tape and bureaucracy in their parents' home country. Also, their interest in Punjab, as such, is quite low.

In spite of all the changes over the decades, the Sikh community bonds strongly through the large network of Gurdwaras. At the same time several Sikh organizations have been doing a remarkable job, and there are many achievements that the community can be proud of.

GROWING UP IN AMERICA

The US is a nation of immigrants who have come from different geographical, ethnic, cultural, linguistic and religious backgrounds. The family structure varies and largely determines how the offspring will progress in their new home in the Americas.

In the book *Growing Up in America: The Power of Race in the Lives of Teens* published in 2010, authors Richard Flory, Korie L. Edwards and Brad Christerson focused on the family structure, parenting pattern, and the capital portfolio of social, cultural, human and religious entities within ethnic groups that make up the US.

Family Structure

In 2010, Christensen and colleagues described the incidence of bio-nuclear families—households with both parents—within various ethnic groups in America. The Asian-Americans reported 67 percent of bio-nuclear families, followed by American white (58 percent), Latino (44 percent), African American (27 percent). No such survey was available for the Sikh community. A cursory look at the Sikh community will, however, reveal that the incidence of bio-nuclear families will be higher than the average Asian-American figure of 67 percent.

Parenting Pattern

In a research article titled *Parental Disciplinary Patterns and Social Competence in Children* published in Sage Journals in 1978, Diana Baumrind speaks of three patterns of parenting among mostly white families, but applies it to others as well. She later adds a fourth pattern, called 'neglectful'.

1. **Permissive**: In this, there is very little parental control, less authority, and more nurturing.

2. **Authoritarian**: This is in stark contrast to 'permissive' and one is more likely to find the 'tiger mother' described by Amy Chua in her 2011 memoir *Battle Hymn of the Tiger Mother*. This type of parenting is characterized by strict parental control, authority, discipline and expectations of high academic standards from the children. There is also nurturing, to achieve laid out goals.

3. **Authoritative**: Parents in this case have reasonable control over children, and conflicts are resolved through discussions, rather than by punishment of any kind. The overall approach is one of reasonable nurturing, considered the best parenting style (Zeltser, 2021).

4. **Neglectful**: These parents take the least amount of interest in the welfare of their children.

Sikh parenting remains less permissive and veers towards being more authoritative and nurturing, both at the same time. Parenting is a complex process and cannot be pigeon-holed into any one type or the other. There is a significant overlap of functions, and variability among families.

Below is a discussion on the childhood-to-adulthood period within various age-groups of immigrant families.

Young children

According to a Yale University Press publication by W. Lloyd Warner and Leo Srole in 1945 titled *The social systems of American ethnic groups*, children of immigrants can be classified into:

1. Foreign-born children of initial parental generation, also known as Parental or P. They are further subdivided into:

P1—Those who entered the US after age eighteen.

P2—Those who entered the US before attaining the age of eighteen. They are also called the one-and-a-half generation or the 1.5 generation.

2. F1 or filial first-born in the US.

Parental (P)

Sikh children who entered the US after the age of eighteen (P1) are the ones who usually follow the pathway of adult immigrants. If they attend college or receive any form of higher education, they tend to adapt to their new surroundings, and at the same time enjoy the language of their homeland, its culture, music and cuisine.

Those who come to the US before the age of eighteen (P2) are known as the one-and-half-generation due to the influence of school and their peer groups. They have a smoother transition from the salad phase to adaptation and assimilation.

Filial First (F1)

Sikh children born in the US (F1) will adapt to their host society right from the very beginning, due to the influence of class fellows and the overall environment. Their way of speaking, linguistic skills, interest in sports, movies and gaming will be in accordance with Americans. Sikh families do make efforts to ensure that their children intermingle with one another. With time, even this engagement will peter out, and the children will grow, adapt and assimilate into the host society.

Adolescence

In the book by Flory, Edwards and Christerson mentioned earlier, the authors have reviewed the growing up of the age-group between thirteen and eighteen years. They developed the concept of a capital portfolio comprising social, cultural, human and religious capital. To some extent it resembles the toolkit described by Swindler (1986).

As adolescents grow into adulthood, the most important aspects of their lives revolve around the subject of family life, religion, school performance, peer relations, dating, sex, drug-use, entertainment, gangs and future aspirations. Patterns may vary within the ethnic groups, but all these factors combine to influence the development of an adolescent individual to adulthood.

CAPITAL PORTFOLIO: SOCIAL, CULTURAL, HUMAN AND RELIGION

Christerson and colleagues have put all the above factors in the growth of youth under the umbrella term 'capital portfolio'. The portfolio consists of four components— social, cultural, human and religious.

1. Social capital relates to activities of adolescents beyond their household with other youth.
2. Cultural capital involves interaction with school teachers and community organizations.
3. Human capital is about individual education and other skills. Educated and successful parents also contribute to this.
4. Religious capital relates to spirituality, faith in religion, and in God.

The youth of various ethnic groups in the US vary in their use of the above capital. Ethnic groups studied include Caucasian-Americans, Hispanic-Americans, African-Americans and Asian-Americans. Sikhs were not studied as a distinct group within the Asian-American subset. All these groups have distinctive characteristics, with some overlapping.

The white American groups are more independent, socialize outwards, and have expectations from school and community organizations. They are less dependent on parents and the extended family. This outward approach helps them in scaling up the economic ladders with the help of outside connections. They also receive personalized attention from teachers.

African-Americans, on the other hand, accept parental authority and depend on extended family and Church. The Hispanic youth give a lot of importance to their parents, extended families and the Church. They do not get too much help from the school which they view as places where they are only taught. They have zilch expectations from their teachers in terms of being tutored by them or being advised by them on their future career.

The Asian-Americans have less communication with parents who expect good grades from them at school and college. Parents themselves are usually well-educated and provide the human capital. Their outwardly interaction, at least in the first two generations, is confined to within their ethnic groups. Their outward thinking is also hampered due to lesser responses from white Americans.

Among immigrant groups, the overall benefits of the capital portfolios move with variable speed. The white Europeans take the lead here, followed by the Latinos, Asian-Americans and shaved Sikhs (the Sikhs have a distinct identity within the Asian-American subset). The African-Americans, even after being in the US for hundreds of years, and ever since the onset of the abominable practice of slavery, have somehow managed to hold on to certain social, cultural and religious practices that came with their ancestors from Africa. Theirs has been a slow march towards being a part of mainstream America. Like African-Americans, Sikhs with their brown skin tones and turbans, may take a long time to assimilate into the mainstream. In fact, they may never shed their cultural and religious paradigms.

The above differences in the use of social capital by various ethnic groups have their own advantages and disadvantages. There is less parental authority over white American youth who have more independence and are generally outward-looking. They are well-bonded with their teachers as can be gleaned from the experience of Mitch Albom and his teacher Morrie Schwartz in the New York Times' bestseller *Tuesdays With Morrie,* translated into over thirty languages. They expect more from their social organizations. Their socializing outwardly is conducive for an upswing in economic and political mobility. On the other hand, their individualistic lifestyles and lack of closeness with the family leads to an emotional deficit that can lead to mood disorders and substance addiction. Many, in fact, become quite indecisive when it comes to taking major decisions about their careers, primarily because of a lack of meaningful input from parents.

On the other side, the Latinos and Asian-Americans lose out considerably on economic mobility, but when it comes to emotional stability and the benefits of a caring family and community, they reap the rewards. African-Americans tend to look inward and carry the deficit of bio-nuclear families, resulting in loss of economic mobility. This has a bearing on their emotional well-being as well.

CAPITAL PORTFOLIO OF SIKH YOUTH

Sikhs make up a fraction of the American population and no survey has been carried out, nor is information available, on how Sikh youth utilize their capital portfolio and transition to adulthood. Most of what is listed below is on the basis of personal observations, and varies with each generation and geographical location. The number of Sikh youths is small and scattered. The current generation of Sikh youths make for three distinct groups:
1.   Sikh youth with turban.
2.   Sikh youth without turban.
3.   Sikh females.

Sikh youth with turban

Social capital: Sikh youth with turbans have a challenging social capital. They usually look for similar turban-wearing youth to socialize with and have an inward-looking attitude. Interaction with teachers is limited, and mostly confined to studies alone. Some become members of various clubs, take part in sports and join debating societies. Due to this limitation, the turban-clad Sikh faces hindrances when it comes to economic mobility.

Cultural capital: For the Sikh youth, this revolves around extended families and the institution of the Gurdwara. It is here that the social capital flourishes and provides golden opportunities to carry out *sewa* or service. Sikh organizations where *langar* (free food) is provided to the poor, hungry and the homeless are avenues for both socializing as well as service.

Human capital: This is a very big asset for Sikh youth. Parents, in general, are highly-educated professionals, or in business. They create the right environment for using stores of human capital from portfolios.

Religious capital: Religion is an integral part of Sikh life. It stands for equality, secularism, hard work and egalitarianism. *Japji Sahib*, the Sikh prayer, is a part of the daily routine of an adolescent youth. Many do this brief prayer before appearing for school examinations, seeking better grades. One will seldom come across a Sikh turbaned youth that is an atheist or an agnostic. They make every effort to visit the Sikh Gurdwara. For a Sikh youth, it is gratifying and an honor to serve *langar*.

Many volunteers opt for cleaning and washing of dishes after weekly *Dewan* (Prayer) and *langar*. *Sewa* for a Sikh youth occupies the pride of place, this is the most important part of Sikh religious philosophy. Spirituality and politics are also an inherent part of Sikh religion, and early leadership skills are acquired at the Gurdwara Sahib. Sikh youth take part in parades brought out on special festivals and on days that have great historical significance. Some do not hesitate to attend interfaith conferences and serve free food to the homeless in the spirit of charity (*Wund Shako*). Sikh youth camps not only impart the teachings of Sikhism, they are also vehicles for cultural capital.

Sikh youth without turban

Social capital: Their social capital is

influenced by parental authority with slight rejection by the dominant community. They are inward looking while interacting with other Indians and Asian-Americans. Even though their parents may be less communicative, they approve of socialization with high-achievers in school, and also expect the youth to have respect for those in authority and for elders. Parents keep a close eye on the wards, especially when it concerns the use of alcohol and other stimulants like drugs. They impose a curfew quite strictly when it comes to late night meetings, and are vigilant about any gang activity.

Cultural capital: The cultural capital of the non-turbaned Sikh youth is confined to the Gurdwara and their related activities. Newer immigrants are attracted to events such as Bhangra dance, Indian movies, cricket matches and those involving visiting singers. The second and third-generation Sikh youth have less interest in these and have mainstream American pastimes.

Human capital: They have the benefit of educated and well-to-do parents.

Religious capital: Their religious portfolio may be a tad less than their turbaned counterparts. But if serving *langar* is taken as a parameter, then the religious capital portfolio is the same.

Sikh women

Sikh girls rarely wear the turban. They are, therefore, like the Sikh males without turbans or like other Asian-American women.

Social capital: In general, when it comes to interacting with their teachers, girls are better. Sikh girls of the current generation seek the company of other Sikh girls. They participate actively in school sports and school clubs.

Cultural capital: This consists of close family and community bonding. They are limited when it comes to looking outwardly due to conservative family values. Attitude towards the opposite sex is quite low key, and secretive mostly. Along with their parents, Sikh girls frequent the Gurdwara Sahib and take part in *sewa* (service and charity). They attend Sikh youth camps and create friendships with other Sikh youth. Sometimes these last a lifetime.

Human capital: Girls take their studies seriously and are also aware of various women's rights movements. They have a clear advantage over other ethnic groups since most of them have parents that are highly educated, and are professionals or are in business.

Religious capital: The religious capital of Sikh adolescent females is the same as the Sikh youth in general.

Success model for Sikh youth
A study conducted in a small community

Since no formal study using the model of Christerson and colleagues is available for Sikh youth, based on my own observations in the greater Pittsburgh area of Pennsylvania where I lived for forty years, I've come up with the following:

Most of the Sikh children living in Pittsburgh were either born in the US, or were brought into the country while still very young. Sikhs came to Pittsburgh in the early seventies and by 1978 there were about twenty Sikh families in Pittsburg. The tradition then was to meet once a week for a Sikh *sangat* (congregation) for afternoon prayers at a Hindu temple building in the Monroeville suburb of the city. The Sikh community was made up of doctors majorly, with some engineers as well. With time we witnessed chain immigration. The new immigrants who came in acquired some fast-food stores. There were, however, unlike today, no taxi drivers or owners of gas stations. The community raised funds and land was purchased in the late seventies and a Sikh Gurdwara came into existence.

This particular community in Pittsburgh was the first to establish a youth camp each year. It enabled children from other states to come and join the camp for two weeks. About fifty children would attend the camp. Gurbani competitions were held every year. The bonhomie at the camps was marvelous. Many struck friendships for life. Everyone started looking forward to the yearly get-togethers. These were the early days for the second generation of Sikh migrants to the US, and for us, "the good, old days" of our life in the US.

I recall that a group of children made a trip to Punjab and had the occasion to meet with the President of India. They spent a few weeks in a school at Dalhousie, at the foothills of the Himalayas, another wonderful experience.

I'll now attempt to fit the above observations in terms of family structure, parenting pattern and capital portfolio, on the lines of Christerson and his colleagues.

Family structure and parenting

My observations lasted between 1980 and 2015. During this period all Sikh families remained bio-nuclear, and the parenting pattern was authoritative and nurturing.

Capital portfolio

Social portfolio: This was limited to the same ethnic and religious group. Interactions were limited with the native white population, and generally remained inward-looking. A few who attended private and boarding schools had outward-looking socializing with all ethnicities, including Anglo-Americans.

Cultural portfolio: This was limited to visits to the local Gurdwara and to nearby friends and families. The Sikh community in Pittsburgh frequently visited India to meet their grandparents, and other members of the extended family. Till the time they graduated from high school and left for college, the Sikh youth attended the two-week youth camp every summer.

Human capital: This was undeniably the strength of the Pittsburgh group. Most Sikh families had highly qualified parents that were financially well-off and comprised doctors and other professionals.

Religious portfolio: This was also a powerful engagement entailing weekly visits to the Gurdwara and attending Sikh seminars,

kirtan competitions. When in India, a visit to the Harmandir Sahib was a must.

The results of children growing under such a vibrant and close-knit environment were indeed amazing. Our young community progressed to fifteen physicians, three outstanding businessmen and three nurses. While this model is not to be expected in all Sikh communities, it does help put in perspective what a wholesome model for children and adolescents can be, so that they can become successful citizens. This model, though, may not hold good for third and future generations of Sikh youth.

Sikh youth are emotionally rewarded by bio-nuclear families and through community bonding. The Sikh youth with turban have a greater social and cultural capital deficit than his counterpart without a turban. But this is more than compensated by human and religious capital. They have the human capital of educated and financially well-off parents.

Almost all Sikh parents want their children to follow the religion their families have practiced through the generations. At this point in time, though, both the Sikh youth and the Sikh elderly are visiting the Sikh Gurdwaras in significant numbers. This is true for the first two generations. The attendance at the Gurdwara has been falling in the third and the fourth generation. It will not be a surprise if generation Z tends to question the role of religion and there is a tendency towards agnostic thinking. But this is what is to be expected, going forward, in many secular societies.

SCHOOL

The school remains the most important institution when children and adolescents of all ethnicities and religious groups are progressing towards adulthood. This path, though, is strewn with some thorns when it comes to turban-wearing Sikh youth. Bullying in school for Sikh children is double that of the national average. Matters can become worse if a school-going Sikh youth is singled out as being brown, while attending a predominantly-white neighborhood school. In school, therefore, the small, minority groups stick together, trying to create safe spaces for themselves as spoken of by Beverly Daniel Tatum in her 1997 national bestseller *Why are all the black kids sitting together in the cafeteria?*

Christerson and colleagues revealed that white kids had a far better equation with their teachers as compared with other American children from the African-American, Hispanic and Asian-American communities. There is an ongoing litigation over how Ivy league colleges and universities, particularly the Harvard University, have shown a bias against Asian-Americans when it comes to the admission process at this august institution. This is in spite of Asian-Americans securing higher scores in the SAT and ACT exams. This bias cannot be ignored in student-teacher relationships in school. Asian-Americans, fortunately enough, are compensated for this bias by the larger quotients of emotional well-being and the higher education levels of parents in bio-nuclear families with distinctive parental patterns of nurturing and authoritative type.

Also, Asian-Americans through high school and college have a clearer guidance and direction about the choice of their major subject, and about their professional preference when compared to their white American counterparts who stay directionless in college for a longer time.

In her 1988 book *Accommodation without Assimilation—Sikh Immigrants in an American High School,* author Margaret A. Gibson did a comparison of white, Hispanic and Sikh high-schoolers in Yuba City. Her observations revealed that Sikh students fared better than the two other groups. She attributed this skill to:
1. Home environment with educated parents with English skills.
2. Better genetic endowment.
3. Parental sacrifice and immigrant challenge.
4. Discrimination and reactive response.
5. Peer pressure.

The white Americans were disadvantaged by the lack of financial help from parents, permissive parenthood, less bio-nuclear families, and the boyfriend-girlfriend culture. The Hispanics on the other hand were limited by less-educated parents who generally displayed a lack of proficiency in English. They had access to less financial resources and overall the teacher-student relationship wasn't too exciting.

The *Journal of American Ethnic History* that reviewed Gibson's book had this to say: "One need not examine only the Japanese approach to education to find models to emulate. There are some immigrant patterns much closer at hand that are at least as relevant. This study of 'accommodation without assimilation' is a very timely case in point and deserves a wide and critical readership."

COLLEGE

College is an important stepping stone to adulthood. Social, political and academic achievements are all important. It is also time when behavioral deficiencies such as addiction and other damaging traits come out in the open and gain visibility. Also, we'll have to wait a while to learn more about the impact that virtual learning, forced upon the world by the coronavirus pandemic, has had on students.

Social life

Undoubtedly, during the days spent in college, adaptation and assimilation pick up speed. It is heartening to know that Sikh children, whether turbaned or otherwise, feel much more at ease in university campuses, than they do in the bullying environs of school. College campuses provide more diversity to the students, and they break-free of the neighborhood school constrictions. But in community colleges in smaller towns, the aggression at the micro levels by local white students, teachers and counselors is doubtless a negative factor. This once again is neutralized by culture, a strong family and community ties (Devere, 2020). Sikhs and other Indian students like to stick together, like peas in a pod. The organization of Sikh

Princeton University Bhangra team

students in colleges and the bhangra dancing teams are helpful when it comes to cementing cultural ties.

Bhangra has in fact pleasantly infiltrated into the social milieu of American colleges and universities and many non-Punjabis, including local Americans, seek permission to get into the teams. My own granddaughter found it tough to qualify for the Princeton University Bhangra team. During weekends, Bhangra certainly provides a great opportunity to get away from drinking parties, and promotes a healthy and robust lifestyle. Money raised in Bhangra competitions goes towards charity.

Bhangra is the traditional folk dance of Punjab. The Sikhs of England brought this on to the world stage, and today there are many professional groups that promote this tradition. Some of them are *Nachda Sansaar*, Lions of Punjab, *Gabru Punjab De*. In addition, there are several Sikh music bands in England such as *Alap, Premi, Hera, Azad, Pardesi,* Golden Star, and others.

Sikhs students feel proud of the Sikh Gurdwara and the institution of *langar*. They do not hesitate to invite their non-Sikh friends to the Gurdwara on weekends, both for socializing and free meals.

Political life

Interest in politics goes up during life on campus. Universities across the US have various organizations that represent a gamut of political philosophies. Most of these institutions, including faculty, are liberal and get criticized by right-wing groups. Sikh students, like other minority groups, lean towards the Democrats. Besides political organizations, there are various religious groups that exist.

Academic life

The caliber of Asian-Americans is quite well known when it comes to academic excellence and also when it comes to gaining national recognition in the National Spelling Bee, National Science Bee and National Geographic Bee competitions. Compared to their peers from white, black and Latino ethnicities, Asian-Americans somehow conjure up a high human capital. They usually come from well-educated backgrounds as well. When it comes to the doctorate level, they by far outnumber other ethnicities, which is surprising considering that they are a fraction of the total US population. They are mostly to be found in stem (science, technology, engineering, and mathematics) programs and are less inclined towards humanities, which may be a disadvantage when it comes to building a political career based on the liberal arts. Asian-Americans are also, by-and-large, not outward thinkers and this can easily be a handicap when it comes to ensuring upward economic mobility.

On the other hand, many white Americans, as well as Asians with white American spouses, do not involve themselves when it comes to decision-making for college bound children. Many such children are caught up in the complex web of choices and do not know which major to pick in college. Children of Indian-Americans and other Asian-Americans, conversely, are guided well, and therefore tend to excel more. About the way things will pan out in the future for Gen Z, we can't quite tell.

Religious life

There is a palpable reduction in the number of Sikh youths carrying out weekly visits to the Gurdwara Sahib. When I was a student at the Sikh National College at Qadian, a small town in Punjab, India, students were expected to visit the in-house Gurdwara in the boys' hostel every evening. Things are not the same, and this needs to be looked into.

Professor Tan Tai Young of the Yale-NUS College—a collaboration between Yale University and the University of Singapore—while delivering an address during the celebration of Guru Nanak's 550th birth anniversary pointed out that it was important to engage Sikh youth who have a different world view, and divergent priorities. As reported in *The Tribune* in November 2019, Young said, "The key is to get them interested and make them take some form of ownership in the preservation of the Sikh religion, traditions and culture."

Peer groups

Studies on adolescents have discussed the subject of social capital and inward-looking and outward-looking attitudes. Many new Sikh immigrants do not have the channels to access outward-looking opportunities. It restricts them initially from climbing the economic ladder. They then tend to use peer groups and community resources to learn more about American business acumen. Peer interactions take place at the Gurdwara Sahib, Sikh youth camps, Sikh parades and other community organizations.

In the US, the current generation of Sikh parents are highly ambitious. They encourage their wards to develop peer relationships in successful families. It is gratifying that the current peer relationships are geared towards upward mobility, and not gang formation, as has been the case in Canada.

Subsequent generations are likely to follow the pattern of other immigrant groups and gradually adapt or assimilate into mainstream America. Their peer groups would be more diverse with less parental control and authority, and they are more likely to demonstrate the outward-looking attitude. It is also possible that with globalization, improved communication, transnational outlook, the assimilation of later generations into the melting pot will get delayed. In countries where the population of Sikhs is less, the youth tend to make a greater use of cyber-socialization.

Drugs and alcohol addiction

The redoubtable Swiss psychoanalyst Carl Jung would say that every form of addiction is bad, no matter whether the narcotic be alcohol or morphine or idealism. Addiction is a global disease and tends to increase in societies undergoing economic and emotional stress. Vodka consumption, for instance, increased substantially after the fall of the communist state in Russia that brought along its own economic and political uncertainty. Likewise, the fallout of the Russia-Ukraine war has to be followed very closely.

Sikh adolescents in the current generation, are fortunately, quite aware of the challenges posed by their new environments. They have accepted parental authority for their own good, and have made every effort to stay out of trouble. They avoid drugs and alcohol consumption. In a small community, any kind of anti-social or delinquent behavior would get noticed very quickly and get amplified.

Twentieth century rural Punjab had a mild addiction to opium and alcohol, and recreational marijuana was common. It wasn't uncommon to find the elderly in Punjab carrying a miniature medicinal box that had small amounts of rounded opium balls. It was also common practice to offer workers small amounts of opium in the harvest season to improve productivity. Even moonshine whiskey was popular, but it did not have any adverse economic or social impact.

In the west, wine was served in abbeys, while a concoction of milk, sugar and marijuana called *bhang shardai* was available for Sikhs and Punjabis, even in Gurdwaras, as an afternoon drink. Today, as I write, Punjab is battling a major problem of drug addiction, especially among the rural youth, resulting in many deaths. Usage of heroin and certain synthetic compounds has become rife. The illicit opium trade that fetches millions of dollars in the western markets has its origin in the Golden Crescent—Iran, Afghanistan and Pakistan. Much of it is trafficked through Punjab, and hence the rise in addiction. Sardara Singh Johal, a leading agricultural economist, during a university seminar pinpointed the lack of education and job opportunities as major drivers of the escalating drug business in Punjab. The problem gets intensified when seen in the context of a general economic malaise, lack of industrial growth, and the pressure of an increasing population. The economic benefits of the green revolution are long gone. The once fertile land of Punjab stands depleted of its natural nutrients.

Even though there are no formal surveys on the incidence of drug addiction in Punjab, several drug-rehabilitation centers report that a staggering seventy-three percent of rural male youth and ten percent of female youth are caught up in the debilitating web of substance abuse. Fortunately, this ruinous habit was not exported to the US when the families migrated to this land.

Addiction in Sikh youth, however, is a major problem in the UK and Canada where Sikhs have significant populations. In the UK, Sikh organizations have stepped up their vigil and are vigorously attacking this serious problem at the very roots. Community discussions and new media are among the advocacy tools being applied to deal with it.

In British Columbia, Canada, the problem has been ongoing, and it has negatively impacted the neighboring US. The trade is facilitated by long-distance truckers that ply between British Columbia and Mexico, via large swathes of US territory. Luckily, Sikhs in the US are as yet away from the clutches of the deadly menace of drug addiction. One of the reasons is that the community in the US is better educated and economically more stable. Newer immigrants, too busy establishing themselves in the US, have no time to acquire a pernicious habit that can drive them down the road of perdition.

Sikh gangs

The occurrence of youth gangs is a common feature in most countries. The northern Latin American and Central American nations have taken gang warfare to a new level with drug cartels involved in international trafficking and frequent, bloody bust ups with law enforcement. Who can forget the fallout of the gang wars in Robert Wise's famous 1961 movie *West Side Story*? The Jets and the Sharks, Polish and Puerto Rican gangs that live on the west side of New York City, battle each other for territory and neighborhood. It ultimately results in the greatest of tragedies.

Over the decades, many armed and dangerous gangs sprouted up in Punjab. Thankfully, the vast majority of these have been eliminated. Sikh youth gangs are active in the UK and Australia, but the most notorious ones are in Canada. The Canadian Sikh Bhupinder 'Bindy' Johal ran one of the most menacing gangs between 1971 and 1998. He inspired others to follow him into his dangerous world, one in which drug trafficking and contract killing in British Columbia had become a norm. Jat Sikh sub-castes with surnames like Dosanjh, Johal, Cheema, Butter, Grewal and Sahota have been a part of various gangs in Canada.

In the US, the Italian mafia still rears its ugly head once in a while, and Chinese and Korean gangs do make their presence felt from time to time. Some not-so-popular Indian groups are active in the New York area but they have not quite dived deep into the world of hard crime. At this point in time there is also no evidence to show that there are any active Sikh gangs, either in big cities or in Sikh enclaves in the US. The Sikh community is well-educated and its per capita income is higher than most other ethnic groups. Evidence of frustration that is visible in unemployed youth is not to be seen among the younger generation of Sikhs. Frustration, and its ill-omened ally, felony, are important ingredients that feed gangs. Mercifully, most of the Sikh youths in the US are better occupied by internet games, biking and cerebral activities that have to do with the computer. Only a handful drift into the dark alleys of misdeed and offence.

Dating

Dating under parental watch has been taking place, and is also encouraged. Sex among adolescents is forbidden and is to be avoided at any cost. Surveys for sex, drugs and alcohol are not practical due to less population of Sikh youth. Also, these subjects rarely come up in discussions among Sikh youth and are kept under wraps. The white, Hispanic and other Asian-American ethnicities are, on the contrary, quite forthcoming on these subjects and willing to have open discussions.

Sikh youth and old-timers

There is an ongoing conflict over values and traditions going on between the Sikh youth born in western nations and their immigrant parents. The parents were raised in a society that had deep-rooted caste equations with subdivisions among Jats, Bhappas, Ramgharias and others. The US-born Sikh youth wants to have nothing to do with casteism. He is more inclined towards meritocracy. At the same time, such youth tend to be more spiritual, less religious and follow modernity and its accompanying practices. The elder generation, on the other hand, is caught in the intricate web of old family values that are not always easy to be put into practice in the host nation. Especially rigid and orthodox are those members of the elder generation that are less educated. Ultimately, something has to give in, and someone has to be the change that they wish to see in this world. Maybe Alfred Tennyson's famous words, "The old order changeth, yielding place to new," will hold true in this case too.

GROWING UP WITH THE TURBAN IN AMERICA

Growing up with a turban is by far the most challenging issue for Sikh boys in western nations. A Sikh boy starts his childhood with a *jurra* where the hair on the head is tied into a rounded-ball configuration. Sometimes a square piece of cloth such as a handkerchief is used to secure the *jurra*. It is anchored with a knot or rubber band. My five-year-old son went to school with a *jurra*. Other children would confuse him for a girl and there were some occasions when, much to his embarrassment, he was asked to use the restroom for girls. This was happening in 1980 in a small town in West Virginia that had not seen Sikhs with turbans and *jurras*. The fallout was that my son became reluctant to go to school. At the same time, he assured me and my wife that he loved his *jurra*.

As they turn about ten-years-old, the *jurra* makes way for the *patka* that is a larger piece of cloth wrapped around the head. In fact, *patkas* are also worn by grown-up men, at times. By the time they enter their teens, Sikh boys are ready for the turban and some families have a religious ceremony to initiate this process.

School admission

According to the *Khalsa Samachar*, back in 1913 three Sikh boys with turbans were not allowed admission in a school in Vancouver Canada. The school's principal William Gourie wrote a 'to whom it may concern letter' and said, "If the three Hindu boys wish to continue school here, it will be necessary for them to remove their turbans and conform to the usual customs of the school." In 1978, Gurinder Singh Mandla, son of Sewa Singh Mandla, was refused admission in a private school in Birmingham, England because he was turban-clad. Recently, the same thing was repeated with five-year-old Sidhak Singh in a Catholic school in Sydney, Australia. The matter had to be resolved by a local court in favor of the turban. France does not allow the wearing of turban, Jewish kippa and the Muslim hijab as part of its constitutional and secular ethos.

Bullying in school

The situation has changed, but things are not better. Turban-clad Sikh boys are allowed admission in schools in the west, but the degree of bullying has not come down. Many a time the Sikh boys face their adversaries by teaming up as a group, and do not give in, or give up. They are heroes fighting their own battles and do not share this with their parents. This assault on a young mind was expressed in detail in CNN in June 2018 by Winty Singh. He spoke about his very first unpleasant experience at the tender age of seven and then went on to recount his tormenting ordeal for the rest of his school life.

While bullying happens in schools in all countries, their rate of incidence varies. About ten percent of children and adolescents are bullied in Swedish schools, the same as in the US and Germany. In Norway it goes up to fifteen percent, while in the UK it rises to an alarming 39.8 percent according to a study in 2008 by R Sansone, a director of psychiatry education at the Kettering Medical Center in Ohio and Lori A. Sansone, medical director of the primary care clinic at the Wright-Patterson air force base. The incident of bullying among Sikh children and adolescents with turban is far higher, and even though detailed survey reports are not available, should be close to double the national average.

Almost every such Sikh child or adolescent is bullied in school. The situation is unacceptable given that every effort is made by the parents to educate other children in the school system about the Sikh faith and turban. The effect that bullying or ragging has on young brains has been addressed in many studies, including by Sansone and Sansone in 2008. Another one was made in 2004 by Minne Fekkes of the Leiden University Medical Center Department of Pediatrics and Child Health, Leiden, The Netherlands.

Bullying has many short and long-term consequences that can result in isolation, feeling of shame, sleep disturbance, anxiety, mood disorders and physical symptoms such as stomach aches, poor appetite, headaches and muscle pain. Long-term effects of bullying can cause adverse mental health issues in adult life.

In spite of the bullying they face, the academic achievement of Sikh children has been compared with that of white and Hispanic children in the Yuba City and Marysville areas. In her 1988 book *Accommodation without Assimilation—Sikh Immigrants in an American High School,* author Margaret A. Gibson says Sikh children fared better than students from other ethnic groups. The question that one has to ask is this, "does bullying better prepare the Sikh youth for future discriminations that may come their way later in life?" Some families have chosen to organize home tutoring as a safeguard against bullying. It is a sad commentary on the state of affairs.

As the Bob Dylan number released back in 1964 says, *The Times They Are A-Changin'.* My own grandchildren today want me to attend grandparents' day proudly with my turban on. *The Sikh Coalition* has taken major steps against bullying and continues to do so. Melania Trump, wife of Donald Trump, has an anti-bullying slogan, 'Be Best'.

Discrimination and hate crime

Discrimination in general (chapter three), and hate crime against turban-wearing Sikhs in particular, have been discussed all along in this book. The local communities are becoming increasingly aware and are honoring the hate crime victims.

Singh and Kaur Park, Elk Grove, California

Marriage and intimacy

It has also been discussed that Sikh young men with turbans have a distinct disadvantage in the marriage market. In general, Sikh and non-Sikh women do not want to enter a relationship or get married to a turban-clad Sikh. It becomes quite a difficult task for devout Sikh families to find grooms who are both qualified and *Sabat Surat* Sikh, the ones with unshorn hair and turbans.

EDUCATION AND SIKHS

Most Sikhs, like other Indians, are well educated. It helps them explain in a more articulate way about who they are and where they come from. It also gives them greater access to interact with the host population. The early Sikh immigrants were mostly farmers and laborers and failed to encourage their children to pursue higher education fearing that they would stray away from the Sikh faith and values. As a result, closed communities developed. The newer immigrants are clearly different, they are highly-educated professionals, and so are their children. Young Sikhs are to be found in all professions. The medical profession, in particular, is the first choice of all new immigrants.

It is worthwhile mentioning in this book that quite a few notable Sikhs failed to get the Nobel prize. Some of those who come to mind easily are Narinder Singh Kapany who is considered the father of fiber optics, Gurdev Singh Khush, nicknamed Hero for his pioneering work in agronomy and genetics,

late Bhagat Puran Singh of Pingalwara (home for the disabled), Ravi Singh of Khalsa Aid, an international charity.

Sikh schools

Sikh schools now exist in the UK, US and Canada. They, like all similar institutions, are more orthodox with a limited world view. Their emphasis remains on Sikh culture, tradition and religion. The plus point is that Sikh students with turbans do not have to face bullying at school.

University chairs in Sikh studies

The Sikh community has actively promoted Sikhism and the Sikh identity in the US through the endowment of Sikh chairs in various universities. Many non-Sikhs, as a result, are in a position today to undertake courses to learn about Sikhism, its identity, symbols, history.

Following is a list that is bound to grow with time.

1. The Kundan Kaur Kapany chair in Sikh studies at the University of California at Santa Barbara.
2. Tara Singh and Balwant Kaur Chattha, and the Gurbaksh Singh and Kirpal Kaur Brar Sikh studies chair at the University of Michigan at Ann Arbor.
3. The Sardarni Kuljit Kaur Bindra chair in Sikh studies at the Hofstra College of Liberal Arts and Sciences, Hofstra University, New York.
4. Sardarni Harbans Kaur chair in musicology at Hofstra University, New York.

| Narinder Singh Kapany | Gurdev Singh Khush | Bhagat Puran Singh | Ravinder Singh Khalsa |

5. Jasbir Singh Saini chair in Sikh and Punjabi studies at the University of California at Riverside.
6. Dhan Kaur Sahota presidential chair in Sikh studies at the University of California at Irvine's School of Social Studies.
7. Sarbjit Singh Aurora chair in Sikh and Punjabi studies at the University of California at Santa Cruz.
8. Sikh and Punjabi studies chair at the California State University at East Bay.

Paul Michael Taylor:
The new face of Sikhism

Sikhs, Punjabis and many other Indian scholars have written about Sikhism and its history. This had become an absolute priority during the Singh Sabha movement. In recent years, monumental contributions have been made by the Punjab University, Guru Nanak Dev University and Punjabi University. In the US, many Sikh chairs as mentioned in the previous segment, have been actively introducing Sikhism to both young Sikhs and non-Sikhs.

With the colonization of India and Sikh migration to the west, many non-Sikh scholars became active in knowing and writing about Sikhism. Ernest Trump, Max Arthur Macauliffe, William Hewat McLeod, Mark Juergensmeyer, Norman Gerald Barrier, Kristina Myrvold, Verne Dusenbery and Eleanor Nesbitt are among some of the leading lights who've furthered the dissemination of knowledge on Sikhs. To this celebrated list, I'm adding the name of Dr Paul Michael Taylor. In addition to being a scholar and a researcher like others, he has contributed to advancing public awareness of Sikh identity in other ways as well.

Dr Paul Michael Taylor is head of the Smithsonian National Museum's Asian Cultural History program and curator of Asian, European and Middle Eastern Ethnology. Based in Washington, DC, he is credited with introducing Sikhism to North America through curating and producing *Sikhs: Legacy of the Punjab*, a major Sikh

Paul Michael Taylor *(Smithsonian institute)*

exhibition at the Smithsonian which later became a traveling exhibit with venues in Santa Barbara and Fresno in California, as well as San Antonio in Texas.

Me and my wife Dr. Jaswinder Chattha, and the late Dr Sohan Singh Chaudry and his wife Kamal Chaudry, were the first Sikhs to ask him to hold a Sikh exhibition at the Smithsonian. We first met him on January 12, 2000, at his office in the Smithsonian in Washington, DC.

Sikh identity (with the turban) at the time was largely unknown in the US. I was exploring the possibility of booking space in museums to promote the subject. I had written letters to the Getty, the Metropolitan and the Smithsonian museums. I got a response only from Dr Paul Michael Taylor of the Smithsonian. I was encouraged, and headed to Los Angeles to discuss this with Dr Sohan Singh Chaudry, a friend active in community affairs.

Along with our spouses, Dr Jaswinder and Kamal, we headed to Washington, DC, on one cloudy morning in January 2000 to meet Dr Taylor. This meeting was the beginning of a strong relationship with the Smithsonian. There were subsequent major Sikh exhibits in Washington DC, Santa Barbara and Fresno, California, and later in San Antonio, Texas.

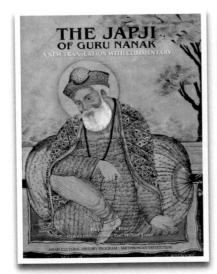

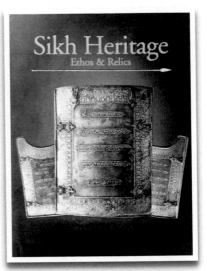

The Japji of Guru Nanak   Sikhs: Legacy of the Punjab   Sikh Heritage: Ethos & Relics

Dr Taylor made two trips to Punjab where he held many workshops to preserve Sikh historical artifacts. Since our first meeting, he has given guidance and authored or edited many books and scholarly papers on Sikhism, and encouraged other authors through his editorial and collaborative work as head of the Smithsonian's Asian Cultural History Program.

The resulting books include:

The Japji of Guru Nanak: A New Translation with Commentary, by Rupinder S. Brar with an Introduction by Paul Michael Taylor Asian Cultural History Program, 2020.

Sikh Art from the Kapany Collection, edited by Paul Michael Taylor and Sonia Dhami (with an introduction and one chapter by P.M. Taylor), Sikh Foundation & Asian Cultural History Program, 2017.

Sikhs: Legacy of the Punjab, by Paul Michael Taylor and Robert Pontsioen. Asian Cultural History Program, 2014.

Sikh Heritage: Ethos and Relics, by Bhayee Sikandar Singh and Roopinder Singh, with an introductory chapter by P.M. Taylor. New Delhi: Rupa, 2012.

Other publications by P.M. Taylor include:

2004 Sikh Heritage at the Smithsonian. Journal of Punjab Studies 11(2):221-236. (Special issue: "Culture of Punjab.")

2006 "Intangible Heritage of the Sikhs: New Strategies for the Future." Poster presentation, XI International UNESCO Forum, University and Heritage: Documentation for Conservation and Development: New Strategies for the Future. (Florence, Italy, Nov. 2006).

2012 Introduction: Perspectives on the Punjab's Most Meaningful Heirlooms. Pp. viii-xi in: Sikh Heritage: Ethos and Relics by Bhayee Sikandar Singh and Roopinder Singh. New Delhi: Rupa.

2016 Sikh Material Heritage and Sikh Social Practice in a Museum-Community Partnership: The Smithsonian's Sikh Heritage Project. Sikh Research Journal (Vol. 1. No. 1)

2017 Exhibiting the Kapany Collection: Observations on the Transformation of Sikh Art and Material Culture in Museums. Pp. 286-309 in: P.M. Taylor and S. Dhami, eds., Sikh Art from the Kapany Collection. Sikh Foundation & Asian Cultural History Program.

2019 Sikh Art and Devotion in the Collection of Parvinder S. Khanuja. Arts of Asia 49(1):107-116 (January-February 2019).

The Sikh community is thankful to Dr Paul Michael Taylor for introducing Sikhism to a broad American public, through his museum exhibits and his writings, at a time when the community became victims of hate crimes due to mistaken identity in an unfortunate atmosphere of Islamophobia.

Professions and businesses

While the early Sikh migrants were in agriculture and lumbering primarily, today

Sikhs are in all professional walks of life. We also have some outstanding Sikhs in agriculture. Didar Singh Bains has substantial land holdings in California. Charanjit Singh Bath is popularly called the Raisin King, while Harbhajan Singh Samra is the Okra King.

The Imperial Valley in California also has many well-to-do Sikh farmers, descendants of the early settlers. Subsequent generations have become accountants, attorneys, doctors, nurses and IT professionals. Many of the Sikh doctors and engineers came to the US after 1965, following favorable immigration laws. Many of the newer immigrants are owners of convenience stores, liquor stores, and fast-food outlets.

Sant Singh Chatwal is a rich hotelier. Ajay Pal Singh Banga has retired as a successful CEO of Mastercard. Aman Bhutani is presently CEO of GoDaddy. It is a matter of great pride that most of them choose to wear the turban. These educated people interact more with local Americans. Many of them are members of non-religious organizations such as Rotary and TiE, thereby helping the Sikh cause and identity. When it comes to billionaire businessmen, though, there are a few in India and in the UK. The US is yet to produce its first Sikh billionaire, but the day may not be far off.

Several Sikhs are taxi and truck drivers. According to an article published in the *Los Angeles Times* in 2019, there are over one hundred and fifty thousand Sikh truck drivers in the US, a staggering number. A few are in the export-import business.

Sikhs in politics

Politics provides a unique opportunity to further Sikh identity. As India's prime minister, Manmohan Singh left behind a legacy for the Sikhs. Likewise, Harjit Singh Sajjan as Canada's former defense minister was a signpost of Sikh identity at an international level. Color and turban remain limiting factors for Sikhs when it comes to holding public office in the US. In spite of these limitations, Sikhs continue to be in local politics. It is laudable,

Nikki Haley   Gurbir Singh Grewal

especially since the Sikh population base in the US is indeed very small.

Dalip Singh Saund was the first Sikh and Indian to become a US Congressman (1957-1963). He served the 29th District of California. Nikki Haley was Governor of South Carolina and US ambassador to the UN, a post she resigned from in October 2018. She was born into a Sikh family and converted to Christianity after her marriage. Manka Dhingra is the first Sikh woman elected to the state legislature in the Pacific state of Washington, home to many of the early Sikh settlers.

Gurbir Singh Grewal, a turban-wearing Sikh was made attorney general of New Jersey in January 2018. He has recently been appointed to a senior position in the security and exchange commission. Preet Didbal is the mayor of Yuba City, California. Ravinder Singh Bhalla is mayor of Hoboken, New Jersey. Parghat Singh Sandhu is mayor of Galt, California.

The Sikh population is on the rise and the second-generation of Sikhs that are highly educated is also politically aware of both national and international developments. This involvement is necessary for Sikh identity and significantly for tackling hate crime.

The list above will change with time. The Sikhs in the US will hopefully catch up with our neighbors in the north when it comes to the political arena. There are many Sikhs in the Canadian cabinet. Some Sikhs in the US are also active in the politics of Punjab. There are organizations that support

Congress, Akali Dal and the Aam Aadmi Party of Punjab.

Eminent scholar Masud Chand in 2012 described the difference between the American melting pot and Canadian multiculturalism. The Canadian model produced more political leaders among the Indian and Sikh diaspora, but income gains were less. The American model created more income gains but less political leaders. The lesser political involvement is a result of the relatively shorter history of the Indian diaspora in North America. With time, this will go up. Most Indians tend to support the Democrats, even though they are religious and conservative. Going forward, more Democrat leaders are likely to appear among the Indian diaspora in future since Democrats are more accepting of minorities.

Indian politicians who are Republicans changed their religion and took advantage of the conservative Christian south. Change is afoot in the Republican Party, and it is unlikely to remain an Anglo-Saxon entity. As people move up the economic ladder, they are more likely to be Republicans. As assimilation takes its natural course, Sikh voters will make decisions at the individual level, rather than at the collective level, as a diaspora.

International organizations

When it comes to disaster relief, the International Red Cross, Doctors Without Borders, Rotary International, few Christian and other charity organizations, have been providing yeoman service in underdeveloped nations as well as in the developed world. The Khalsa Aid Society also has been very active and has provided food and clothing to no less than sixteen locations in the world at the time of natural calamities and wars.

Sikh organizations

Sikh organizations are very active and have been successful in the fight against discrimination and hate crime. There are over a dozen such organizations that deal with the issues of the community. The organizations

Baba Sewa Singh
Khadur Sahib

Balbir Singh
Seechewal

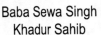

that should count among the pioneering ones are United Sikhs, Sikh Coalition, National Sikh Campaign, Sikh Net, Sikh American Legal Defense and Education Fund.

The Sikh institution of *langar* (free food) has been around since the very inception of the Sikh religion. In the US, *langar* is provided in many cities to the homeless, and those looking for meals during the coronavirus pandemic.

Eco Sikh is collaborating with the United Nations to create green spaces by planting trees (Baba Sewa Singh) and cleaning waterways (Balbir Singh Seechewal).

Sikh interaction with host community

The Sikh community is involved actively in local host activities. Sikhs are members of Rotary clubs and other organizations. Sikh professionals and businessmen are members of professional organizations. They actively

Darsh Singh

Nov Bhatia Toronto Raptors basketball team Superfan to be at the new gallery Basketball Hall of fame

participate in interfaith meetings and are at the forefront of charitable work. Politically, they are more inclined towards the Democratic Party.

Nov Bhatia, a turban-wearing Sikh businessman and a superfan of the Toronto Raptors basketball team, was inducted into the Naismith Memorial Basketball Hall of Fame in Canada. The Bhangra Empire entertained fans at the halftime show during a Warriors basketball game in Los Angeles.

Sikhs are active in sports. Paul Singh Dhaliwal was the first Sikh wrestler in the US. Now Jinder Mahal a.k.a. Yuvraj Singh Dhesi from Canada has turned out to be another outstanding wrestler. Monty Khela has played basketball for Case Western Reserve University. Satnam Singh and Sim Bhullar are recognized basketball players.

When he stepped into the NCAA court in 2014, Darsh Singh became the first-ever Sikh-American basketballer the league had seen. But because he was a turbaned Sikh, memes came up on social media. One of his friends, Greg Worthington, defended him, writing, "He's not Arab, he's Punjabi. He's not even Muslim, he's a Sikh. His name is Darsh Singh and he's a US citizen, born and bred. That jersey he's wearing in this pic, it currently sits in a Smithsonian Museum in Washington, DC because he made US history as the NCAA's first turbaned Sikh-American basketball player for Trinity University in my hometown of San Antonio."

Samrath Singh became a varsity baseball player for the South Jersey Elite. He told an interviewer, "Growing up as a Sikh is a blessing in and of itself. I have always enjoyed being outside and playing sports. I have been discriminated against because of my appearance, especially because I choose to only wear my turban while playing, and not a baseball cap."

Sikhs celebrate Christmas, Saint Valentine's Day, Thanksgiving, Labor Day, Memorial Day, Independence Day and more than ten other festivals. Many Sikh homes have Christmas trees with gifts under them.

Cultural exchange

Cultural, religious and scientific interaction is not a one-way street. You give some, you take some.

Historically, most advances in science and culture did not start with the US, Canada or even the entire western hemisphere. The printing press and pyrotechnics were innovated in China, geometrical finesse was a feature of the Ottoman empire, infinity as a concept had its birth in India, indisputably.

The west's contribution to science is certainly a hallmark of the modern world. Steam engine, telecommunication, IT, space exploration, vaccination and other medical advances are noteworthy and exceptional. Democracy and eugenics are a boon to humanity.

The Age of Enlightenment transformed Europe in the 18th century. It was a philosophical movement that advocated ideals like liberty, progress, tolerance, among others.

The early Sikh migrants, mostly farmers, lumber and construction workers, were at the fringes of American society, mainly due to their small numbers and also due to the exclusionary tactics of the local white population. Sikh contribution to the host society began in earnest following the Luce-Celler Immigration Act of 1946 and then the amended Immigration Act of 1965 signed by President Lyndon Johnson. As the Sikh population legitimately found its moorings, and the numbers grew, it became a model minority (Richwine, 2009).

The filial piety to be found in the community is the envy of the host society. The upbringing of youth with the authoritative and nurturing models is a lesson for the American parenting style.

Fiscal discipline, Bhangra dance and curry are other gifts to the US. Also, the Sikhs brought in the practice of cremation, and now the host society has been able to understand its advantages.

The Sikhs have received a lot more from America. They came to the North American shores for a better life. They achieved better living standards by the virtues built into a free society—democracy, secularism, religious freedom, rule of law, rights of citizens, meritocracy, make-your-own destiny and absence of superstitions. Values like truthfulness, love-thy-neighbor, cleanliness, human dignity and that of labor, are typically western gifts to the world. America is also the largest donor to charities around the world. American institutions receive very large endowments from their alumni, particularly the ones that have become very rich.

Small wonder then that even if the early Sikhs had entertained thoughts of returning to India, they vanished quickly. They chose to stay in North America. The virtues they saw and felt in a free society united and encouraged them to liberate India from British rule, and hence the Ghadar movement. The immigrants are slowly transmitting these American values to their home country.

To be where they are today, Sikhs had to sacrifice some of the symbols of Sikhism. In spite of cultural differences between Sikhs and local Americans, the fundamental *Punjabiat* traits of hard work, adventure and entrepreneurship are the same as those to be abundantly found in the host nation. Sikhs, much like the Yankees, were called *The New Frontiersmen* by G.S. Aurora in his 1968 book.

Sikhs and other religions

Sikhism respects all religions and no effort is made to convert others to Sikhism. This is at a time when India is embroiled in religion, and at the moment there is no separation of the religion and the state. The majority community is keen to legislate against the conversion of Hindus to other religions, and against 'love jihad' where Hindu girls marry Muslim boys. The caste system in India does not shadow the Sikh community in the US. Here, Sikhs get along with all religions.

Sikhs, Punjab and India

Sikhs in general are well-respected in India. They have made their marks in all walks of Indian society, with major contributions to the Indian army. India has had a Sikh president and a Sikh prime minister, numerous judges in the Supreme Court and the higher courts, chief ministers, members of Parliament, a national team cricket captain, a national team soccer captain, many superstars in hockey, many business magnates, TV show stars, film stars, marshal of the air force, army generals, police chiefs, and distinguished lawyers, doctors, engineers, journalists, diplomats and much more. India's current ambassador to the US is a Sikh.

The Indian Government has not given dual citizenship options to its citizens. Special lifelong visas known as the overseas citizen of India card have been granted to Indians and Indian origin people residing in about one hundred plus countries in the world. The card, however, does not give voting rights to its immigrants and does not permit contesting elections for attaining public positions. In the book *Nations Unbound—Transnational Projects, Postcolonial Predicaments, and Deterritorialized Nation-States*, editors Linda Basch, Nina Glick Schiller, Christina Szanton Blanc point out how Filipinos and the Caribbean islanders give special status to their diaspora. Cory Acquina was a US citizen when she became the president of the Philippines. Likewise, Grenada's ambassador to the US was an American citizen.

The current generation of Sikhs maintain strong ties with Punjab and are sympathetic to its causes. For instance, Sikhs overseas used all their means to support the cause of the farmers during the recent agitations. They also approached local politicians to come to the aid of the farmers.

The generation of new immigrants has a pattern of transnationalism (Bosch). They are doing well in North America, and their heart aches for Punjab. They are people with feet in two societies (Chaney, 1979).

The Sikhs overseas made an attempt to change the political landscape of Punjab by supporting the Aam Aadmi Party unsuccessfully in 2017. But five years later, that support fructified into gratifying results, and the AAP swept to power with complete majority in the state elections of 2022.

One stumbling block in the relationship with Punjab has undoubtedly been the large pro-Khalistan lobby in Canada. The Indian state has blacklisted many such leaders in Canada who support the formation of Khalistan, and even Sikh cabinet ministers in that country are given the cold shoulder when they visit India.

Even though the Indian Government invited the diaspora to invest in the country, those who did became frustrated with the red tape and bureaucracy in which administrations are still mired. Many who were interested, therefore, pulled out of investments.

Immigrants abroad may not contribute to the economy of Punjab but they do transmit some of the virtues of western societies. Good, secular, transparent democracy is missing in India and migrants can relay those values for the overall good of the country, now embroiled in communal politics with rampant corruption at all levels. One bright spot, though, is that many organizations in the US are busy doing charity work in the field of education and healthcare in Punjab and for the Sikhs.

New immigrants

In the last few years there has been an upsurge in Sikh youth leaving Punjab for higher studies to Canada, US and Australia with a clear intention of settling down in these countries. This migration is economics-related at the level of education and skills. The reduction in birth rate in the west is a blessing for Sikhs overseas, as more will migrate.

The benefits of the green revolution in farming have disappeared and prices of commodities did not keep pace with inflation, particularly since the cost of fertilizers, insecticides and pesticides have shot up. Punjabi farmers, mostly Sikhs, were economically hit very hard. A

recent article on Thalli economics (Sharma, 2020) points out a glaring irony—while there is a food price relief to the Indian population, in general, the farmer is not benefitting from it, in fact he's getting poorer due to an increase in cost of production. The lethal combination of drug addiction and farm debts results in farmers claiming their own lives. And when industrial growth does not keep pace with population growth, any state will have to stare down the abyss of unemployment. Punjab is no exception.

There is a sense of déjà vu. The way things are playing out at present are similar to the way things were in the latter part of the 19th century and the early 20th century. Those were the days of the British Raj, and as families expanded there was a corresponding reduction in land holdings. We are still stuck in the same morass, only made worse by drug addiction and politicians who are out to fleece the taxpayers' hard-earned money.

In an article of December 31, 2019 in *The Tribune,* author Bachan Jagat broached the subject of large-scale youth exodus from Punjab at the cost of leaving behind an elderly population in most villages. In another article in the same newspaper on February 3, 2020, Kamaljit and Rakshinder Kaur of the Punjabi University mentioned that a recent survey in Punjab shows that a whopping seventy percent of the youth in the state belong to farming families. The best

way to pay for tuition in colleges abroad is by mortgaging or selling the limited farmland they possess. Punjab's travel agents are having a field day as a result of the exodus to foreign lands.

Sikhs continue to immigrate to the US using every means possible. Most are a part of chain migration. Many who come as students become residents in the US, or move to Canada, where they have a better acceptance. While a small percentage gets citizenship through birthright, the number of H-1B working visas for specialty occupations is on the decline. Very few Sikhs, on the other hand, avail the HB-5 immigrant investor visa. And next to the Hispanic group, Indians, including Sikhs, comprise the largest number of those who've illegally entered the US or have overstayed in the country and have disappeared.

The most recent US Census tells us that the US population growth is almost negligible. At the same time there is a growing population that is making a shift from the working age-group to the elderly age-group. There is a growing labor shortage in all sectors of the economy. If the US must keep pace with the world, and keep its economy growing, then immigrants will need to fill in vacancies all around. This should be a harbinger of good news for those who wish to immigrate to the US. ∎

CHAPTER 8

SIKH CHALLENGES TODAY

"Nothing is so painful to the human mind as a great and sudden change," said Mary Shelly in *Frankenstein*. The large increase in immigration after the new act in 1965 passed by President Lyndon Johnson was a sudden change for many. It left little time for adjustment.

I have earlier discussed the challenges early Sikh settlers faced in North America. The issues related to citizenship, owning property and Sikh Hispanic marriages have been resolved. The color bias is declining gradually. America is becoming less religious. But even though some issues have been resolved, matters related to the turban have become worse. The anti-Sikh violence in the early 20th century was a result of labor disputes. The current one is a result of Islamophobia. The mistaken identity with militant Islam has made Sikhs vulnerable to hate crimes.

All these issues have been debated in chapter five. Currently, Sikhs face the following challenges:

1. Sikhism.
   A. Theology.
   B. Sikh turban, *Keshdhari* and *Amritdhari* Sikhs.
   C. Offshoots of Sikhism.
   D. Punjabi language.
2. Interfaith marriages.
3. Color.
4. Adaptation and assimilation.

The aforementioned points can be classified either as challenges or as problems that need resolution. These can also be changes for the good or for the worse. But one thing is for sure, the change is constant and continuous.

Many of the above aspects of the Sikh community have changed since the time Bakshish Singh Dhillon and three other Sikhs landed in San Francisco, US, in 1899. Further changes will continue in future according to the demands of the societies of the future.

These challenges and changes may not be perceived universally by all Sikhs, at home and abroad.

Change
*It is not the strongest of species that survive,
nor the most intelligent that survive.*

Punjabi Market during the Vaisakhi Parade of 2017 in Vancouver

It is the one that is adaptable to change.
Charles Darwin

Kitna Badal Gaya Insaan
(How much humans have changed)
Song in Indian movie *Nastik*, 1954

Religion and change

The rise and the fall of religion and the debate about the existence of God has been discussed earlier (chapter three). The world is gradually becoming more spiritual than religious. The existence of God, omnipotent creator without shape and form as mentioned in *Japji Sahib* (Sikh script), has been the subject of discussion even before Sikhism came into existence.

Human thinking keeps on changing and could be Darwinian social evolution brought about by enlightenment, science, modernity, globalization or detraditionalization. The change occurs in all spheres of life but is debated and challenged most in religion. The change is universal but variable in different religions.

Below is a sample of changes, reform or upgrade of some organized religions including Sikhism.

Reform Judaism (Liberal Judaism, progressive Judaism) appeared in the mid-19th century in Germany. This denomination believes in the evolving nature of faith with ethical superiority over ceremonial one and with human reason and intellect. It believes in inclusion, acceptance and individual responsibility.

Christianity went through changes of its own with many sub-groups and denominations like the Catholic Church, Protestantism, Eastern Orthodox Church, Oriental Orthodox Church, Nontrinitarian Restorationism, Independent Catholics and few others.

Catholic Church faces many challenges and is borrowing time to change. Sexual abuse, celibacy of priests, birth control, abortion and denial of priesthood to females, remain challenges. These controversies are not new. Bruno, philosopher, mathematician, poet and cosmologist theorist, was burned alive on February 7, 1600 in Campo de' Fiori in Rome as he did not believe in the trinity and divinity of Christ and the Virgin Mary. This will not happen in Christianity now but is possible in few other religions like Islam.

Hinduism has four main denominations—Vaishnavas, Shaivas, Shaktas and Smartas and around sixteen sub-groups. Most pertinent for Sikhs is the Arya Samaj movement in North India.

Islam refuses to change and this rigidity in thinking has its own consequences.

Salman Rushdie, Ayana Hirsi Ali are under death threat (*fatwa*) for pointing out reprehensible writings in the Quran.

The office of French satirical magazine Charlie Hebdo was attacked on January 7, 2015, killing twelve people for the publishing of cartoons of Mohammed to the dislike of Muslims.

Sikhism

The issue of the existence of God and the fall of religion in general was discussed in chapter three. Mool Mantar, the important component of Sikh theology related to the relevance of God in Sikhism, is under challenge. Same is the case with all other religions. There is an increase in the number of agnostic and atheist Sikhs as revealed in a small survey of Sikhs.

According to a *British Sikh* report there has been a reduction in the numbers of *Keshdhari* and *Amritdhari* Sikhs. The baptized Khalsa has lost its role in the defense of Sikhism and other oppressed people. Kirpan is not the weapon of choice.

The young Sikhs in the second and the third generations are not literate in Punjabi language, the media of Sikh scripture and have low attendance in the Gurdwara Sahib.

This could further precipitate the fall of Sikhism.

The offshoots of Sikhism face a bigger problem. They are inconspicuous to start with and are likely to become extinct in the US. Modernity, detraditionalization, advances in science and Darwinian social evolution are powerful forces to counter and are responsible for the downfall of all religions.

All above does not cheer up Sikhism. But *Kirit Kar*, *Wund Shako* and *Sarbat da Bhala* have their own virtues. The role of the Gurdwara in the everyday life of a Sikh holds great significance.

Sikh Turban—Keshdhari and Amritdhari Sikhs

This is the most important challenge facing Sikhs in the US. Young, turban-wearing Sikh boys have had difficulties getting admission to schools. Once admitted, they face bullying in school. Adult women in general, who are both Sikh and non-Sikh, are reluctant to marry or have intimacy with turban-clad Sikhs.

They face job discrimination and become victims of hate crime due to the mistaken identity with Islam. The Iranian hostage crisis was followed by the attack on the twin towers in New York City. Islamophobia is on the rise since militant Islam continues to foment violence in the western world. David Amess, British MP, was stabbed to death last year. This mistaken identity has been responsible for many injuries and even death of innocent *Keshdhari* and *Amritdhari* Sikhs.

Turban hinders upward mobility in all spheres of life, including in public office. No immediate solution to this issue is at hand. Time, though, can be a great healer. Sikh organizations are doing their best and have been successful in recruitment of turban-wearing Sikhs in police and defense services. As turban is accepted in other western countries, one hopes the US will follow. The recent upsurge in activities of white supremacist groups like the Ku Klux Klan, Proud Boys and the great replacement

> [There is an increase, as well as more acceptance of, interfaith marriages in North America. The acceptance of interfaith marriages increased from 20 percent in 1978 to 43 percent in 1998 (Gallup Poll, 1998)]

theorists are not good signs for colored and immigrant people.

Interfaith marriage

There is an increase, as well as more acceptance of, interfaith marriages in North America. The acceptance of interfaith marriages increased from 20 percent in 1978 to 43 percent in 1998 (Gallup Poll, 1998). Pew Research (February 7, 2013) revealed that twelve percent of Asian Americans had spouses of different races and ethnicities. This is painful for new immigrants. There are not too many choices for educated Sikhs when it comes to endogamy. The arranged marriages of the past are now history.

Color

The color bias is gradually fading away in spite of a recent upsurge in replacement theory. The US will be a white minority nation in future (Poston and others, 2019).

Adaptation and assimilation

This is a slow process. Adaptation is preferred over melting pot. The Sikh enclaves are the places to slow down adaptation and assimilation, while amalgamation will speed them up.

United States or Canada
(Tale of two countries)

The early Sikh migrants did not differentiate between the two countries and moved across undefined borders, depending on job opportunities, immigration laws and attitude of the host country. When they initially arrived, the US was a free nation and Canada a British dominion. Now both nations are free and relations are friendly between them. There are border checkpoints in place. Sikhs feel and find Canada less challenging due to their higher percentage in the total population as compared to the US. They have a greater voice in the nation's democracy and there is more multiculturalism in Canada, thanks largely to the multiculturalism act of 1988.

Chand (2012) has made an observation that East Indians in Canada have less income but more representation in the cabinet. This is quite opposite to the situation in the US. Which is better? Canada does beat the US in the happiness index. Canada for Sikhs, therefore, has become home away from home.

To sum it up, all immigrants face some problem or the other. Sikhs stand out in the crowd due to their religious symbols and turban and pay a price. In spite of the above challenges, the community can afford to pat itself on the back for the laudable progress made in many spheres.

America, though, has sadly been beleaguered by a dangerously spiraling out-of-control gun culture. But the daily deaths as a result of indiscriminate shootings will not be tolerated for too long. American Sikhs are happy and are making a headway along with other East Indians. They are very much an integral part of a highly-qualified, model minority (Richwine, 2009). ∎

CHAPTER 9

> 66
>
> *Change is the only constant in life"*
> —**Heraclitus**

SIKH CHALLENGES IN FUTURE

We know what we are, but not what we may be
—**Hamlet**

Future of human being

The future is what follows this moment in time. Its duration is infinite. Any change that takes place in humans takes decades and centuries. Evolution of man has happened over seventy thousand years. There is a Punjabi saying, *"Kall kin dekhia"*. It means, who knows what tomorrow holds for us. The famous lines by the American actress Dorris Day say,

> *"Que sera, sera*
> *Whatever will be, will be*
> *The future's not ours to see*
> *Que sera, sera*
> *What will be, will be..."*

And yet, even though I'm not a futurist, I'm deeply aware that things do change with time. This change is in every sphere. Some changes are natural, some man made. Volcanoes, tsunamis, avalanches, hurricanes are natural phenomenon, while changes in the political landscape, invention of new technologies, newer eating habits, changes in culture, language and religion are brought about by human beings who themselves are constantly evolving in accordance with the Darwinian theory of social and evolutionary adjustment.

The Ionian philosopher Heraclitus had said that the only constant in life is change. Change is good for humanity, but it is nonetheless quite challenging in the beginning. Are we, for instance, not challenged by newer technologies every day, even though they may be for our own good?

Many sociological changes may occur in the future. Spirituality could override religion. Gender and income equality could prevail. Robots could replace humans. Universal minimum income may become reality. More elderly could be roaming the world, while less numbers of the younger population will work to support them. The institution of marriage could give way to partnership, and even just friendship. Birth rates may fall. Some current customs and behavioral patterns could return to the pre-civilization times and newer ones may be born. Homo sapiens will be the only race for humans. There could be a growing number of atheists and agnostics, challenging the very foundations of religion. All this, eventually, can combine to make things better than the 'good ol' days' and the Sikh community will be a part of it.

Before we start looking at the future of Sikhism, it would be worthwhile discussing the definition of a Sikh of the future.

Defining the Sikh of the future

The definition of a Sikh has changed many times since the very beginning of the Sikh faith. Different organizations and individuals have in the past attempted to define a Sikh. Since most Sikhs in North America are shaved, there is a need to redefine a Sikh in North America.

Bhai Gurdas was a Sikh scholar during the Guru's period and defined Sikhs differently from Hinduism and Islam. Sikhs were identified as the ones who would stick to the fundamentals of the faith, that is *Nam Japna, Kirt Karna* and *Wund Shako*. There were no external symbols of Sikh identity. Those were the days of Nanak Panthi Sikhs, before the Khalsa was created and Guruship was bestowed on the holy Guru Granth Sahib (*Guru Manyo Granth*).

The Gurdwara Act of 1925 provided a formal definition of a Sikh, one who believed in the Guru Granth Sahib, and the ten Gurus prior to that. The Sikh had no other religion. The Shiromani Gurdwara Parbandhak Committee (SGPC) altered the definition in 1950 and baptized Khalsa as the one who is a Sikh. In 1971, the Delhi Sikh Gurdwara Bill added that the Sikh is the one with unshorn hair—*Keshdhari*.

Professor Chahal (2002) went at lengths to define a Sikh. After reviewing all earlier available definitions, he suggested that, "a person who follows Sikhi (Gurmit/Sikhism) that is based on Gurbani incorporated in the *Aad Granth Sahib* by Guru Arjan and Guru Gobind Singh, the fifth and tenth Gurus in succession to the house of Nanak, is a Sikh. Consequently, such a person is solely a follower of Sikhism, and does not practice any other religion simultaneously."

Professor Chahal did not explicitly consider hair, baptizing or turban in the aforementioned definition. I'd like to go a step further and define a Sikh as such: "A person who claims to be Sikh, considers Guru Granth Sahib as the current Guru, and practices no other religion." This definition is similar to the one in the Gurdwara Act of 1925 and brings us closer to the teaching of the founding father and his philosophy of Nanak Panthi Sikhism.

Future of Sikhism

The survival and changes in a religion depends on many factors. The changes are determined by its theology, Darwinian survival, advances in science, modernity, detraditionalization and attitude of the host society. Sikhism will change. Many of these changes are already in progress as outlined in chapter eight. The changes, in future, are likely to be in Sikh theology, baptism of Khalsa, religious symbols, offshoots of Sikhism, Sikh *maryada*, marriage, and finally impact of adaptation or assimilation in the host country.

Sikh theology
Mool Mantar

Nam Jap | *Kirt Kar* | *Wund Shako*
Prayer | Hard work | Charity
Nam Jap pertains to the prayer of God.

"*Rab ik gunghal dar bugart,*
Rab ik gorakh tandha
Kholan Laghian pech ase
Dey Kaffer ho jai banda"
(God's existence is very complex to understand. The more you explore, the more you get agnostic)
—Professor Mohan Singh

The existence of God and the institution of religion has been the subject of discussion since the very beginning. Lately, Richard Dawkins (2008) and others have rekindled this debate. The idea and concept of God or Akal

Mool Mantar

Purakh along with prayer has been the mainstay of Sikh theology. There is praise of God in the first lines of *Japji Sahib* as there is in almost every page of the holy scripture, the Guru Granth Sahib Ji.

At the same time the growing presence of agnostic and atheist Sikhs (newer Sikhs) has been recognized before. Their numbers are likely to increase, especially among the educated Sikhs in the western world where agnosticism, atheism and humanism are gaining speed. A small survey among the educated Sikhs in the US further showcases this present and clear concern.

Agnostic thinking among some Sikhs is a challenge to *Nam Jap* (prayer to God) in *Mool Mantar*, the basic theology of Sikhism. The two other components of Sikh theology, *Kirit Kar* and *Wund Shako* will, however, prevail in future.

One wonders if in future God and religion can come back strong? Maybe, if there is a big catastrophic event. Maybe if another Guru Nanak is born? Maybe, if there is a miracle which can occur only by the will of God?

The complements of Sikh theology such as equality of humankind and gender, the crushing of one's ego, pride, lust, greed, anger will remain key to Sikhism. Likewise, partaking in fellowship, *sangat* (congregation) and *pangat* (eating together on the floor) are disciplines and excellent rules of civil society and they will prevail going forward. But some may opt for membership in non-religious clubs. The complements discussed have a commonality with other religions.

Baptized Khalsa

The baptized Khalsa and religious symbols were the need of the time when the tenth Guru created the Khalsa. He had a definite purpose and need for this transformative movement. He was aware that religions cannot survive without political power. The plundering of wealth and mass conversion to Islam by the Mughals and Muslims invaders could only be countered by force. Khalsa is also called Akal Purkh di Fauj (Army of God). Khalsa, in future, will, however, not have any other purpose except furthering love and dedication to the tenth Guru.

The baptized Khalsa Sikh has to navigate a challenging obstacle course and comply with numerous rules and traditions of baptism. Uncut hair, turban, frequent prayers, keeping the sword, are all impediments when it comes to being successful in business and the global corporate world, and yet the Khalsa must abide by them. Small wonder that according to the *British Sikh report (2019)*, there has been a fair reduction in baptized and other turban-wearing Sikhs in the UK.

What is likely to replace the Khalsa in the future? Plato had said that our need will be our real creator. Sikhs will invent what is needed—higher education, wealth creation, charity, unity and political involvement. This will be the new Khalsa that will promote and protect all religious, cultural and complimentary ethics of the Sikh society that have been mentioned earlier.

Turban

As a symbol of Sikh identity, the turban has been discussed at length in chapter five. While it remains the most important symbol of Sikhism, it is also the reason why Sikhs have had to cope with numerous hate crimes and discriminatory practices. The turban is going through a tough phase, but as the original Persian adage goes, this too shall pass. As the world becomes less religious, more educated, and interdependent, the turban will become increasingly acceptable everywhere. It is well recognized in all Asian countries, Great Britain and our next-door neighbor, Canada. The other symbols are largely conspicuous by their absence in North America and many other nations, barring, of course, the sword.

This change is not going to take place through a mandate or order. It is a simple Darwinian principle of achieving a goal by expending the least amount of resources. What is not needed, loses its utility and disappears. I'm sorry to say that in the western world all the components of 5Ks will not survive, even though the number of Sikhs are likely to increase. A multicultural society like Canada will provide a brief reprieve.

Sikh *Maryada*, Sikh *Rehat Namas*, Sikh tradition and customs

Sikh *Rehat Namas* or Sikh codes of conduct were initiated by Guru Gobind Singh Ji. He gave fifty-two *Hukams* or rules of conduct that he asked his followers to formalize. Sikh scholars and dignitaries have further penciled them down as their own versions. The various versions are the *Rehat Namas* by Bhai Nand Lal, Bhai Dessa Singh, Bhai Chaupa Singh, Bhai Daya Singh and Bhai Prahlad Singh.

There were some variations among these, hence the SGPC updated the final version in 1945.

I have divided these codes of conduct into two parts, the one which is likely to survive in future and the other which will gradually wither away.

Group A
Old traditions and *Maryadas*

1. Langar or free kitchen.
2. Sharing (charity) and *Daswand*—Charitable giving is universal in all religions, and has been specially emphasized in Sikhism. *Daswand* or giving ten percent of one's income to charity was a one-time guideline, but not mandatory.
3. *Sangat* or congregation as a democratic, decision-making body.
4. *Pangat*—eating together on the floor, or now on chairs, representing equality.
5. *Sewa* or service to society. This includes focusing on the needs of the weak and the downtrodden.
6. Sikh shrines—visit to the Harmandir Sahib and other religious sites will increase as curiosity and the desire to find one's roots go up.

Newer traditions—*Maryadas* of the future

1. Political involvement—This will be emphasized as the most important *Maryada*. This will become the modern defensive weapon for the protection of Sikhism and will replace the baptized Khalsa. Political involvement will gradually increase as has already happened in Canada, our next-door neighbor.
2. Eco Sikh—This may not typically be considered a new *Maryada* but there is a new emphasis on it today and will continue to be there in future.
3. LBGTQ community—acceptance.
4. Same sex marriage—acceptance.
5. Helmet: This is not being accepted universally by Sikhs, nor is it being applied uniformly. Certain Sikh leaders have been advocating that the wearing of a helmet is against the tenets of Sikhism. It is true that helmets were non-existent during the time of the Gurus, or even when the *Rehat Namas* were written. But today's world is different. You have fast-moving traffic, and busy construction sites where workers go up skyscrapers. Human life is more important than a religious diktat. If one dies of head injury at a construction site, or during a highway bike accident, for not wearing a helmet, will the Sikh leaders who campaign against it provide financial support to the family of the deceased? Those who die due to a head injury are not categorized as shaheeds, or martyrs. So, there is no point in following antediluvian diktats. Sikhs in future will adopt helmets and could even come up with an improvised one that can be worn over a turban.

The above traditions will flourish in future, and more will be added in conformity with the needs of the time.

Group B

The *Maryadas*, traditions and customs in group B are less likely to continue in the future for the reasons outlined below.

1. Daily Prayers

As per the code of conduct or *Rehat Maryada*, Sikhs are expected to pray at least three times a day. This is, however, only on paper. During a long flight to India alongside several other Sikh passengers I did not find anyone opening a *Gutka* (prayer book) or saying a quiet prayer. Instead, I found a Muslim passenger asking me about the direction of the geographical west as we were flying. He then turned in that direction, placed a mat on the floor, and prayed, all while the aircraft was zooming in the skies at an altitude of forty thousand feet. He was facing Kaaba, the sacred Muslim shrine in Mecca.

2. Sitting on the floor

Traditionally, one has had to sit on the floor for prayers and for *langar* at the Gurdwara Sahib. This is in deference to the Guru Granth Sahib. It is also a symbol of humility. Of course, as people age, it becomes physically challenging to sit on the floor and that is why chairs are available for senior citizens in most Gurdwaras. A time may come when the Guru Granth Sahib will be kept on an elevated platform and there will be a chair to sit for everyone attending a *sangat*.

3. Akhand Path

This is a special prayer that lasts for three days at a stretch. It is a ritual that is carried out by Granthis, more as a paid service for a Sikh family.

4. *Massia* and *Sangrand*

This is a tradition of visiting holy places at the start of the month for offering prayers and taking a dip in the holy tank. To get family issues resolved, many Sikhs in the past would regularly undertake a monthly visit and offer prayers to Waheguru, as God is called in Sikhism. My father paid a visit to Harminder Sahib to seek help for a truant grandson who did not forgo the slightest opportunity to bunk school. My father took a pledge called *Massia Sukhni* or a pledge for the truant grandson. To my father's delight, his efforts of waking up at four in the morning to take the train to Harminder Sahib for the spiritual visit bore fruits. My nephew started attending school regularly and took his classes far more seriously than before. This monthly visit, in the past, provided an opportunity to leaders of the Sikh faith to meet and keep everyone abreast of developments concerning the community. There are better ways of communication now.

5. *Parkarma*

This is a tradition of going around the periphery of the Harmandir Sahib or other Sikh shrines. My doctor friend who was on blood thinners slipped on a patch of wet marble and started bleeding. He was hospitalized, and needed a blood transfusion. And once my grandson was like a cat on a hot tin roof while walking on the scorching marble during a summer month. I am not too sure if the *Parkarma* will appeal to every Sikh in the future.

6. Dip in Holy Tank (Ashnan)

Oil on the surface of the holy water stuck to me when I was a young boy taking a dip in the holy tank. It belonged to hundreds of people taking their bath. Very few, I believe, will take a dip now, even though water purification equipment is in place.

7. Chuli

Taking a sip of holy water from the sacred tank has been in vogue among Sikhs visiting the Harmandir Sahib or other holy shrines. Some also collect the water in bottles and take it back for family members to drink. This ritual may not be a healthy one.

A doctor (Gawande, 2014) took his deceased father's ashes to be submerged in the river Ganges and took a sip of holy water. He developed an infection with Giardia in spite of prophylactic antibiotics.

8. Ashes of deceased

Traditionally, the ashes of the dead are taken to Kiratpur Sahib in Punjab for immersion in the local river. As outlined by Tarlochan Singh Dupalpur, this is against Sikh tenets. He noted that many families, some from overseas, had met with serious accidents, even resulting in death, while travelling to Kiratpur Sahib to submerge the ashes of loved ones who had passed away. In my own case, when I took my father's ashes to Kiratpur Sahib after his demise, sharp bones that had piled up from previous immersions at the place injured my feet as I was entering the shallow river.

This is not an accepted *Rehat maryada* and is not part of the Sikh tenets. Ashes of one of my deceased relatives were immersed in the Pacific Ocean in the Bay Area of Northern California. Was this even necessary?

9. Granthi

The clergy in Sikhism are known as Granthis. They interpret *Gurbani*, the spiritual writing. Baba Buddha was the first Granthi at the Harmandir Sahib. It is not easy these days being a priest, a mullah, a rabbi, a Granthi or a Gyani. The salaries are relatively low and, therefore, the job is not as appealing as it could be. Many Gyanis quit their job as preachers and pursue other professions. Today there is a shortage of priests in the western world that is the home of Christianity. Congregations are reducing. I met Father Thomas in a small town in Ohio. He was fast-tracked during immigration as the local Church did not have any priests. During a trip to Germany, I visited a famous Church that did not have a priest or any clergy.

In time, the physical presence of Granthis will become unnecessary. Recorded kirtans can be beamed live onto a television screen. Sikhism in future will be learnt online from courses offered by Sikh chairs and not the less-educated Gyani. Zoom and Skype conferences will further make them dispensable.

10. Hemkund trip

High on the mountains of Uttarakhand in India is the Gurdwara Shri Hemkund Sahib Ji. It is considered the place where tenth Guru Gobind Singh Ji prayed in his previous life. This is a debated issue (Inder Singh Ghagga). This is a place which many a devout Sikh wants to visit as part of a pilgrimage to holy places of the Sikhs. But it is a difficult place to reach.

11. *Jathedar*

Jathedar was the status given to a devout Sikh in the past who functioned as a local leader in a community. The *Jathedars* have no role in a secular democratic society except the *Jathedar* of the Akal Takht who is supreme and is followed in hierarchy by the *Jathedars* of four regional Takhts.

12. Sword

It is my thinking that the sword as a symbol of Khalsa and Sikhism will gradually disappear in North America and in the west in general. A small symbolic one, attached to the comb, will continue to be there.

13. Reincarnation and Afterlife in Sikhism

As mentioned in the subsection on Hemkund Sahib in Uttarakhand as part of Sikh *maryadas* and traditions, the tenth Sikh Guru Gobind Singh Ji is said to have meditated in his previous life at this high Himalayan place. This, though, has been a subject of much debate among Sikh scholars. The concept of reincarnation and afterlife is a myth and not an educated delight.

14. Sant, Mahants, Cults and Deras

In the last fifty odd years there has been a surge in these organizations and traditions. Educated Sikhs will find a way past them and they'll be discarded in the longer term. Ceremonies and customs inherited from Hinduism such as the Nag Puja (cobra worship), marriage constraint for widows, praying for rain are no longer in practice. Islamic practices like wailing for the dead, putting a veil on the face, have stopped. Ceremonies involving the naming of a new born (*naam karan*), turban initiation (*dastar bandi*) and the much-hyped arrival of a groom on a horseback for marrying, are traditions that are already on the wane. With time, it looks like they'll completely disappear.

Punjabi language and the Gurmukhi script

The Guru Granth Sahib, the Sikh religious holy book, has been written in Punjabi and follows the Gurmukhi script. The first-generation immigrants to North America post-1965 are able to speak and understand the Punjabi language. Many of them are able to read and write Gurmukhi as well. The second and third generation Sikhs, however, have neither picked up the language, nor the script, and are unable to read and understand the Guru Granth Sahib through direct reading. They are dependent on its English translations that are available with several Gurdwaras across the US and Canada. But as is evident, the translations are usually a poor substitute for the original text.

The reasons for the decline of the Punjabi language and its relevance to Sikhism has been discussed in chapter five. The demise, if at all, will be slow. Languages, after all, take their time to be born, and are even slower to die. Sikhs and other Punjabis have a responsibility to save their mother tongue, also the medium of the holy Granth.

More recently, though, many Sikh Gurdwaras, Sikh chairs in various universities, and Sikh charter schools, have started giving out lessons in the Punjabi language and the Gurmukhi script to the newer generations of Sikhs born abroad. Would all this save Punjabi and Gurmukhi script?

Nanak Panthi Sikhism

The term Nanak Panthis, in the broader sense, applies to those who follow the teachings of Guru Nanak. This includes all those who claim to be Sikh. Some progressed to become Sikhs that were associated with the external identity of 5Ks. They came to be known as *Keshdhari* Sikhs. Later the baptized Sikhs came to be known as Khalsa or *Amritdhari* Sikhs.

But those who are not *Keshdhari* or Khalsa can be classified as Nanak Panthis. In the past, the term was used in a narrower sense, that is for a specific category of Sikhs. According to Karnail Singh Panjoli, member of the SGPC,

Sikligarh, Vanjaarey, Lubaney, Johri, Satnamiye Udaasiyas and the early Sikh communities of Bihar, Madhya Pradesh, Gujarat, Haryana, Assam, Uttar Pradesh and in some other locations have been considered Nanak Panthis.

How about Sikhs in the west who are neither *Keshdhari* nor *Amritdhari?* I consider them to be Nanak Panthi even though I'm aware of the fact that there are many who will differ with me. This category will constitute the vast majority of Sikhs in the west. Their numbers would swell if we were to include all the offshoots of Sikhism discussed earlier.

Sikh community is not homogeneous now and nor will it be in the foreseeable future. The Nanak Panthis will outnumber the *Amritdhari* and *Keshdhari* Sikhs.

Relationship with Punjab

The love and affection that Sikhs have for Punjab is enduring. After all, Punjab is the birthplace of Sikhism. A visit to Harmandir Sahib and other holy places will remain a burning desire of all Sikhs abroad. This desire can be compared to the one that Muslims have for visiting Mecca, and the Jews and Christians have for visiting Jerusalem.

The newer pattern of transnational immigrants with one foot in each society (Chaney 1979) will improve relations with the mother country. A lot, however, depends on the prevailing social, political and economic climate in the home country.

Love fatigue could occur in subsequent generations. I met an elderly Greek immigrant some years ago. He had absolutely no love for his mother country and said he'd never again visit Greece. He carried unpleasant memories from the past about his homeland. In stark contrast, his physician son, born in the US, has made many trips to Greece, primarily in search of his roots. I'd call it more curiosity, or perhaps unrequited love.

Punjab—The Sikh Israel

At the outset, let me mention that by this I do not mean a separate Sikh country but a homeland of Sikhs.

There are numerous similarities between Sikhs and Jewish people. Judaism had its birth in areas around Palestine. Apparently, at least twelve Jewish tribes took off for various places on the planet. Due to their runaway success in entrepreneurship, business, sciences and the arts, the Jewish people are loved and hated in equal measure. The last emotion resulted in severe antisemitism and eventually culminated in one of the greatest crimes in the history of mankind, the holocaust.

The thought of a Jewish homeland appeared in the mind of Theodor Herzl (1860-1904), an Austro-Hungarian Jewish journalist, sometime during the First World War. It became a reality after the Second World War. Israel is an independent nation with its own sovereignty. The credit for the birth and magnificent progress of Israel goes to the Jewish people scattered in different parts of the world. Education, hard work and relentless innovation has also turned Israel into a veritable oasis in a desert.

Similar is the story of the Sikhs. They too have dispersed to destinations near and far from their homeland Punjab. There is hardly a family in Punjab which does not have kith and kin overseas. It is likely that in future they'll become more affluent than Sikhs in India. Till Punjab stabilizes economically, human capital will move abroad. These immigrants will continue visiting the Sikh holy places in Punjab on both sides of the Ravi river. Amritsar for the Sikhs will be like Jerusalem to the Jewish folks.

The Jewish people have invested heavily in the desert state of Israel, almost magically transforming it to a highly advanced nation in the Middle East. Will something similar happen in Punjab? I would tend to think so. Punjab will flourish and the Sikh diaspora will handhold it to prosperity. This is evident from the support provided to the farmers during their long-drawn agitation in India. At the moment, the economic climate is not favorable for investments in Punjab. Till such time it does become favorable, Punjab will continue to benefit from the tourist economy and the charitable giving from its diaspora. All this bodes well for Punjab.

Sikhism and future technology

While futurists are busy predicting the impact of new technology on human beings, I'll just focus on Sikh teaching and prayer. Students at schools and colleges have benefited from virtual learning during the coronavirus pandemic. *Kirtan* (spiritual prayer) has been relayed all over the world from the Harmandir Sahib in Amritsar. Prayers and functions can be carried out with ease these days over the Zoom media. The *Kirtan Sola* (prayer for departed souls) was recently done virtually without the physical presence of a Gyani (Sikh clergy).

Physical therapists in medicine are looking at the connection between a computer and the human brain in order to move artificial and paralyzed limbs. How about connecting the emotional brain, prayer and human behavior? Will we need physical schools and colleges in future? How about temples, mosques and Gurdwaras?

Facing the future

Social, religious and cultural shifts will happen in an educated and globalized world. All religious and ethnic groups are vulnerable to this shift, the Sikhs being no exception. As has been our subject of discussion at many places earlier, Sikhs face many challenges. Following are suggestions for the success of Sikhs, going forward. These methods have been tried and tested by the earlier immigrants.

1. Population density: In greater numbers lies greater strength. More immigration will be helpful. Sikhs should move to bigger cities and concentrate on Sikh enclaves. Before them are their own examples like in Yuba City and Marysville in California. There are also the examples set by the Chinese, Jews, Cubans and others.

2. Business and self-employment: Sikhs should be encouraged to start their own businesses, rather than being at the mercy of employers who may at times look disparagingly at turbans. A Sikh business council is the need of the hour.

3. Education and wealth: People that are

both educated and wealthy are respected more and face less discrimination.

4. All Sikhs should actively participate in politics at all levels and join Sikh organizations in order to fight against discrimination and other challenges faced by the community.

5. Gurdwaras should be made attractive for the youth who in turn should be encouraged to get involved in their management. The early Sikh leadership was a product of the Gurdwara Sahib. The concept of *Sewa* and *Wund Shako* should be prioritized and given utmost importance.

6. Free group tours for young Sikhs to visit Sikh shrines in India should be arranged. Similar tours to Israel have been undertaken by Jewish organizations like the Birthright Israel Foundation.

7. All Sikhs should learn about Sikhism. There are enough online portals and channels that can provide free education. Likewise, there are Sikh chairs set up in various universities that can be very useful. Punjabi language courses also are offered by many US universities. Chartered Khalsa schools, Sikh youth camps, children's books, videos of Sikh history, turban-tying competitions, all contribute in a big way in keeping Sikhism alive in the west. Sikh goodwill through charitable giving, *langar* and *sewa* (service) for the needy and homeless will continue to improve the Sikh image, identity and awareness.

8. Retirees should be encouraged to wear the turban in case they had to remove it while they were working.

9. All Sikhism offshoots should be welcomed by the mainstream. This can help them in embracing Sikhism as preached by the founding fathers of Nanak Panthi Sikhism.

Futurology of Sikhism summarized

Sikhism is bound to face challenges in future. There will be those who will question the concepts of Waheguru and *Mool Mantar.* There will be a rise in atheism and agnosticism. Turban-wearing Sikhs will be on a decline, as will be the case with symbols of Sikh identity, mainly the 5Ks. Majority of the Sikhs will be *Mona* or clean shaven, and without the turban. There will, therefore, come a time when the definition of a Sikh male will have to be revisited, at least in the US.

The Sikh Gurdwara will continue to be the most important Sikh organization in future. *Sangat* (congregation), *pangat* (the concept of equality by eating together, preferably on the floor), *langar* (free kitchen) and charity will continue, and keep providing strength to the Sikhs. Some old Sikh *Maryadas* (customs and traditions) will nevertheless disappear, and new ones will take their place. Interfaith marriages will go up. The Punjabi language and the Gurmukhi script will face challenges with a decline in their usage.

Sikh organizations in Punjab will no longer be relevant to the Sikhs in the US. Local organizations will develop to promote the Sikh cause in the US. Like other citizens, Sikhs will be active in politics. Americanization will entail greater adaptation, and the melting pot factor will be reduced. The Sikhs in future will follow the language, culture, sports and festivals of their new home. Discrimination on the basis of color, race and religion will reduce.

The demand for engaging Sikh clergy or Gyani will come down. Many Sikh events will be virtual. Sikh education will be mostly online. Established chairs in Sikh studies in various universities will stay, and will be enough to fulfill the need to know more about Sikhism.

The offshoots of Sikhism are unlikely to survive in the US and will be a part of universal Sikhism, with Nanak Panthi as the basic philosophy. Sikhs overseas will be better educated and richer. Punjab will be the Sikh Israel. There will be an increased desire to visit Sikh holy places, and for searching for roots.

Every religion is fighting for its future. The Singh Sabha movement played an important role in the promotion of Sikhism in the last century. Local Sikh organizations will play a similar role in future. I've outlined some of these suggestions in the lines above. ∎

SUMMARY OF SIKH CHALLENGES

(Past | Present | Future)

Happiness is a common goal of life for all human beings. This begins with basic needs of life as depicted in Maslow's pyramid. They involve food, clothing and shelter, or as the Punjabis would say, "*Kulli, Julli, Gulli.*" The 1974 Indian movie *Roti, Kapada Aur Makaan* (food, clothing, shelter) is also on the same theme. To meet these basic needs, humans take many steps, and migration is one of those.

The host society or the new place of domicile or the adopted land may or may not be welcoming for new immigrants. Some degree of initial discrimination is almost given. Color, race, religion, culture and competition for making a living become crucial for migrants. Discrimination, though, is generally on a decline as a result of increased education levels and globalization. It also reduces as there is greater assimilation in the host society. Will the competition for jobs reduce with greater automation? Time will tell.

Sikhs were the first among Indians to enter the US and Canada. There used to be frequent to-and-fro movement across the porous borders for the early Sikhs. The migration was economic in nature, facilitated largely by the fact that Sikhs, declared a martial race, were recruited in large numbers in the British army and came in contact with soldiers of western countries at various locations. Originally when they entered North America, Sikhs were sojourn migrants. Later, they chose to make it their permanent home.

Life in North America was far from smooth, though, for the early Sikhs, and they faced stiff hurdles. For one, the color of their skin drew pejorative remarks from the white society. That they came from an enslaved nation did not do their cause any good. Much to their hurt, the turban became a thing of scoffing and contempt. Many, therefore,

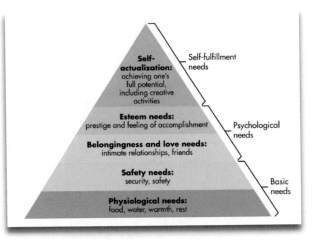

Maslow's pyramid

sought shelter in Sikh enclaves in Sacramento and the Imperial Valley of California. They faced riots along with Chinese and Japanese immigrants in Vancouver and Bellingham, just fifty-five miles apart in the Pacific West. Local hatred resulted in the enactment of unfavorable immigration and citizenship laws.

Sikhs and East Indians were barred from owning land in California. American citizenship was denied to them. Many ended up marrying Hispanic women since re-entry to the US could turn out to be impossible in case they went to Punjab in search of a bride. At the same time their interfaith marriages and hybrid children became unacceptable to both the Hispanic and Sikh communities. Many of the children adopted the mother's religion, Christianity, and were forever lost to the Sikhs.

The early migrants faced all these hostile conditions and hardships with grit and determination. Their most important weapon was their hard work with which they opened the doors for others to follow them into North America. Their love for the freedom of their mother country from the oppressive, stifling and pillaging British rule led to historic events such as the Komagata Maru ship journey and the Ghadar movement. Many were killed, hanged, and sentenced to life imprisonment and left to rot and die in the inhuman conditions of the cellular jails in Kalapani, as the Andaman and Nicobar Islands were called. These Sikhs who gave their lives for the cause of their nation were the real heroes of the independence movement.

The favorable immigration law enacted in 1946 and further amended by President Johnson in 1965 allowed many Indians and Sikhs to emigrate to the US. Currently, the Sikh community is better educated and is progressing well. There are approximately 500,000 Sikhs in the US, and a similar number in Canada. But their overall say in Canadian society is much more since the Canadian population is about 38 million as compared to the US's 330 million. The presence of the Sikhs in the top echelons of Canadian politics is heartening. There are eighteen Sikhs in the Canadian Parliament, five more than in India. Also, four of them became ministers in the Canadian cabinet. At the provincial level, there were eight Indo-Canadians, many Sikhs were elected to the British Columbia assembly in 2020.

With time, as discussed earlier, color bias will reduce. There will be more colored and brown people in the US as the population of Hispanics and Southeast Asians rises, and at the same time there is a perceptible dip in the fertility of the white population. Sikhs are adopting many traditions of the host country that include speaking the English language with greater proficiency, adapting to the food habits of North America, and greater assimilation when it comes to dating, sports, festivities, politics and national holidays. It's also heartening to note that all the important features of the Sikh *Rehat Maryada* are being followed, albeit with some modifications.

Turban is the most important symbol of Sikh identity but at the same time carries peril and prejudice (Chattha, 2020). This results in job discrimination and hate crimes due to mistaken identity related to Islamophobia. Recent surveys reveal that a large majority of recent immigrants and the subsequent generation has chosen to live without the turban. Sikh organizations are working hard to save the turban. Sikhs with turban are now recruited in police and defense services in many western countries.

In spite of the shortcomings and challenges, this is the golden period for Sikhs in North America. Their per capita income is well above the national average. Sikh education, financial well-being, charity (*Wund Shako*), *Sarbat da Bhala* (doing good to all) have become emblems of a model minority in the US.

Like every other ethnic and religious group, Sikhs will be benefited through the advancement in science, modernity and globalization. The Sikhs will spread all over the world due to a demographic transition in many developed countries.

One can only, at best, make an educated guess about the future of Sikhism. The world is well connected today, and thought processes move in tandem. All religions change with time, and there will be possible changes in Sikh theology, traditions and rituals, as the future unfolds.

The Sikh religion believes in the existence of God as is formulated in the *Mool Mantar*, the basis of Sikh theology. The current agnostic movement perpetuated by advances in science are not in consonance with the *Mool Mantar*. The Bhakti movement, that was a spiritual renaissance, was at its very height when the Sikh faith began. It was a time when science was in its nascency. Today, things have changed. The number of atheist and agnostic Sikhs will rise, as has been the case with all religions.

Even this small group that I've termed as cultural Sikhs or new Sikhs will contribute to Sikhism by virtue of participation in all other activities that lead to the good of humanity. *Kirit Kar, Wund Shako, Sarbat Da Bhala* and other virtues of Sikhism will flourish.

Baptized Sikhs or Khalsa may not be relevant in future. Nihang Singhs, the Sikh warriors, are fast disappearing. The 5K symbols of the Khalsa are not being used. The three-feet sword has been reduced to a one-foot dagger. Today it is a tiny one attached to a small comb in only a symbolic way. This too will disappear in future. The concepts of reincarnation, afterlife, soul as distinct from the human body, heaven and hell are no longer part of the belief system of educated Sikhs.

Due to the mistaken identity with Islamic

terrorists, the turban as a symbol will continue to draw negative attention and even some form of violence. Sikhs in the majority will be without turbans, a painful reality in the west. But they will continue to be the flag-bearers of the religion. The identity of a Sikh itself will be redefined. Nanak Panthi philosophy will reunite all Sikhs. They will embrace new changes with open arms, including respect for the LBGTQ community, issues related to same-sex marriage, surrogate motherhood and other advancements in fertility. Interfaith marriages will have more acceptance.

The long queues in inclement weather will be a discouraging factor for devotees to visit the Harmandir Sahib. Some rituals will disappear in the future. The *Parkarma*, walk around the Sanctum Sanctorum, will not remain necessary. The marble walkway gets very hot and can be slippery, resulting in injuries.

A dip in the holy tank and small *chuli* (drink) of holy water is unhygienic and not necessary. Taking a sip of holy water from the sacred tank has been in vogue among Sikhs visiting the Harmandir Sahib or other holy shrines. Some also collect the water in bottles and take it back for family members to drink. This ritual may not be a healthy one. Very few, I believe, will take a dip now, even though water purification equipment is in place.

Many have been injured while making a trip to Hemkund Sahib, believed to be the prayer site of tenth Guru Gobind Singh in his previous life. The entire story has been questioned and has commercial value only. Also, it will not be necessary to carry the ashes of the dead to a river in Kiratpur. Traditionally, the ashes of the dead are taken to Kiratpur Sahib in Punjab for immersion in the local river. As outlined by Tarlochan Singh Dupalpur, this is against Sikh tenets. He noted that many families, some from overseas, had met with serious accidents, even resulting in death, while travelling to Kiratpur Sahib to submerge ashes of loved ones who had died.

Many older traditions, detailed earlier, will disappear and be replaced by new ones. The helmet and the hard hat, for instance, will become more acceptable to the Sikh community.

For future generations, the relationship with Punjab and India will change. This will be one that will lean more towards curiosity, and the search for roots. It will remain the eternal wish of every Sikh to visit the Harmandir Sahib and other holy Sikh places in Punjab and India. The Akal Takht, SCPC, Akali Dal will not be relevant to the Sikhs overseas. Sikhs have their own organizations for today, and for tomorrow.

Any changes that a religion undergoes cannot be measured in terms of months or years. Rather the changes take place over centuries as is evident in religions older than Sikhism (see chapter eight). The turban, 5Ks, baptizing to Khalsa will not be the only parameters for measuring the rise or fall of Sikhism. One must keep in mind that Sikhism was born as a stream of philosophy that believed in Nanak Panthi, and there were no symbols at the time. The majority of Sikh women do not have any Sikh symbols, nor are they required to wear the turban. But they too remain faithful Sikhs.

Modernity, globalization and detraditionalization will have their own knowns and unknowns. Homo sapiens and all other living species on planet earth follow the laws of evolution. Survival is on the basis of the least amount of energy expended. Sikhs are no exception to his universal rule, and follow the path of happiness, longevity and prosperity. The discrimination on the basis of color, creed, race and religion is ignorance and an unintended and undesirable consequence of the fast pace of migration and globalization. In future, there will be a bigger and better Sikhism.

I humbly beg to differ with all those who have expressed pessimism on the future of Sikhs in the US in no uncertain terms. Confucius, the Chinese philosopher, said that one must study the past in order to define the future. For me, if past history is any guide, Sikhism will flourish with and without the evolving changes in Sikh thoughts and appearances. The Khalsa of the future will march ahead with its own *Naggara* (percussion instrument) and its widely known clarion call, **Bole So Nihal Sat Sri Akal.** ■

GRATITUDE AND ACKNOWLEDGEMENT

As an octogenarian in his mid-eighties, I must admit at the outset that I didn't mind the ample help I received from many sources as I ventured into writing my third book.

I remain ever so grateful to my life partner of sixty years, Dr Jaswinder Chattha, for her encouraging words that allowed me to complete this book, and for keeping me active and cognitively stable.

To my three gracious children, Geetinder, Sonia and Vijay and their respective spouses, Eldan Eichbaum, Harvinder Sandhu and Archana, my gratitude. They were happy to see me remain quite busy with the book, and at the same time refrain from interfering in their kitchens and bars. My grandchildren, Yasmin, Anju, Josh, Alexi, Arjan, Rani, Amrik, Taj and Jaia who during this time did not insist that I entertain them with any family story-telling. They aided me generously on the IT front, much to my liking.

My gratitude to my elder brother Ajit Singh Chattha (IAS, retired) who has always encouraged me to expand my horizons and explore a newer world beyond my medical profession.

To my many friends who during informal conversations helped shape my thinking during the course of writing this book. Some of them provided key inputs on the early settlers in North America they had known personally. Gina Brar, for instance, narrated the life story of Mayo Singh, the 'lumber king' from Vancouver Island, Canada. Dr Jagtar Singh Sandhu and Dr Piara Singh Pannu knew Santa Singh Pannu personally. Dr Jaswant Singh Sachdev, MD, introduced me to Rala Singh from Phoenix Arizona. More details on Rala Singh were provided by Daljit Singh Gill, his relative, also from Phoenix. My late friend Dr Nirmal Singh Mann, MD, gave me valuable insights personally from the book he'd written on Pakher Singh Gill.

I am thankful to the late Tejinder Singh Sibia for creating *Sikhpioneers.org*. Likewise, I am grateful to Samip Mallick and Michelle Caswell for creating the *South Asian American Digital Archive* (SAADA). I extensively used material from these valuable resources. When the world shut down due to the coronavirus pandemic, it was good old Google that came to my rescue time and time again, not to, of course, forget Wikipedia. I'm grateful to Manorama and Dr Brijinder Singh Kochher, Mohinder Singh Chattha, Kirpal and Tripit Grewal and Ajit Singh Chatha from Sunnyvale, California for their help in the survey, and to Dr Manohar Singh Grewal, Dr Gurpal Singh Kingra, Dr Kulwant Singh Dhaliwal for their inputs and reviews of the script. The book is based on the sharing of personal experiences of numerous friends who migrated to North America more than fifty years ago. All of them are *keshdhari* Sikhs.

Experienced editor Sayantan Chakravarty put my thoughts in proper perspective for the readers. He has himself written books on the *Ghadar* movement and on the diaspora extensively and was conversant with Sikh immigrants to North America. I owe my gratitude to him for his patience, hard work, search of archives and writing skills.

My wonderful doctors from UCSF ensured that I worked through this beautiful phase, bringing to life another book, in the best of physical and emotional health.

My heartfelt thanks go to all.

SUGGESTED READING

❖ *The Biology of Skin Color: Black and White*
From Discover, Vol. 22, No. 2, February, 2001. Gina Kirchweger/© 2001. Reprinted with permission of Discover.

❖ *Being Mortal: Medicine and What Matters in the End*
Atul Gawande, 2004

❖ *The God delusion*
Richard Dawkins, Houghton Mifflin, Boston, 2008

❖ *Detraditionalization*
Paul Heelas (Editor), Scott Lash (Editor), Paul Morris (Editor), Wiley-Blackwell, 1995

❖ *The New Frontiersmen: A Sociological Study of Indian Immigrants in the United Kingdom*
Gurdip Singh Aurora, Popular Prakashan, 1967

❖ *Indian Americans: The New Model Minority*
Jason Richwine, Forbes February 24, 2009

❖ *Assimilation in American life: the role of race, religion, and national origins*
Milton M Gordon, Oxford University Press, New York, 1964

❖ *Incorporating diversity: rethinking assimilation in a multicultural age*
Peter Kivisto, Paradigm Publishers, Boulder, Colo, 2005

❖ *Ghadar Movement - Ideology Organisations Strategy*
Harish K Puri, Guru Nanak Dev University Press, Amritsar, January 1, 2013

❖ *Ghadar Centennial Commemoration 90th Anniversary*
June 1, 2003, organized by GOPIO International

❖ *Khalsa Samachar*
November 20, 1907 (page 5) and November 20, 1913 (page 2)

❖ *This is what a Sikh child faces in America*
Winty Singh, CNN opinion, June 25, 2018

❖ *Bully Victims: Psychological and Somatic Aftermaths*
Randy A. Sansone, MD and Lori A. Sansone, MD, Psychiatry (Edgmont). 2008 June; 5(6): 62–64.

❖ *Bullying behavior and associations with psychosomatic complaints*
Minne Fekkes 1, Frans I M Pijpers, S Pauline Verloove-Vanhorick, J Pediatr. 2004 January; 144(1):17-22

❖ *Accommodation without Assimilation Sikh Immigrants in an American High School,*
Margaret A. Gibson, Cornell University Press, Page 88-110, 1988, Ithaca & London

❖ *Sikhism in the United States*
Wikipedia

❖ *Turban*
Wikipedia

❖ *Bulletproof turbans for Sikh cops*
Times of India, May 8, 2009

❖ *Turban Myths: The Opportunities and Challenges For Reframing Sikh American Identity In Post-9/11 America*
Chris Bennett, Margarita Quihuis, and

Giovanni Rodriguez, Saldef and Peace Innovation Lab, Stanford, December 14, 2013

❖ *The Tide of Turbans*
Herman George Scheffauer, Forum Publishing Company, 1910

❖ *Young Sikh Men Get Haircuts, Annoying Their Elders*
Amelia Gentleman, March 29, 2007, The New York Times

❖ *Why Democracy Is Troubled (and How to Fix It)*
Gerald F. Seib, January 19, 2020, The Wall Street Journal

❖ *Nations Unbound: Transnational Projects, Postcolonial Predicaments and Deterritorialized Nation-States*
Linda Basch, Nina Glick Schiller, Cristina Szanton Blanc, Published November 3, 1993 by Routledge

❖ *The World Economy and Contemporary Migration*
Elsa M. Chaney, SAGE Journals, first published June 1, 1979, Page 204-212, Vol. 13

❖ *Punjab's exodus without an end*
Gurbachan Jagat
The Tribune, India December 31, 2019

❖ *Mental health implications of migration: a review of mental health community studies on Russian-speaking immigrants in Israel*
Julia Mirsky, Israel Social Psychiatry 44 (3) 179-187 September 2008

❖ *Bret Harte*
Overland Monthly and Outwest Magazine, Vol 20, Page 254, 1892

❖ *Encyclopedia of Wars*
(3 Vol. Set) Phillips Charles and Alan Axelrod, Facts on File, 1 January 2010

❖ *70% student visa aspirants from farming families: Study*
Vishav Bharti, Tribune News Service, Chandigarh, February 3, 2020

❖ *'Thalieconomics' gets it wrong*
Devinder Sharma, The Tribune, India, February 08, 2020

❖ *Wilhelm Wundt, Philosophische Schriften*
Vol 111 (1883) quoted by M F Ashley Montagu, 1947

❖ *UNESCO ad hoc expert group on endangered languages*
Paris, March 10-12, 2003

❖ *The Religion of Plato*
Paul Elmer More, Princeton University Press, 1921

❖ *Making Ethnic Choices: California's Punjabi Mexican Americans*
Karen Isaksen Leonard, Temple University Press, May 29, 1992

❖ *The Sikhs of Northern California: A Socio-Historical Study*
Bruce Wilfred La Brack, Syracuse University, 1980

❖ Dr. Alvin Poussaint, associate professor of psychiatry at the Harvard Medical School, participant at a symposium on *Psychosocial aspects of children of mixed marriages* in 1980.

❖ *Darwin's Dangerous Idea*
Dennett Daniel, Simon and Schuster, July 1, 2014.

❖ *God Is Not Great: How Religion Poisons Everything*
Christopher Hitchens (Author, Narrator), Hachette Audio (Publisher), May 1, 2007

❖ *The Philosophical Basis of Theism: An Examination of the Personality of Man to Ascertain His Capacity to Know and Serve God, and the Validity of the Principles Underlying the Defence of Theism*
Samuel Harris, Charles Scribner's sons, 1883

- *Enlightenment Now*
  The Case for Reason, Science, Humanism, and Progress
  Steven Pinker, Penguin Books, 2018

- *The British in India: A Social History of the Raj, 2018*
  David Gilmour, Picador, 120 Broadway, New York, 2018

- *A People's History of the United States*
  Howard Zinn, Harper Perennial Modern Classics 2001, recent edition 2009

- *The diary of William Bentley (1759-1819)*
  Salem, Mass: Essex Institute, 1905-14.

- *Salem And The Indies*
  James Duncan Phillips, Published by Houghton Mifflin, Boston, 1947

- *The East India Marine Society and the Peabody Museum of Salem: a sesquicentennial history*
  Walter Muir Whitehill, 1905, Published: Salem: Peabody Museum, 1949.

- *"California and the gold fields." Translated from the German of Frederick Gerstäcker 1854.*
  UC Santa Cruz, University Library

- *The Making of Asian America: A History*
  Erika Lee, Simon & Schuster, August, 2015

- *How many undocumented immigrants are in the United States and who are they?*
  Elaine Kamarck and Christine Stenglein, November 12, 2019, Brookings Institution

- *Yogi Bhajan Turned an L.A. Yoga Studio into a Juggernaut, and Left Two Generations of Followers Reeling from Alleged Abuse*
  Stacie Stukin -July 15, 2020, Los Angeles Magazine

- *The coming end of Christian America*
  Kristian Bonnie, Opinion, The Week, October 20, 2019.

- *'Black Is King' by Beyoncé Review: Visions of Paradise*
  Mark Richardson, August 3, 2020, The Wall Street Journal

- *Has Indian migration led to a brain drain or a gain?*
  Sasha Cherian, June 29, 2020, The Startup

- *The brain drain: Old myths, new realities*
  Cervantes, Mario; Guellec, Dominique, OECD Observer, Paris, January 2002.

- *Ghadar, Historical Silences, and Notions of Belonging: Early 1900s Punjabis of the Columbia River*
  Johanna Ogden, June 2012, Oregon historical quarterly. Oregon Historical Society 113(2):164-197

- *Pioneering Punjabis Digital Archive*
  University of California at Davis

- *Bhai Mewa Singh Lopoke – the immortal martyr of Canada*
  Sohan Singh Pooni, Bhai Mewa Singh Lopoke Journal publishing service, UVic 2019

- *Martyr or Murderer: Mewa Singh and the Assassination of William C. Hopkinson*
  Erin Chewter, Journal Publishing Service, UVic, 2019

- *Where will the next decade take religion? Experts predict the future of faith*
  Aysha Khan, Religion News Service, June 12, 2020

- *Marriage and Domestic Partnership*
  First published Saturday, July 11, 2009; substantive revision Wednesday, July 14, 2021 in the Stanford Encyclopedia of Philosophy

- *The Future of Marriage: Changing demographics, economics, and laws alter the meaning of matrimony in America*
  Harbour Fraser Hodder, Harvard Magazine, November - December 2004

❖ *Sikhs in America: A History of Hate*
A.C. Thompson, ProPublica, August 4, 2017

❖ *When Americans Say They Believe in God, What Do They Mean?*
April 25, 2018, Pew Research Center

❖ *What to do about ethnic enclaves in Canada?*
Alex Sangha, The Georgia Straight, Vancouver, May 8, 2012,

❖ *Circuitous Assimilation among rural Hindustani In California*
Yusuf Dadabhay, Semantic Scholar, December 1, 1954

❖ *Democracy versus the melting-pot—A Study of American Nationality*
Horace M. Kallen, The Nation, February 25, 1915

❖ *The social systems of American ethnic groups*
W Lloyd Warner; Leo Srole
Publisher: New Haven, Yale University Press; London, H. Milford, Oxford University Press, 1945.

❖ *Same-sex marriage in presence of Guru Granth Sahib invites Akal Takht's ire*
GS Paul, Tribune News Service, Amritsar, October 19, 2020

❖ *Growing Up in America—The Power of Race in the Lives of Teens*
Brad Christerson, Korie L. Edwards, and Richard Flory, Stanford University Press, April 28, 2010

❖ *Legacies: The story of the immigrant second generation*
Alejandro Portes, Ruben G. Rumbaut, Russell Sage Foundation, University of California Press, Berkeley, 2001

❖ *Asian American Youth—Culture, Identity and Ethnicity*
Jennifer Lee, Min Zhou, Routledge, 2004

❖ *Pope Francis Backs Civil Unions for Gay Couples, in Shift for Vatican by Francis X. Rocca*
The Wall Street Journal, October 1, 2020

❖ *German Catholic Leaders Support Blessings for Gay Couples, Challenging Pope Francis*
Francis X. Rocca, The Wall Street Journal, October 1, 2021

❖ *In U.S., Decline of Christianity Continues at Rapid Pace*
Pew Research Center, October 17, 2019

❖ *Religiosity and happiness: A comparison of the happiness levels between the religious and the nonreligious*
Warren J Sillick, Bruce Stevens, Stuart Cathcart, The Journal of Happiness & Well-being, Vol. 4 (1), Page 115-127, published by the Charles Sturt University in 2016

❖ *Paldi remembered: 50 years in the life of a Vancouver Island logging town*
Joan Mayo, Priority printing, 1997

❖ *The Making of Little Punjab in Canada: Patterns of Immigration*
B. Archana Verma, Sage India; First edition (May 2002)

❖ *A Half-Century Appraisal of East Indians in the United States*
Jacoby S. Harold, The Sixth Annual College of the Pacific Faculty Research Lecture May 21, 1956

❖ *The tree man of Punjab on a green mission*
Anil Sharma, Hindustan Times, June 6, 2018

❖ *Other Sikhs: A View from Eastern India*
Himadri Banerjee, Manohar Publishers and Distributors, January 1, 2003

❖ *Atlas of the world's languages in danger*
UNESCO, Christopher Moseley and

Alexandre Nicholas, UNESDOC Digital Library, 2010

❖ *Women in Sikhism*
Wikipedia

❖ *Guru Nanak Charity*
www.SearchSikhism.com

❖ U.N. World Happiness Index 2018

❖ *The Mormon Church Amassed $100 Billion. It Was the Best-Kept Secret in the Investment World*
Ian Lovett and Rachael Levy, The Wall Street Journal, February 8, 2020

❖ *Diaspora Experiences in Multicultural VS Melting Pot Societies: Lessons from the Indian Diaspora in the U.S. and Canada*
Masud Chand in the Business and Management Research, Sciedu Press, Vol. 1 (1), pages 2-12, March, 2012

❖ British Sikh Report, London, 2019

❖ *The West and the Hindu Invasion*
Agnes Foster Buchanan, published in the Overland Monthly, April 1908

❖ *Becoming American: The Journey of Early Sikh Pioneer Kehar Singh | Nomachar, Punjab to Clovis, CA*
AIISF

❖ *The US white majority will soon disappear forever*
Dudley Poston and Rogelio Sáenz, The Chicago Reporter, May 16, 2019

❖ *Studying community: Culturally Jewish — proud of heritage but not religious*
Toby Tabachnick, Pittsburgh Jewish Chronicle, February 20, 2020

❖ *From Bhagat Singh, Atheist, To Agnostic Khushwant: Mapping Sikh irreligiosity*
Robin Rinehart in Sikh Formations Religion Culture Theory 11(1):1-14, April 2015

❖ *The Sikh Turban in America: Pride & Prejudice*
Amrik Singh Chattha, Publisher: Personal History Productions (May 21, 2020)

❖ *Sikhs Living Beyond Punjab in India*
Himadri Banerjee, Edited by Pashaura Singh and Louis E. Fenech, The Oxford Handbook of Sikh Studies in March 2014

❖ *The Lost Sikhs of Biranchipur*
Anil Dhir in Odisha Bytes on September 13, 2017

❖ *The Political Economy of Human Happiness: How Voters' Choices Determine the Quality of Life*
Benjamin Radcliff, Cambridge University Press, March 25, 2013

❖ *The US white majority will soon disappear forever*
Dudley Poston and Rogelio Sáenz in The Chicago Reporter of May 16, 2019

❖ *The "Bad Is Black" Effect*
Daisy Grewal on January 17, 2017 in the Scientific American

❖ *Second-Generation Americans—A Portrait of the Adult Children of Immigrants*
Pew Research Center on February 7, 2013

❖ *The New Third Generation: Post-1965 Immigration and the Next Chapter in the Long Story of Assimilation*
Tomás R. Jiménez, Julie Park, Juan Pedroza, published in the International Migration Review on December 18, 2017.

❖ *Forever Foreigners or Honorary Whites?: The Asian Ethnic Experience Today*
Mia Tuan and published by the Rutgers University Press; March 1998

❖ *Punjabi language is not dying; Punjabi language will not die, but...*
Jagmohan Singh, The World Sikh News 2019

❖ *Economic inequality*
Wikipedia

❖ Wealth distribution and income inequality by country
Global Finance, November 26, 2018.

❖ Color terminology for race
Wikipedia, Johann Friedrich Blumenbach, 1779

❖ Some Aspects of Social Stratifications Among the Immigrant Punjabi Communities of California
Littleton, C. Scott in Culture Change and Stability (Ralph L Beals, editor), published by the Department of Anthropology, University of California, Los Angeles, 1964, pp. 105-116.

❖ The Hindus of Uppertown
Denise Alborn in Sikhpioneers.org

❖ Century of Struggle and Success—The Sikh Canadian Experience
Sandeep Singh Brar in Sikhs.org in 1997

❖ Avicenna and the visionary recital
Henry Corbin and published by Spring Publications in Irving, Texas in 1980

❖ Understanding Early Formation of Punjabi Diaspora: Causes and Dispersions
Hardeep Kaur, Journal of Sikh and Punjab Studies, Vol. 27 No. 1, 2020

❖ Bicultural accommodation: A critical examination of the academic and social experiences of Sikh American college students
Daniel J. DeVere, Sikh Formation Religion, Culture Theory Vol. 16 Issue: 4, 2020.

❖ Defining a Sikh
Devinder Singh Chahal, Institute for Understanding Sikhism, Vol. 4 No. 2, January 2002

❖ Tryst with Trees—Punjab's Sacred Heritage
D.S Jaspal, January 1, 2012

❖ Sarbat da bhala
Sikhiwiki.org

❖ Sikhism & Democracy
Sikh Missionary Society (U.K.)

❖ Does Having Children Make People Happier in the Long Run?
Nicholas H. Wolfinger, Institute for Family Studies, December 10, 2018

❖ Financial Aid
Mark Kantrowitz in fastweb.com, August 8, 2009

❖ The Gain from the Drain: Skill-biased Migration and Global Welfare
Costanza Biavaschi, Michal Burzynski, Benjamin Elsner, Joël Machado published by the Center for Research and Analysis of Migration, Department of Economics, University College, London, October 7, 2016

❖ Brain drain from developing countries: how can brain drain be converted into wisdom gain?
Sunita Dodani and Ronald E LaPorte, J R Soc Med., 98(11): 487–491, November 2005

❖ A Vindication of the Rights of Woman with Strictures on Political and Moral Subjects
Mary Wollstonecraft (1792), The third edition Printed for J. Johnson no. 72 St. Paul's Church-yard 1796.

❖ The Subjection of Women
John Stuart Mill in 1869, London: Longmans, Green, Reader & Dyer, 1869.

❖ The Laws of Manu
Wendy Doniger, Penguin India; Reprint edition, October 14, 2000

❖ An Inquiry into the Nature and Causes of the Wealth of Nations Kindle Edition
Adam Smith, Publisher: University of Chicago Press; Facsimile of 1904 edition, May 16, 2012

❖ Science and Sikhism - Conflict or Coherence
Devinder Pal Singh, Amritsar, Punjab,

India: Singh Brothers, 2018

❖ *The Book of the City of Ladies*
Christine De Pizan, Publisher: Persea; Revised edition, September 20, 2013

❖ *Some reflections upon marriage*
Mary Astell, Printed for John Nutt near stationed-Hall 1700, London

❖ *A psychologist shares the 4 styles of parenting— and the type that researchers say is the most successful*
Francyne Zeltser, Contributor, CNBC.com, Published June 29, 2021

❖ *What Makes an American Hero?*
Adam Kirsch, October 1, 2021, The Wall Street Journal

❖ *History of Punjab,* Wikipedia.

❖ *The Viking Heart: How Scandinavians Conquered the World*
Arthur Herman, August 3, 2021, Publisher: Houghton Mifflin Harcourt, Boston, New York, 2021

❖ *Indian American: The new model minority*
Jason Richwine, Forbes, February 24, 2009

❖ *The US white majority will soon disappear forever*
Dudley Poston and Rogelio Sáenz, May 16, 2019, The Chicago Reporter

❖ *Religion's Sudden Decline: Why It's Happening and What Comes Next*
Ronald F Inglehart, Amy and Alan Lowenstein Professor Emeritus of Democracy, Democratization and Human Rights, and Research Professor Emeritus at the Center for Political Studies, University of Michigan, December 10, 2020

❖ *Indians in Malaya: Some Aspects of Their Immigration and Settlement, 1786–1957*
Kernial Singh Sandhu, Cambridge University Press, 1969

❖ *British Sikh Report,* 2018 ∎

ABOUT THE AUTHOR

Amrik Singh Chattha, MD, was born on September 1, 1937 in village Chattha Chak No. 46, undivided Punjab in British India, today located in Pakistan. His educational journey took him through the Sikh National College at Qadian and the Government Medical College in Patiala, both in Punjab, India. In the US, he was with the Drake Memorial Hospital in Cincinnati, Ohio; New York Medical College, New York City; Boston Children's Hospital and Mass General Hospital, Boston, both affiliated to the Harvard Medical School where he was a fellow in neurology, and remained the rare turban-wearing Sikh to be accepted into that program. He spent five years in Boston training in neurology.

Dr. Amrik Singh Chattha

He and his family then moved to Weirton, West Virginia, where he practiced neurology for forty-one years, before finally calling it a day and retiring in the San Francisco Bay Area. He was honored by his Alma mater by the distinguished alumnus award. After his marriage to Dr. Jaswinder Kaur Brar in 1961, the couple journeyed together and are parents to three successful children. He was a member of various professional organizations including the American Academy of Neurology and a past president of the Sikh Council of North America. In honor of their parents, the couple has endowed a chair in Sikh studies at the University of Michigan.

Other books by the author
Safar: A Child's Walk to Freedom During the Partition of India (2018)
The Sikh Turban in America Pride and Prejudice (2020).

Price: US$ 40

ISBN No. 978-81-958108-1-9